A TRAILS BOOKS G

Lake Michigan Travel Guide

Nina Gadomski

TRAILS BOOKS
Madison, Wisconsin

Library of Congress Control Number: 2008922959
ISBN: 978-1-934553-09-1

Editor: Melissa L. Faliveno
Designer: Kathie Campbell
Maps: Magellan Mapping Co.
Photography: All photos by Nina Gadomski unless otherwise noted.
Cover Photo: Lake Michigan and the Ludington Lighthouse at dawn
Back Cover Photo: Sailboats on the blue water of Grand Traverse Bay, Michigan

Printed in the United States of America.
13 12 11 10 09 08 6 5 4 3 2 1

Trails Books, a division of Big Earth Publishing
923 Williamson Street • Madison, WI 53703
(800) 258-5830 • www.trailsbooks.com

To my mother, Stella, who once crossed an ocean.

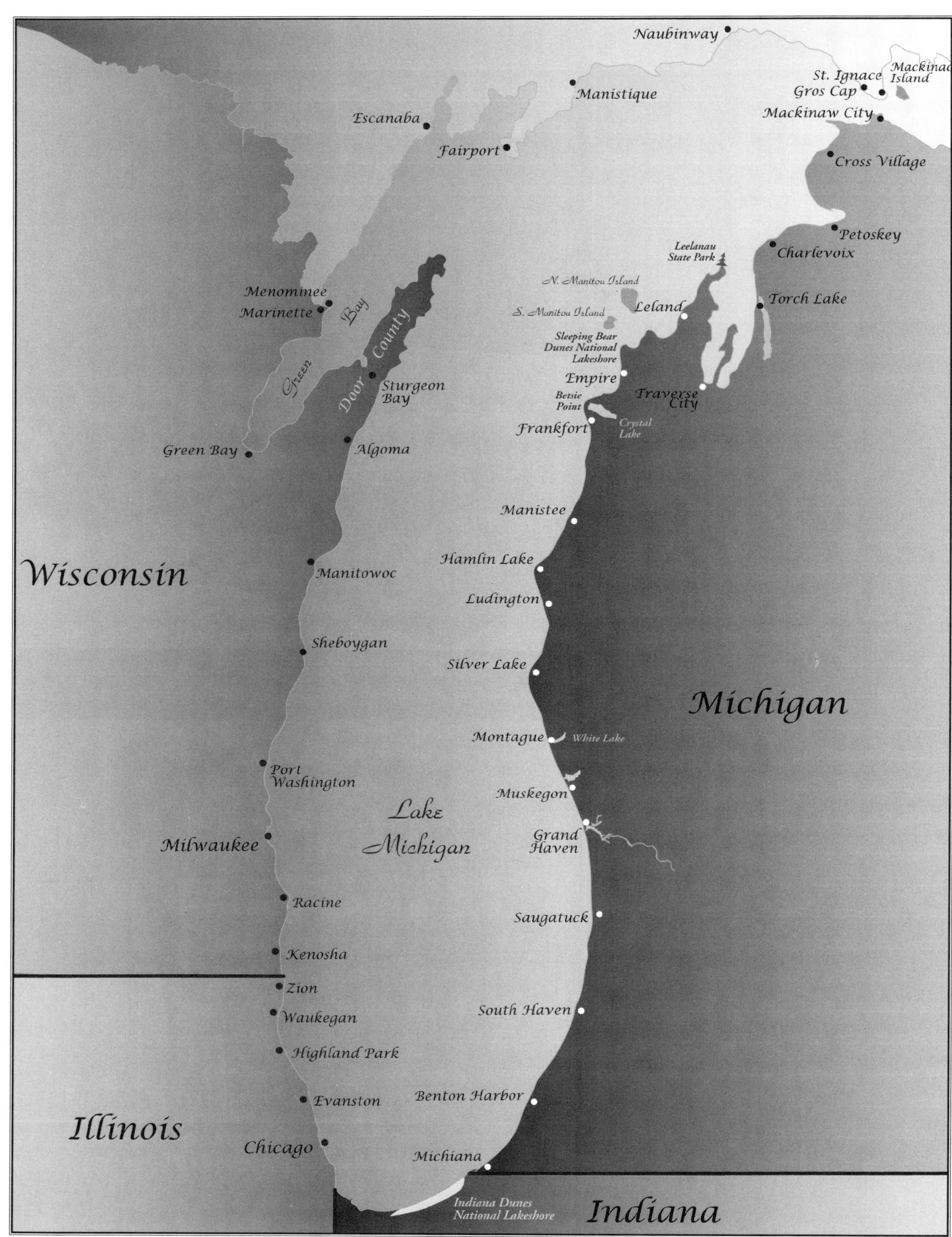

Naubinway
Mackinac Island
St. Ignace
Gros Cap
Manistique
Escanaba
Mackinaw City
Fairport
Cross Village
Petoskey
Leelanau State Park
Charlevoix
N. Manitou Island
Menominee
Marinette
Green Bay
Door County
Torch Lake
S. Manitou Island
Leland
Sleeping Bear Dunes National Lakeshore
Empire
Sturgeon Bay
Betsie Point
Traverse City
Frankfort
Crystal Lake
Green Bay
Algoma
Manistee
Hamlin Lake
Wisconsin
Manitowoc
Ludington
Sheboygan
Silver Lake
Michigan
Montague
White Lake
Port Washington
Muskegon
Lake Michigan
Grand Haven
Milwaukee
Racine
Saugatuck
Kenosha
Zion
Waukegan
South Haven
Highland Park
Benton Harbor
Evanston
Illinois
Chicago
Michiana
Indiana Dunes National Lakeshore
Indiana

Table of Contents

Acknowledgments

I WOULD LIKE TO extend a very special thank-you to the great people who helped make this book possible, and whom I am privileged to know:

From the home port, Stella, Elizabeth, and Steve. Also Desiree, who would have been there for my writing breaks if she could. Dennis, too, who has been an anchor for all these years.

Eva Šolcová of Big Earth Publishing for recommending me for this book even before the ink was dry on *Great Midwest Country Escapes: Farms, Foods, and Festivals.*

My aids to navigation: Michelle Fischer of Boelter + Lincoln, Milwaukee, Wisconsin (for Travel Wisconsin), who is amazingly thoughtful and thorough; Timothy Meloche of Marx Layne & Company, Farmington Hills, Michigan (for Travel Michigan), who opened doors to another grand adventure; Kirsten Borgstrom of Travel Michigan, for providing assistance along the way; the lakeshore CVB and Chamber of Commerce people who are not only knowledgeable, but also gracious, bright, and just plain fun.

Special thanks to the cross-lake ferry people: Kay Collins, *Lake Express*; Lynda Daugherty and Kari Karr, SS *Badger*.

My thanks also to the local historians and experts who gave their time and shared their passion for Lake Michigan. In Oconto, Wisconsin, Dick Doeren. In Marinette, Wisconsin, Frank Lauerman III. In Montague-Whitehall, Michigan, Roger P. Scharmer. In Holland, Michigan, Geoffrey D. Reynolds, Bob Vande Vusse, Randall P. Vande Water, and Bob & Lois Sligh. Also Bob's brother Charlie for his laugh that can light up an entire restaurant. In Grand Haven, Michigan, George F. VerDuin. In Sheboygan, Wisconsin, William F. Wangemann. On Mackinac Island, Robert M. Tagatz.

Finally, I wish to thank the hundreds of other great people I met along the way, people who make their piece of the lakeshore that much more rewarding to visitors. People like Bill and Jane Carpenter of The Lamplighter Bed & Breakfast in Ludington, Michigan, for whom hospitality is a way of life. Marilyn Fischer in the UP, who never forgot it when an old lighthouse keeper took her by the hand and showed her around the place. Ken Koyen of

Washington Island, Wisconsin, who knows what to do with old wood and fresh fish. Joel Lefever of the Holland Museum in Holland, Michigan, for his ability to make a century of time make sense. Fred MacDonald in Manistee, Michigan, who knows how to throw out the welcome mat. Johnny Martinez of the Washington Park Zoo in Michigan City, Indiana, who said, "Sure, I've got time to talk," even when I showed up unannounced. John Scholtz of the Ottawa County Parks in Grand Haven, Michigan, who watches over the dunes for the rest of us. Ronald Wood of Historic White Pine Village in Ludington, Michigan, who opened the gates to the village and its magical windows to history.

Introduction

Before there were sandboxes, there was the beach. Before waterparks, there was the lake. It is said that Lake Michigan has been around since the Ice Age. How many years has it been since you built a castle from its sand, or made a memory of its sparkling water?

IF EVER THERE WAS a perfect time to take that Lake Michigan vacation, the time is now. Maritime museums are expanding with each new story they have to tell. Lighthouses are getting fresh coats of paint and becoming beacons of discovery. Classic passenger steamers are getting a good polish and showing visitors what shipboard style was all about. Underwater shipwrecks are getting land-based signage so non-divers can explore them without ever getting wet. With sails billowing into the wind and masts pointed to the skies, replica schooners are plying these waters as if it were once again the nineteenth century. But the reawakening is not just cultural; it's environmental as well. Great efforts are underway to address the threat of invasive species. State parks are finding new ways to preserve their old dunes. Former manufacturing sites are becoming green parkways and gathering spots for fishermen and beach-strollers alike.

This book will lead you to all of these adventures and more. Take your choice of 20 geographically-segmented tours around the four states that border Lake Michigan: Wisconsin, Michigan, Indiana, and Illinois. Across most of their land areas, these are Midwestern states full of farms and small towns. But where they touch Lake Michigan, they are states of the Great Lakes, where silos give way to sails, and small towns transform into harbor towns.

Tours take a clockwise spin around Lake Michigan, beginning in Wisconsin, circling around the magnificent Upper Peninsula, heading south along Michigan's sunset coast, and finishing through the short but significant stretches of lakeshore in Indiana and Illinois. Thanks to the two cross-lake passenger ferries, you can do a variety of smaller circles around parts of the lake that you find most appealing. Whatever shape your Lake Michigan journey takes, you will surely find perfection along this route. And, since circles have neither a beginning nor an end, you will probably find that after you leave the lakeshore, it will never truly leave you.

As you embark upon your journey, do not disregard the rivers that drain into Lake Michigan. The first settlers certainly did not. What the rivers lack in sandy shores they make up for in significance: settlement typically occurred at the mouth of a river, and those old settlements are the great cities and towns of today. Long ago, Lake Michigan was the freeway of commerce, and the rivers supplied the access points for the loading and unloading of cargo.

Those were the days of three-masted schooners and, somewhat later, passenger steamers that carried the wealthy city people to summer resorts. As you visit these same ports today, you can relive those days aboard replica schooners and real steamers at the few grand resorts that remain, at the new ones that have come up in the traditional style, and at the maritime museums.

LAKE MICHIGAN IS…

A brilliant ice sculpture. It was formed during the Ice Age by the retreat of the Wisconsinan Glacier about 11,800 years ago.

The second-largest of the five Great Lakes by volume and the sixth-largest lake in the world.

The third-largest of the five Great Lakes in surface area, covering 22,300 square miles. It is about 300 miles long, an average of 75 miles wide, 118 miles across at its widest point, and up to 925 feet deep. It is the only of the Great Lakes that lies wholly within the United States. Its shoreline is over 1,600 miles long.

The largest body of freshwater in the United States.

Linked to the four other Great Lakes, the St. Lawrence River, and the Atlantic Ocean via the St. Lawrence Seaway. Along this 2,340-mile navigable waterway, iron ore, coal, grain, and manufactured products are shipped between lake ports and overseas.

Home to the world's largest freshwater dunes and the world's longest annual freshwater race.

Known throughout history as many things: Michig-gama, Grand Lac, Lake of the Stinking Water, Lake of the Puants, Lac St. Joseph, Lac Dauphin, and Lac des Illinois.

A graveyard for ships. No one knows for sure how many schooners, steamers, and other vessels have gone down, but of an estimated 10,000 on all five of the Great Lakes, about 700 are thought to have sunk in Lake Michigan.

Closing in on its 400th birthday. It was discovered by French explorer Jean Nicolet in 1634.

NAUTICAL DÉCOR

You do not have to be an avid sailor, a retired U.S. Coast Guard officer, or the proud owner of a lake cottage to enjoy the nautical gifts that are sold at shops up and down the lakeshore. You need only to appreciate the range of feelings these objects evoke. A certain breeziness, a simplicity of line in the sail of a decorative boat, a cleanliness of the color blue are all so universally appealing. The placement of a simple wood-and-canvas sailboat upon a coffee table will catch the eye and stir up memories of fine summer days. A funky fish, complete with lips and teeth, will make people smile. Kids, too, can be inspired by nautical décor, such as an antique binnacle that could lead to a whole new world of discovery. Whatever the particular items and whatever their style, nautical décor touches us in a way that is as elemental as our connection to water. So go ahead, visit the shops, and splurge a little. This stuff—even a fish with lips—will never go out of style.

CROSSING THE LAKE

Whether by ferry or under sail, it is still a thrill to cross Lake Michigan. We have the stately SS *Badger* and the speedy *Lake Express*, and who knows how many more ferries will take to these waters in the future? Drama, romance, and tradition swirl around the Chicago to Mackinac Race that has, since 1898, been connecting sailors with the elements of wind and water, and enthusiasts with the spirit of adventure. Indeed, the Mac is the longest annual freshwater race in the world. Advanced technology is making it easier than ever for spectators to follow its progress every knot of the way.

ENVIRONMENT

Lake Michigan looks so pretty—how can it be in trouble?

The troubles that plague Lake Michigan are the same that increasingly threaten lakes across the country: pollution, water quality, beach closings, waves of invasive species, and native fish unable to reproduce.

What can we do about this? The folks at Wisconsin-based Great Lakes Forever say that a visit to the lakeshore is the best time to start doing something. And what they suggest is so easy it can be summed up in three words: "leave nothing behind." Here are their suggestions:

Plan ahead by bringing things with you instead of buying disposable products once you arrive, because it all adds up to pollution. Skip the bottled water and bring a container to refill from taps and fountains, the water you get will be from Lake Michigan;

Leave nothing in or around the lake, including cigarette butts and other waste material;

Clean up pet waste; it improves the environment for bacterial organisms, but certainly not for us;

Stamp out invasive species by cleaning boat rudders, trailer wheels, and even feet and water shoes before you put them into different bodies of water; do not dump live bait into the water, as bait can sometimes be exotic or invasive species;

Respect wildlife by not feeding it. It is lovely to interact with wild ones, but feeding them can disrupt their natural way of life. By giving them something, we have also taken away what makes them special—their wildness. Also, too many droppings in a concentrated area often contributes to beach closings. Respect hunting and fishing regulations.

FROM THE GALLEYS . . . TO THE DOCKS

Travel can be tiring, so within the book you'll find brief listings of recommended places to eat and stay along each tour. "From the Galleys" lists and describes selected restaurants, most of which feature fish on the menu and often a waterfront view. They range from casual to fine dining, and there is even an occasional 1950s-era drive-in.

"To the Docks" lists suggested accommodations. Most are on the water or have lake views, while others invite guests to celebrate the spirit of the lake with nautical décor. There are many lodging styles to choose from: bed and breakfasts, boutique inns, resorts, cottages, hotels, motels, condotels, and boatels. Heck, you can even bed down on the occasional submarine cot.

AIDS TO NAVIGATION

Travel planning resources are listed at the end of each tour to ensure smooth sailing on your journeys around Lake Michigan. Each tour concludes with a short list of the convention and visitor bureaus and chambers of commerce in the area. There are also detailed maps for each tour. Finally, a comprehensive list of Web sites will take you to the lake even before you leave the home port.

WAVING GOODBYE

As you read this book, you may find yourself thinking, "We haven't been to places like these since the kids were little."

But then you remember how much you enjoyed yourself at those places.

And you realize you would love to go again—for yourself this time.

But if you need one more reason to go back to the lake, take the following piece of advice from children everywhere. Best yelled at the top of your lungs while running down the length of a wooden pier glistening with footprints, it is this: "Last one in is a rotten egg!"

WISCONSIN

WISCONSIN'S MOST celebrated stretch of shoreline is the Door County Peninsula. Here, with water on two sides and a classic resort character, you are sure to enjoy yourself. But if all you saw of Wisconsin's shoreline was Door County, you would be missing a lot. Each harbor town along Lake Michigan has a unique story to tell, a unique maritime heritage to share, and unique vistas to show you. From Kenosha in the south to Marinette in the north, it is an intriguing collection of ports that are so much fun to explore, whether that means sunbathing on a beach or marveling at the boatbuilding traditions. Milwaukee, of course, is the big city where the possibilities for fun and exploration seem never to end.

But everywhere, things are changing. As the industrial lakefront becomes a recreational playground, boaters and landlubbers are finding more and more ways to enjoy the lake. Right now, Sheboygan is on a roll, and if you have not yet seen its massive Blue Harbor Resort, you need to put it on your calendar. While you're at it, climb a lighthouse tower or two, and hop a tour boat from one exciting destination to another. For divers, Wisconsin Maritime Trails, which is a partnership of the Wisconsin Historical Society, the University of Wisconsin Sea Grant Institute, and the Wisconsin Coastal Management Program, is making it easier than ever to explore fantastic shipwrecks while protecting them for future generations. Non-divers need not feel as if they have been stranded on shore; recently, Maritime Trails posted signage on land sites near the wrecks, so that land-dwellers, too, can experience this fascinating part of maritime history.

Kenosha to Racine

"There really isn't any place you can go in the Midwest and catch the fish that we catch. It's really that way up and down the lake. We take a lot of people from Iowa, downstate Illinois, and they fish rivers and ponds and inland lakes, and they come out here and they're just blown away by what we can catch in just a half day."

—Captain Dave Scott, Kenosha Charter Boat Association, Kenosha

WISCONSIN'S southernmost stretch of lakeshore is fast becoming a popular lakefront destination. It begins in Kenosha, which is roughly halfway between Chicago and Milwaukee—about 50 miles either way—and within viewing distance of Racine.

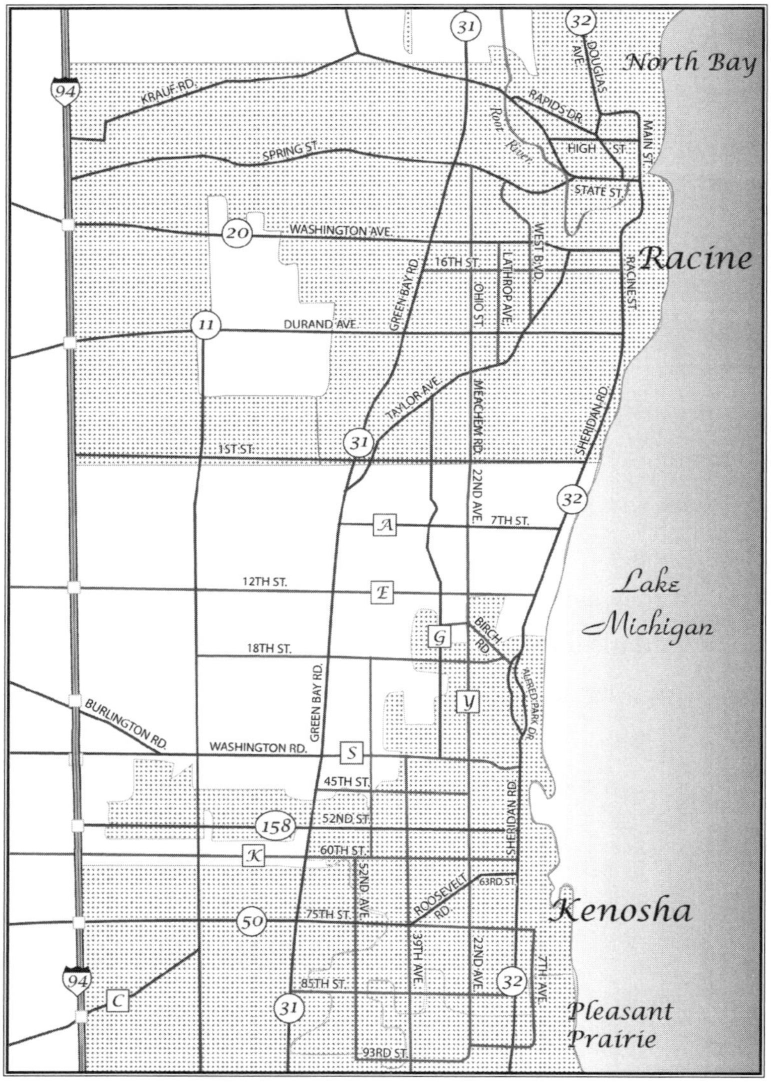

Kenosha

In the city from which sleek sedans once rolled off the assembly line, today the Kenosha lakefront belongs to salmon fishermen, dog walkers, museum-goers, lighthouse lovers, boaters, and others who know how free time is best spent. Join them across acres of shoreline that offer plenty of recreational excitement and peaceful seclusion.

Kenosha was once called Southport because it represented Wisconsin's southernmost port.Today the city is embracing its lakefront past in order to craft a present-day experience unlike anything that came before. Hop a trolley and plunk down a coin for a ride to the many exciting attractions along the lakefront. Five colorful streetcars transport you on a two-mile loop that includes Southport Marina, Harbor Park, and other points of interest.

Just across the harbor, the cream city

brick tower of the **Southport Light Station**, Simmons Island Park, 50th Street and Lighthouse Drive (4th Avenue), Kenosha, Wisconsin 53140, (262) 654-5770, points 55 feet into the sky, as it has since 1866. Cream city brick tops the stone foundation. Enjoy the two-story keeper's quarters (small houses typically adjacent a lighthouse where the lighthouse keeper lived), recently opened as a maritime museum, including a tower tour up 72 steps. Down a grassy slope from the lighthouse is the **Kenosha History Center**, 220 51st Place, Kenosha, Wisconsin 53140, (262) 654-5770, www. kenoshahistorycenter.org. Here you can stroll the streets of old Kenosha, where life-size facades replicate period buildings. View gleaming cars from the Rambler automaking era. Nearby, the new 56,000 square-foot **Civil War Museum**, 5400 First Avenue, Kenosha, Wisconsin 53140, (262) 653-4140, www.thecivilwarmuseum.org, opened with a bang in the spring of 2008. Immerse yourself in the experience of that conflict as it affected the settlers of Wisconsin, Michigan, Indiana, Illinois, Minnesota, and Iowa. Drop into their towns before the war, follow soldiers into battle, and return home with them to a changed Midwest. Life-size exhibits, personal papers, photographs, weapons, currency, and uniforms all help visitors understand the local story.

The past takes on mammoth proportions inside the glacier-inspired architecture of the **Kenosha Public Museum**, 5500 First Avenue, Kenosha, Wisconsin 53140, (262) 653-4140, www.kenoshapublicmuseum.org, where you can trace the timeline of life around the area from trilobite beginnings to settlement. The towering woolly mammoth is a replica, as is the one not faring so well at the hands of Paleo Indians who are rapidly turning it into dinner. But the woolly mammoth bones lying at your feet are the real thing, carbon-dated to 12,500 years old. Some of the bones bear cut marks, indicating that the animal was butchered by humans. But this legacy would have been left one thousand years before man is supposed to have been in the Americas.

Get more lake views just to the south in the Third Avenue Historic District, where the **Durkee Mansion**, Kemper Center, 6501 Third Avenue, Kenosha, Wisconsin 53143, (262) 657-6005, offers a peek into gracious living and the largest suspension stairway in Wisconsin. While running around town, look for the Fish Mosaic at Simmons Island Fish Cleaning Station, the Sailing Ship Sculpture at Harbor Park, and the Fish Bowl at Tot Park.

River pirates, voyageurs, military troops, a ship-to-shore battle with real cannon fire—it's either the 17th century or the annual Pike River Rendezvous on Simmons Island (www.kenosha.org). Attend this free event in early August and enjoy the swashbuckling bluster along with great food, including buffalo burgers and Indian fry bread. Be sure to grab a meat pie at the Kenosha Public Museum. Visit the wigwams and tents of re-enactors' camps, and watch blacksmiths, tinsmiths, and woodworkers ply their trades. Put the kids to work grinding corn.

Wind Point Lighthouse, Racine, Wisconsin

A mile northwest of the Durkee Mansion, make tracks for the new **Dinosaur Discovery Museum**, 5608 Tenth Avenue, Kenosha, Wisconsin 53140, (262) 653-4460, www.dinosaurdiscoverymuseum.org, which is housed in a Beaux Arts building that is a relic in itself. Visitors of all ages will enjoy this new museum. Here you can discover the link between ancient dinosaurs and present-day birds. A great series of life-size replica casts of Tyrannosaurus rex, Ceratosaurus, and others of their kind will thrill the kids. Find out why dinosaur fossils cannot be found in Wisconsin. Interact with bones and fossils, and observe real paleontology students at work in their on-site paleontology lab, where they prepare and conserve specimens unearthed during recent field school expeditions that will ultimately be displayed. Or unearth your own prehistoric finds on a Family Fossil Trek, which is only one of the Kenosha Public Museum's many outstanding programs.

Need a break from all that history for lunch? A stop at **Tenuta's**, 3203 52nd Street (Highway 158), Kenosha, Wisconsin 53144, (262) 657-9001, www.tenutasdeli.com, will set you up with delicious Italian specialties from marinated mushrooms and bulk olives to cheeses, sandwiches, and dessert pastries—perfect for packing a picnic or just grabbing a midday snack.

Getting out onto the water is as easy as calling the **Kenosha Charter Boat Association**, (800) 522-6699, www.kenoshacharterboat.com, whose 14 member captains will take you up to four miles offshore for some of the best salmon fishing on Lake

Michigan. Feel the thrill of fish strikes and the slap of waves beneath a craft that is all yours for a half or whole day. Depending on the time of year and other conditions, you may be able to reel in Chinook (King) or Coho Salmon, or Brown, Lake, or Rainbow Trout. While on board, learn as much or as little as you want—such as what a dipsy diver does —and don't forget to pack sandwiches and snacks. No experience is needed, and both individuals and groups are welcomed. Back on land, they will either fillet or gut your catch for you. Afterward, a short drive north of the marina through Simmons Island takes you to Kiwanis Park and the rocky lakeshore on your way up to Racine.

End your day on a sweet note by touring the **Jelly Belly Visitor Center**, 10100 Jelly Belly Lane, Pleasant Prairie, Wisconsin 53158, (866) TOUR-JBC, www.jellybelly.com. It is located eight miles southwest of the Harbor Park attractions in neighboring Kenosha. If you need convincing, take note that the next closest one is in California; and better yet, everyone rides in a little train and gets free samples at the end of the line. Needless to say, the kids will want to do this; but just remember that these are *gourmet* jelly beans, so the adults can get just as excited.

Ready to move on to Racine? It is just 10 miles north of Kenosha.

Racine

Extravagant power yachts and sailboats glide across the water. Jagged rocks keep the lake at bay while also lending it a ruggedly handsome shoreline. Out on the farthest breakwater and above the Racine Reef that had once been so treacherous to maritime vessels, people fish and, if they are lucky, put the nearby fish cleaning station to use. Here in Racine, home of the Great Lakes' largest privately owned marina, you will know it's July when **Big Fish Bash** (formerly Salmon-A-Rama) fever hits town. The world's largest freshwater fishing tournament, Big Fish reels in over a

KNOT A PROBLEM

Why is the Racine Danish Kringle shaped like a racetrack? To answer that, you have to go back to the Danes' ties to the sea. Seems that the word *kringle* is an old Danish nautical term for certain knots, and the true Kringle shape involves overlapping the dough in the center, in the way of a knot or pretzel. Fast-forward to the 1940s when customers of the Danish bakeries in Racine began to request that their Kringle not be tied up in knots, so that they could get more filling per slice. It was tinkering with tradition that the bakers were willing to go along with; but, hey, this was America.

"A pretzel-shaped Kringle requires the pastry have three points of overlap. Each overlap requires double the pastry and a significant reduction of the filling. Here in Racine, Kringle has metamorphosed to the oval shape and there is no interest in changing back to the pretzel shape," said Eric Olesen of O&H Danish Bakery.

One thing the family bakers of O&H would never change, however, is their amazingly flaky pastry. Olesen explained why it takes three days to achieve it.

"The dough is alternately rolled and rested so that a light, tender, flaky pastry is achieved. Multiple layers of butter and margarine create the texture and flavor of the wonderful Kringle dough commonly referred to as wienerbrod by Danes. When shortcuts are taken the dough can easily become butter-flavored bread lacking the flaky texture our Kringle fans adore."

And shortcuts are taken, but not in the Olesen family kitchens. "Few people have the patience and commitment necessary to bake great Kringle. The Olesen family has it!" affirmed Eric Olesen.

It is not an overstatement. You really can taste the difference. So race to Racine for flaky, racetrack-shaped Kringle, but don't take any shortcuts along the way.

thousand fishermen from all over the country, who try to win big prizes including boats, fishing gear, and cash. This is a serious contest that involves polygraph testing to ensure compliance with rules, including when the fish was caught and that it was by hook and line. Contestants may register in either shore or boat categories, and prizes are awarded to the largest fish by weight. The concurrent Family Festival keeps everyone happy with live music and all kinds of food, from butterfly pork chop sandwiches to a deep-fried candy bar on a stick. If it's August, the competition heats up during the **Sand Castles** festival; teams of up to 10 build sand sculptures to entertain visitors at this family event.

Continue driving north from the Racine harbor to experience three outstanding shoreline sites. First up is **North Beach**, 1501 Michigan Boulevard, Racine, Wisconsin 53402, (262) 636-9233, www.cityofracine.org, which has received recognition and even awards for its cleanliness. If you have little ones along on the trip, they might not let you get past the Kids' Cove wooden play structure, which reels them in with colorful, beach-themed allure. Less than a mile north is the **Racine Zoological Gardens**, 2131 North Main Street, Racine, Wisconsin 53402, (262) 636-9189, www.racinezoo.org. Pretty perennials greet you alongside paths that wind around to the homes of 250 animals representing 76 species. An inquisitive emu would love to get closer to visitors if only that pond was not there, but a jaded lioness cannot be bothered to turn her head. The zoo's newest habitats showcase biodiversity hotspots that are considered to be the most biologically rich and threatened places on earth. Here, heated dens and private breeding caves enhance the inhabitants' experience of zoo life.

The third stop is **Wind Point Lighthouse**, Lighthouse Drive (between Three and Four Mile Roads), Wind Point, Wisconsin 53402, (262) 639-3777. Tucked in among civilized homes about three miles north of the zoo, this immaculate white beacon was built in 1880 and is still active today. Forest green trim and a bright red roof decorate the adjacent keeper's quarters, which serves as Wind Point's village hall, police headquarters, and caretaker's residence. You are welcome to pick up a brochure and walk the grounds to the outbuildings and to the lovely beach below. "Tours to the Top" of this 108-foot tower are scheduled several times throughout the year.

Let's drive back into downtown Racine now for a little museum-hopping. The **Racine Heritage Museum**, 701 Main Street, Racine, Wisconsin 53402, (262) 636-3926, www.racineheritagemuseum.org, is housed within an intriguing stone building that just bursts with the story of Racine. Head upstairs for a little perspective on "Our Maritime History." The luxury boats you see in the marina outside? They are just the latest chapter in Racine's long-time maritime tradition. As the exhibit explains, Racine was the Great Lakes' fifth-busiest shipping port by 1848, and boat-building began here in 1878. View a sleek early-model Old Town Canoe on display at the museum; and if you want to buy your own canoe, head just a couple blocks down the road to the **Johnson Outdoors Retail Store**, 555 Main Street, Racine, Wisconsin 53402, (262) 631-6700.

After leaving the store, cross the street to the sand-colored **Racine Art Museum**, 441 Main Street, Racine, Wisconsin 53401, (262) 638-8300, www.ramart.org. This is not your traditional art museum, and not because it showcases contemporary paintings. It is because art is viewed a little differently here, and it is not all about what can be hung on the wall. Forget paintings and think pottery—gorgeous pots that blur the line between sculpture and function, gloriously impractical pots that hold nothing but your attention. Here, craft is art, and your contemplation of it is time well spent.

Where to next? The folks at the downtown store, **Dover Flag & Map**, 323 South Main Street, Racine, Wisconsin 53403, (262) 632-3133, (866) 266-6277, can tell you where to go. Their mountains of maps are displayed like greeting cards and are backed by this guarantee: "If you ever get lost, just call, and we'll tell you where to go!" Shop for navigation charts and nautical gifts, including charming resin lighthouses, and greet a resident cat or two.

But you will not need a map to find the next stop. Just follow the locals to **O&H Danish Bakery**, which has two locations in town: 1841 Douglas Avenue, Racine, Wisconsin 53402, (262) 637-8895; and 4006 Durand Avenue, Racine, Wisconsin 53405, (262) 554-1311, www.ohdanishbakery.com. What comes out of the O&H ovens is Old World pas-try that is buttery and flaky and generously filled and iced. The flaky part is critical to the Kringle; and here, they get it just right, as they have since 1949. Pecan and Raspberry always top the bestseller list, but the Olesen boys offer plenty of other addictive choices, such as cherry-cheese and chocolate.

On your way up to the excitement and vibrancy of Wisconsin's largest city—Milwaukee—drink in the peaceful views from **Cliffside County Park**, 7320 Michna Road, Racine, Wisconsin 53402, (262) 886-8400, www.racine.org, and have a bite of that Kringle.

FROM THE GALLEYS

Boat House Pub & Eatery, 4917 7th Avenue, Kenosha, Wisconsin 53140, (262) 654-9922. Nautical décor, rich woods, brass fixtures, and lakefront views get you in the mood for clam chowder, delicious fish and seafood specialties, and summertime shore lunches. Bring your own catch from a charter run, and they will fry, bake, or broil it, and serve it to you with fries, a roll, and coleslaw. Complementary docking for diners' boats up to 50 feet in length.

HobNob Restaurant & Cocktail Lounge, 277 South Sheridan Road (State Highway 32, between Kenosha and Racine), Racine, Wisconsin 53403, (262) 552-8008, www.thehobnob.com. Traditional lakeside dining since 1954. Take a cocktail onto the lakeside terrace and relax to the rhythm of the waves. Seafood choices include sea scallops over a bed of rock salt, and farm-raised salmon with crunchy, curly, shoestring sweet potatoes.

Lucarelli's Docks Waterfront Restaurant, 2 Christopher Columbus Causeway, Racine, Wisconsin 53403, (262) 633-6990. Dine indoors or out on seafood, steaks, and specialties while feasting your eyes on the beauty of the harborfront.

TO THE DOCKS

Best Western Harborside Inn & Kenosha Conference Center, 5125 6th Avenue, Kenosha, Wisconsin 53140, (262) 658-3281. Harborside rooms offer panoramic views of the Harbor Park and yacht club scenes, along with the lighthouse and U.S. Coast Guard station. Continental breakfast, indoor pool, and whirlpool.

Radisson Inn Harbourwalk, 223 Gaslight Circle, Racine, Wisconsin 53403, (262) 632-7777. Luxury boats snooze in quiet waters, and the 9.8-mile Lake Michigan Pathway passes just steps from the hotel. The indoor pool and hot tub overlook the harbor through floor-to-ceiling windows that bring the outdoors in. Deluxe continental breakfast includes heavenly slices of Danish Kringle.

AIDS TO NAVIGATION

Kenosha Area Convention & Visitors Bureau, (800) 654-7309, www.kenoshacvb.com.

Racine County Convention & Visitors Bureau, (800) 272-2463, www.racine.org.

Milwaukee Lakefront

"People gathered in Milwaukee forever because it had three rivers coming in to the lake."
—Mary McAndrews, Tour Guide, Historic Milwaukee

COME EXPLORE THIS major Great Lakes port that is reinventing itself by folding the past into the present. Here a worker polishes a brand new RiverWalk sign. Old brick manufacturing plants have become stylish stages for hot restaurants, sizzling specialty shops, and cool condominiums. An array of tour boats, charters, and ferries makes Lake Michigan ever more attractive and accessible. How about a lighthouse tour, followed by lunch and latté in a nineteenth-century river flushing station that now houses the popular Alterra on the Lake café? Now is the time to explore Wisconsin's largest city and its 1,200 acres of lakefront parkland. Find it all about 30 miles north of Racine and about 60 miles south of Sheboygan.

It is a celebration of the lake, and when it opened in 2006, it made a splash on the Milwaukee lakefront. Welcome to **Discovery World at Pier Wisconsin**, 500 North Harbor Drive, Milwaukee, Wisconsin 53202, (414) 765-9966, www.pierwisconsin.org. What is this place? Part public science lab, part aquarium, part lakefront gathering place, and part architectural destination, Discovery World defies categorization. But this much is clear: Discovery World is about water. It starts at the dock where the 137-foot, three-masted schooner ***S/V Denis Sullivan*** sets sail throughout the summer with up to 50 passengers on day sails, and up to 18 for overnight adventures. Built in 2000 to replicate a 1800s sailing vessel, the S/V *Denis Sullivan* is a sight to behold on the Milwaukee lakefront. Those aboard thrill to the elements of wind and waves, and also help hoist a sail or two.

High-flying cow and other kites redefine Milwaukee skyline from lakefront park, Milwaukee, Wisconsin

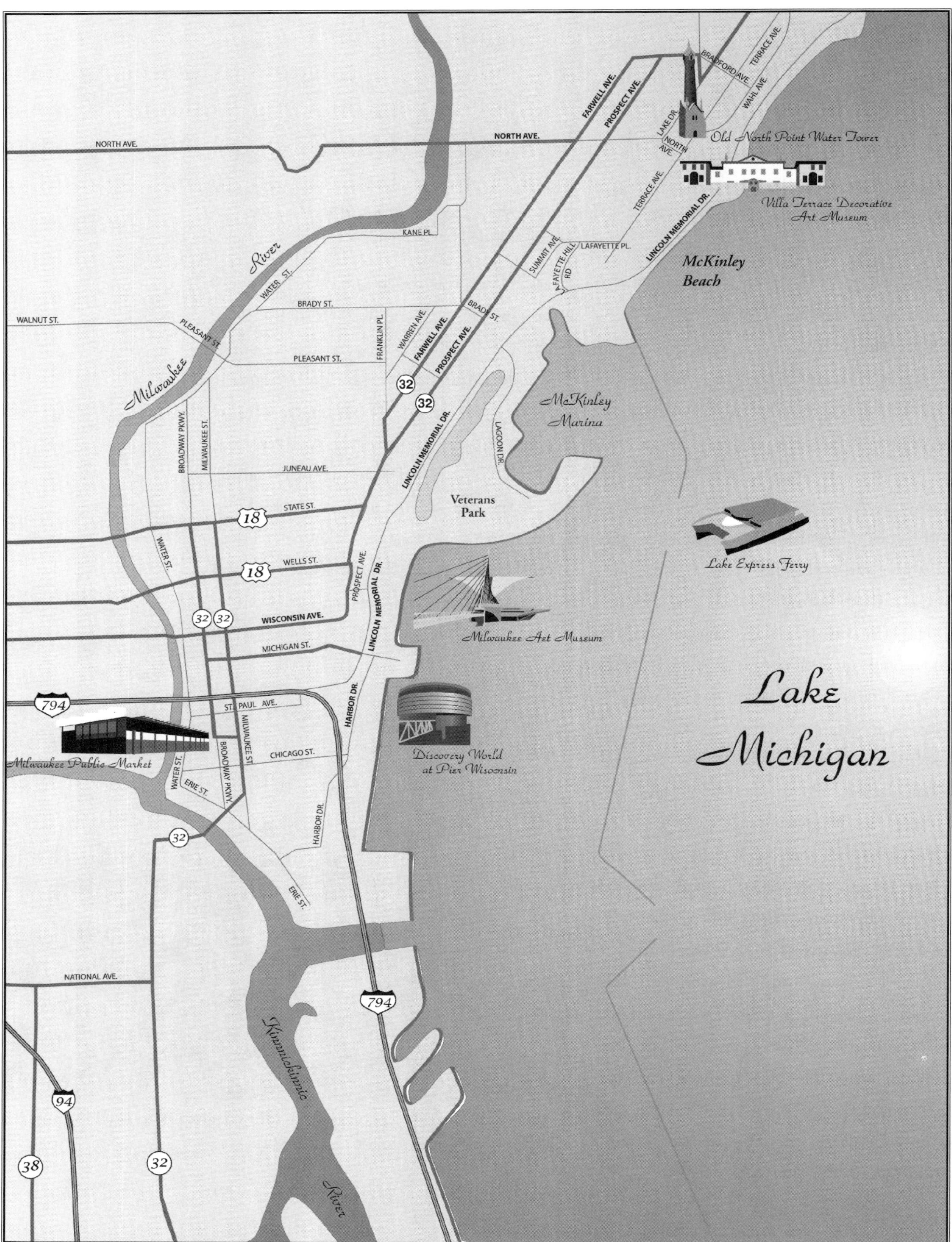
Lake Michigan
Old North Point Water Tower
Villa Terrace Decorative Art Museum
McKinley Beach
McKinley Marina
Veterans Park
Lake Express Ferry
Milwaukee Art Museum
Discovery World at Pier Wisconsin
Milwaukee Public Market
Milwaukee River
Kinnickinnic River
NORTH AVE.
FARWELL AVE.
PROSPECT AVE.
BRADFORD AVE.
TERRACE AVE.
WAHL AVE.
LAKE DR.
KANE PL.
WATER ST.
BRADY ST.
WALNUT ST.
PLEASANT ST.
FRANKLIN PL.
WARREN AVE.
SUMMIT AVE.
LAFAYETTE HILL RD
LAFAYETTE PL.
LINCOLN MEMORIAL DR.
LAGOON DR.
BROADWAY PKWY.
MILWAUKEE ST.
JUNEAU AVE.
STATE ST.
WELLS ST.
WISCONSIN AVE.
MICHIGAN ST.
ST. PAUL AVE.
CHICAGO ST.
ERIE ST.
HARBOR DR.
NATIONAL AVE.
18
32
794
94
38

Thanks to on-board distance learning equipment, those on shore can explore the waters through which the ship sails, all the way to her winter home in the Caribbean. Inside Discovery World, fresh and saltwater aquarium exhibits and a research lab make it easy to study the differences between these marine environments. Other interactive opportunities include City of Freshwater, with its Liquid House that explores the water system within your own home; the Sea of Sustainability that harnesses chemistry, biology, and atmospheric science to study water; and Great Lakes Future, a scale replica of the Great Lakes Watershed, complete with live aquatic creatures.

Less than half a mile away is the **Milwaukee Art Museum**, 700 North Art Museum Drive, Milwaukee, Wisconsin 53202, (414) 224-3200, www.mam.org, which has become the city's most recognizable landmark and a true celebration of the shoreline. The building's creator, Santiago Calatrava, drew inspiration for his architectural masterpiece from maritime culture. Look for such influence in the 200-foot mast that soars above the cabled pedestrian bridge, the galleria that curves like a wave, and the moveable sun screen that spreads like the wings of a bird. The sun screen, called the Burke Brise Soleil, spans 217 feet, which is comparable to that of a Boeing 747 aircraft. The museum houses nearly twenty thousand pieces of art dating from antiquity to the present. The ancient artworks were first collected to demonstrate art's evolution, but are now recognized in their own right. European masterworks from the seventeenth through the twentieth centuries include works by Rembrandt,

View of *Denis Sullivan*, Milwaukee, Wisconsin

STEPHEN BEAUMONT

Milwaukee Art Museum

Renoir, Degas, and Monet.

Follow the **LakeWalk** footpath north from the museum for endless views of soft green grass, the city skyline, and the water. Have a picnic lunch, rent a paddleboat or bicycle, fly a kite, or hire a fishing charter or sailboat. If you want to save your strength, you can park near the lagoon for the paddleboat rental; the other recreational opportunities are clustered near the lakeshore. The entire parkland offers plenty of parking options.

SEE THE LIGHT

Stone lions guard the lighthouse that has kept watch over all the mariners who have passed by this shore since 1855. This is the **North Point Lighthouse**, Wahl Avenue and Terrace Avenue (park at Lake Park Pavilion), Milwaukee, Wisconsin 53201, (414) 332-6754, www.northpointlighthouse.org. Decommissioned in 1994 and now open only to visitors, the tower, which is uniquely built of bolted cast iron, measures 74 feet and rises an impressive 160 feet above the waves that crash against the shoreline below. A wild tangle of plants clings to the ravines that lead up to the tower. The keeper's quarters, which has been reconnected to the tower by a covered passageway, houses an exhibition gallery that includes the tower's original fourth order Fresnel lens. Surrounding the lighthouse and its attendant lions are the green grasses and recreational pathways of Lake Park, which was laid out by Frederick Law Olmsted during the Gilded Age of the 1890s.

Lincoln Memorial Drive whisks you north to McKinley Beach with its sand wrapped in the arms of two breakwaters. Behind the beach and up on a bluff, the **Villa Terrace Decorative Arts Museum**, 2220 North Terrace Avenue, Milwaukee, Wisconsin 53202, (414) 271-3656, www.cavtmuseums.org, poses to artful advantage like an Italian beauty queen. Her exquisite garden-gown, which is adorned with petals and leaves, cascades all the way down to the level of the lake. Visit this grand lady and her collection of fine and decorative arts that hail from the fifteenth through eighteenth centuries. Afterward, it is worth a quick stop to drive or walk north to North Avenue at the University of Wisconsin-Milwaukee campus, where the 1873 **Old North Point Water Tower** rises 175 feet in Gothic splendor and overlooks the lake in the way of a lighthouse. The tower's cut Niagara limestone and patina-green roof form a most elegant sheath for the wrought iron standpipe that is hidden within. Signage explains how this historic tower served a crucial purpose during Milwaukee's bitterly cold winters.

Now drive north to the **Schlitz Audubon Nature Center**, 1111 East Brown Deer Road, Milwaukee, Wisconsin 53217, (414) 352-2880, www.schlitzauduboncenter.com, where 185 acres of ponds, ravines, woodlands, and prairies are a haven for wildlife and nature-lovers on the shores of Lake Michigan. Enjoy six miles of trails where the Joseph Schlitz Brewing Company draft horses once grazed. To get your bearings, know that the nature center is located 13 miles north of the art museum.

Head back into town to catch up with some fascinating walking tours. **Historic Milwaukee, Inc.**, 828 North Broadway, Suite 110, Milwaukee, Wisconsin 53202, (414) 277-7795, www.historicmilwaukee.org, supplies intrepid guides for a variety of forays such as **Lake Drive Mansions**. This tour showcases residences that were built in a privileged enclave during the city's Gold Coast era from the 1890s to the 1920s. In this area north of downtown, mature trees shade long driveways, notably on the lakefront side of Lake Drive. But don't expect to see much of the lake from Lake Drive—that pleasure is reserved for the homeowners and is indeed part of the mystique for the rest of us. Today some of the Lake Drive mansions have the highest property values in the county. The tour begins at the English Tudor style Alumni House of the University of Wisconsin-Milwaukee, which is said to be the largest mansion within the city limits. Originally a private residence, it has 18 bedrooms, a beach, an Olympic-size pool, formal gardens, and a tunnel that leads nowhere. Don't miss the house whose garage has a turntable so that vehicles could be driven out facing the right way. Another of the Lake Drive mansions was relocated and rebuilt here in 1928 when the city wanted to tear it down for parkland. Stone by stone and piece by piece, it was taken apart and numbered. At more than 124,000 square feet, that must have been some jigsaw puzzle.

Join Historic Milwaukee's **RiverWalk** tour to find out why Gertie the Duck became famous, and look up to see the neon fish swimming across the side of a building. Called "Dream with the Fishes," this delightful public sculpture glows at night and reflects its colors into the water. Learn how a century-old architectural principle helped make today's RiverWalk experience not only delightful but also possible, and learn why many Milwaukee bridges span the river at angles rather than straight across.

SUZANNE TUCKER

Historic Third Ward and Public Market, Milwaukee, Wisconsin

After this tour, you may wish to continue on your own along the RiverWalk past waving prairie grasses and right into the **Historic Third Ward**. This reinvented neighborhood bordered by the Milwaukee River, the city's downtown, and the lakefront park is where all those great ethnic and music festivals blast off each year. This hot up-and-coming district boasts stylish new storefronts and hip restaurants amid vintage manufacturing buildings. Enjoy the creative ambience of galleries, boutiques, eateries, and architectural details restored to vintage perfection. While in the neighborhood, fill your picnic basket with the goodness of regional farms and ovens at the deliciously new **Milwaukee Public Market**, 400 North Water Street, Milwaukee, Wisconsin 53202, (414) 336-1111, www.milwaukeepublicmarket.org. This year-round indoor market is the future of the past, as the Third Ward was historically a center for produce vendors. As you explore the ward, look for the markers that tell the story of how it came to be. You'll find it's got quite a history: In the nineteenth century, Irish immigrants populated the ward; they were among those killed in 1860 when the *Lady Elgin* sank in Lake Michigan off Winnetka, Illinois. Then, in 1892, a devastating fire destroyed 16 square blocks at an estimated cost of $5 million. After the fire, though, rebuilding began in earnest and was accomplished in a relatively short period of time. This is precisely why the ward you see today retains such a cohesive, and delightfully authentic, appeal.

Next is a tour that concentrates on a maritime story that is as fascinating as it is obscure. Led by a different group, **Urban Anthropology**, (414) 271-9417, www.urban-anthropology.org, it is called "The People Nobody Knew: The Kashubes of Jones Island." It involves lunch, a fishing boat, and an island, and it's more an adventure than a tour. Not surprisingly, it sells out every time, so plan ahead. Meet your anthropologist at the corner of Bay/Becher Street and Kinnickinnic Avenue for a 2.5-hour jaunt that opens with information about Indian settlements and later migrations. It continues at Barnacle Buds Fish, which overlooks Jones Island. There you can enjoy lunch and watch Urban Anthropology's own documentary that features some surviving members and descendants of the extinct fishing village. Board a fishing boat to circle the island while the captain tells stories of what happened there so long ago.

In Milwaukee, you can also get out on the water aboard a variety of cruises and day-sails. **Riverwalk Boat Cruises**, (414) 283-9999, www. riverwalkboats.com, is big on cocktail cruises, but if you want to learn something, too, try their Educational/Historic Tour. It includes museum time and teaches about the biology of the Milwaukee River, architectural points of interest, history of the area, and the latest developments of modern-day Milwaukee. The Educational/Historic Tour is offered on weekdays only, and requires a minimum of 25 passengers.

Or try the ***Blue Chip***, which docks at McKinley Center Marina, G Dock, Slip 1, (414) 687-3203. This 34-foot sailing yacht takes you to where breezes and sunshine and a little spray off the water are all you need for a good time on the lake. Are the stars out tonight? Then board the ***Edelweiss I*** or ***II*** at 1110 North Old World Third Street (Third and Juneau), Milwaukee, Wisconsin 53203, (414) 272-0330, www.eidelweissboats.com, for a dinner cruise that takes you down the river and out to the Lake Michigan harbor for magnificent skyline views.

The 1892 **Pabst Mansion**, 2000 West Wisconsin Avenue, Milwaukee, Wisconsin 53233, (414) 931-0808, www.pabstmansion.com, is located a wee bit farther inland, but it bears a timeless connection to the lake in that its original owner. Captain Frederick Pabst, was in fact a captain on Lake Michigan ships before he became a beer baron. Apparently, though, he never lost his love for the lake, for he retained the title of captain throughout his entire life. As you take the guided tour of his Flemish Renaissance Revival mansion, you will notice other signs of his lifelong love affair with the lake, such as the oil painting of a nineteenth-century side-wheeler on the door of the home safe, and other paintings depicting scenes of the sea.

Isn't it time to join those who still gather by the waters in Milwaukee?

FROM THE GALLEYS

Alterra at the Lake, 1701 North Lincoln Memorial Drive, Milwaukee, Wisconsin 53202, (414) 223-4551, www.alteracoffee.com. Who knew that a river flushing station built in 1888 would have just the right nooks and crannies for a cozy coffee and lunch spot? At the time of its construction, the station's pump was the largest of its kind in the world. It is still operational, but only used for general maintenance purposes. Specialty coffees are the specialty of the house, but you cannot go wrong with a Milwaukee-made Sprecher gourmet soda. Select from the small but super-fresh soups, sandwiches, and wraps that come with a choice of chips.

Coast, 931 East Wisconsin Avenue, Milwaukee, Wisconsin 53202, (414) 727-5555, www.coastrestaurant.com. Coast is perfectly situated near the lake and the art museum, and specializes in American fare from coast to coast. It features a good selection of seafood choices such as the New England Lobster Roll and the Floribbean Grilled Grouper with tropical flavors.

Pieces of Eight, 550 North Harbor Drive, Milwaukee, Wisconsin 53202, (414) 271-0597. Located on the lake, Pieces of Eight offers fresh seafood and steaks, prime rib, and a Friday seafood buffet

Third Street Pier, 1110 North Old World Third Street, Milwaukee, Wisconsin 53203, (414) 272-0330, www.wegmke.com. Their fresh, exciting seafood menu changes weekly (check menu online) and may include grilled Chilean salmon, pecan-crusted trout from Idaho, baked Alaskan halibut, Norwegian Dover sole, or other delightful choices, always freshly prepared. Enjoy great service, riverfront ambience, and the neighboring specialty shops of Old World Third Street. (You've been wanting to try Usinger's Famous Sausage, so why not try their Yachtwurst—coarse-cut lean pork shoulder blended with finely chopped beef, pistachios, and just enough garlic.)

TO THE DOCKS

Brumder Mansion, 3046 West Wisconsin Avenue, Milwaukee, Wisconsin 53208, (414) 342-9767, www.brumdermansion.com. If a friendly atmosphere in an antique-filled setting (with chocolate chip cookies thrown in for good measure) sounds like your cup of tea, then make Brumder Mansion your home for the night. Common areas set the stage for guests to thumb through antique books and photo albums before a massive oak fireplace, perhaps with a complementary glass of wine or soft drink in hand. Breakfast included.

The Knickerbocker on the Lake, 1028 East Juneau Avenue, Milwaukee, Wisconsin 53202, (414) 276-8500. Expect service that you thought went the way of white gloves in this grand dame hotel, which opened in 1933. Elegant lobby, well-appointed rooms, suites with home-size refrigerators and stoves, and an old-hotel atmosphere. Enjoy people-watching from outdoor seating at The Knick restaurant.

Comfort Inn & Suites Downtown Lakeshore, 916 East State Street, Milwaukee, Wisconsin 53202, (800) 328-PARK, (414) 276-8800, www.choicehotels.com. The lakefront is at the forefront of a stay where the rooms are beautifully appointed and the Aqua lounge and restaurant bubble with excitement. It is lovely to be outdoors on the rooftop patio, accompanied either by sunrises and church bells or sunsets and stars. Laid out before you from this vantage point is a view not unlike that found in Chicago's fashionable Lincoln Park, with serious runners, green space, and a generous stretch of lake. Here, though, you can also find parking—not to mention a fitness center and continental breakfast.

AIDS TO NAVIGATION

Visit Milwaukee (Greater Milwaukee Convention & Visitors Bureau), (800) 231-0903, www.visitmilwaukee.org.

Port Washington to Sheboygan

"I can safely say we're the only lighthouse in the United States whose tower and lantern arrived by FedEx."

—Linda Nenn, Historian and Co-director, Port Washington 1860 Light Station

"No matter how hot it gets, you can always go into Lake Michigan and turn blue if you want to."

—Jim Buchholz, Kohler-Andrae State Park

JUST 27 MILES NORTH of downtown Milwaukee you'll find Port Washington; and another 30 miles north on I-43 will take you to Sheboygan. From the seven hidden staircases of Port Washington to a shipwreck that was hauled out of Lake Michigan for permanent display in Sheboygan, this stretch of lakeshore boasts its own brand of maritime merit, and two of the most charming harbor towns around.

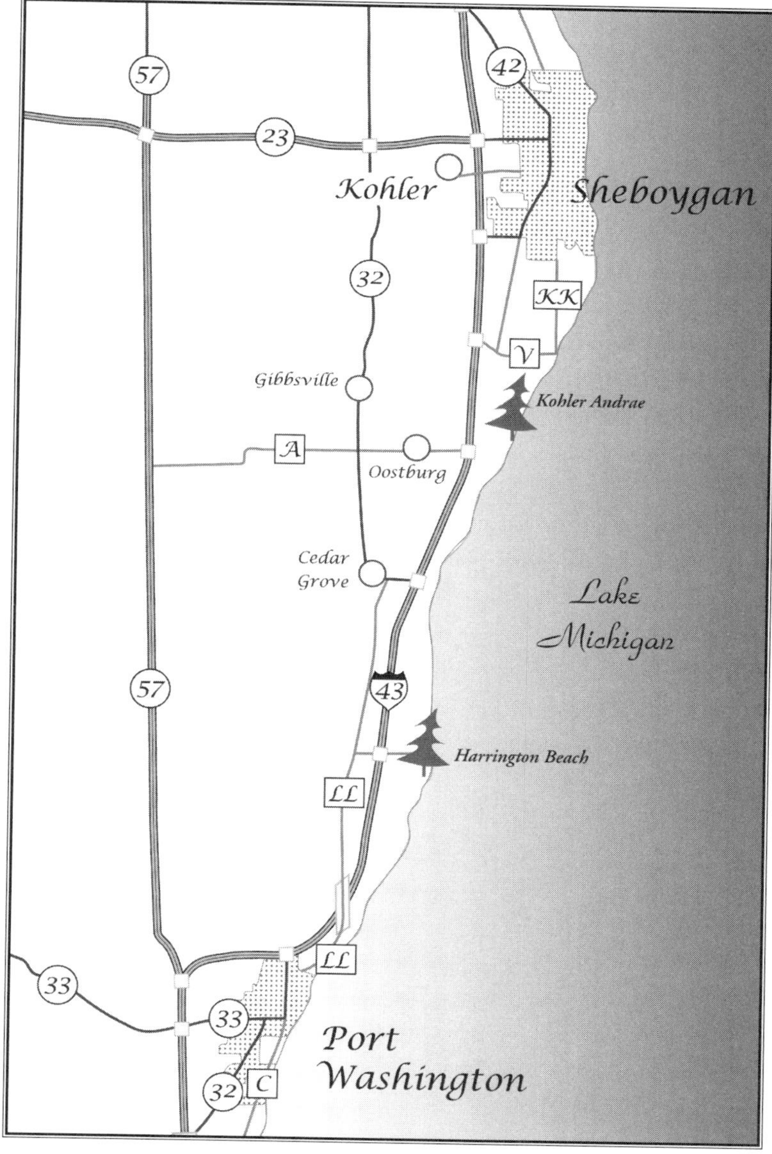

Port Washington

Despite the lack of both a river and a natural harbor, the settlers of Port Washington managed to craft a nautical heritage that today's residents celebrate in the form of light station tours, a unique art deco lighthouse, a storied seafood house, a large sportfishing fleet, a commercial fisherman's memorial, and fish festivals. Join them in April for the **American Legion Smelt Fry**, return in July for the **World's Largest One Day Outdoor Fish Fry** on **Fish Day,** tour tall ships during the **Maritime Heritage Festival** in July or August, and catch all the sailboat races and fishing derbies in between. Many events take place at the **Port Washington Marina**, 106 North Lake Street, Port Washington, Wisconsin 53074, (262) 284-6606, www.ci.port-washington.wi.us/Marina.html, which serves boaters with 244 slips and offers courtesy dockage to those stopping for lunch (for up to three hours, advance reservations accepted).

Port Washington harbor and art deco lighthouse sparkle from fourth-floor room in the Holiday Inn, Port Washington, Wisconsin

Birds on the beach, Kohler-Andrae State Park, Sheboygan, Wisconsin

Let's start at the **Port Washington 1860 Light Station**, 311 Johnson Street, Port Washington, Wisconsin 53074, (262) 284-7240, www.portlightstation.org. Perched on a hill that overlooks downtown Port Washington, the light station can be reached by one of seven hidden staircases or by car. This cream-brick building with tower inside has recently been restored—a project that has become the latest chapter in a long history.

"There was another lighthouse here in 1849, but it was built poorly and had to be replaced," notes curator and co-director Richard Smith. "But when we gutted this cottage, we started seeing evidence that they had reused part of the 1849 structure, so when you look right underneath the crown of the windows, you'll see a line of demarcation." The tower was rebuilt in 2002 by craftsmen from Luxembourg, after the U.S. Coast Guard decommissioned the station and lopped off the original tower in 1934. The tower and lantern room, which visitors ages six and above can climb, only rise 14 feet; but to get the harbor view and bragging rights, you'll have to climb three ladders beyond the staircase.

Back outside, visit the site's tiny museum that is housed in the generator building. The museum includes commercial fishing and shipwreck history, an intact lighthouse keeper's toolbox, and artifacts of an old Port Washington brewery that cheekily billed its product as "The Beer That Made Milwaukee Furious." Check out the lifeboat that was discovered in the remains of the carferry *Milwaukee* wreck of 1929. When it was first found, the lifeboat contained the bodies of four men who had died of hypothermia.

Let's make the short trek toward downtown now and get a closer view of the Port Washington harbor along the **Historic Maritime Harborwalk**. It was first dredged to attract maritime commerce in the 1870s, making it the first man-made harbor in North America. Consider the massive effort that was required to shape all this as you follow the picturesque, two-mile walkway that traverses it.

Stop at the **Port Washington Fishermens' Memorial** in Rotary Park, Grand Avenue, next to the marina. With a pipe in his mouth and a sturgeon on his back, the bronze fisherman forever hauls in his catch. Interpretive signage lists the names of local commercial fishermen, their boats, and those who were lost at sea. Farther on beneath a curved archway, the ***Niagara* Historic Marker** honors the "palace steamer" era of 1844–1857, and commemorates the steamer that was lost to fire in 1856, about 10 miles north of Port Washington off the present-day Harrington Beach State Park. Over 60 people were killed in the fire.

If the wind is calm and waves are not breaking over the 2,534-foot-long north pier, you can walk out to Port Washington's **1935 Pierhead Lighthouse**. Characterized by a distinctive art deco design, this 51-foot tower sits atop a 16-foot concrete base. Fully automated in 1976, its active red beam is visible for 16 miles.

William F. Wangemann at Wreck of *Lottie Cooper* as brought up from lake bottom, Sheboygan, Wisconsin

THE WRECK OF THE *LOTTIE COOPER*

April 9, 1894

as told by William F. Wangemann, Historian, City of Sheboygan

"When the ship was off Sheboygan, it ran into a heavy storm and the seam started to open and take on a little bit of water. They signaled for a tug to come out, but it was dark and apparently nobody on the shore saw the light. So they rode out the storm during the night. There used to be a lifesaving station down where the Blue Harbor Resort is now, and it had a tower on top. In the morning a guy climbed up [the tower], looked down at the lake, and they were flying their flag upside-down, which is an international signal for distress. So they started going out to the ship; but before they got out to it, it capsized, and she laid right over on the side, dumped all the lumber in the water. The men were in between it, getting all beat to pieces. So they came back in for a heavier boat, and at that time a tug came along, pushed through the lumber, and managed to rescue—they had a crew of seven. One of the guys tried to swim ashore, and he was lost in the storm."

Three more maritime sites are must-sees in Port Washington. The striking **Pebble House**, 126 East Grand Avenue, was built by Edward Dodge in 1848. Dodge and his wife combed the shores of Lake Michigan to find just the right pebbles, then carefully arranged them by size and color to create an incredibly intricate and very rare example of cobblestone construction designed in Greek Revival style. The Dodge's masterpiece is now home to the Port Washington Visitor Center, where you can pick up the "Historic Walking Tours" brochure for greater detail.

SHEBOYGAN MEN'S ROOM

There is a place in Sheboygan where the décor draws its entire inspiration from the lake and water-related sites about town. Such a tribute has not been paid in quite this way anywhere along the vast lakeshore. The ladies among us, however, will not be privy to this spectacle, as it lies entirely within the confines of the Sheboygan Men's Room at the John Michael Kohler Arts Center.

This is not just a bathroom; it's a phenomenon. Richly painted in blue and white and vaguely reminiscent of blue-patterned china, every last surface is a work of art. From the tiles to the toilets, beautifully crafted scenes depict views of Lake Michigan, a local carwash, a community swimming pool, supermarket shelves lined with bottled water, a water treatment plant, and Sheboygan homes with sprinklers and swimming pools. And ladies: if your curiosity gets the best of you, just head to reception and ask to take a peek. "Please knock first" is most likely what you'll hear.

To find such style in your home, look no further than Wisconsin's very own Kohler Company. Located just west of Sheboygan in a village all its own, Kohler happily puts its people to work on tubs and toilets that are not just functional fixtures, but works of art.

You can't miss the 1954 Colonial Revival style **Smith Bros. Restaurant Building**, 100 North Franklin Street; and as long as you're learning about this local legend, check out the **Smith Bros. Fish Net House**, which sits to the south across the west slip and represents the last testament to local commercial fishing. Built by the Smith Brothers between 1922 and 1938 to house equipment, the site now serves as a charming portal to the past for surrounding condos.

Leaving Port Washington, take I-43 north to Exit 107 through sleepy Lake Church and into **Harrington Beach State Park**, 531 County Road D, Belgium, Wisconsin 53004, (262) 285-3015, www.dnr.state.wi.us. The drive from Port Washington is just under 10 miles. Swim and sunbathe along the park's mile of beautiful sandy beach set against a backdrop of trees. On busy days you will have to board the park shuttle down to the lake, but don't let that stop you. If taking it easy is your style, pack a lunch and view the anchor of the sunken freighter *Niagara* at the Point Picnic Area. Or, for the more adventurous, grab your scuba gear and head toward the mooring buoy for an 80-foot dive to see the wreckage firsthand. But Harrington Beach State Park has more surprises in store: a bit inland around Quarry Lake you can find the remnants of Stonehaven, a turn of the twentieth-century limestone mining settlement where people not only worked, but also lived.

Sheboygan

Sixteen miles north of Harrington Beach State Park is another beautiful beach park, the thousand-acre **Kohler-**

Andrae State Park, 1020 Beach Park Lane, Sheboygan, Wisconsin 53081, (920) 451-4080, www.dnr.state.wi.us/org/land/parks/specific/ka. Kick off your shoes and dig your toes into the gorgeous white-sand beach surrounded by dunes, cottonwoods, and white pines. Climb atop the park's Sanderling Nature Center observation deck where astronomers hang out after dark, or select a video to watch inside the spacious auditorium. Learn about the Archaic and Copper Culture Indians who traded fish hooks and spear points here around 3500 BC. Outside, see part of a keel from the 87-foot schooner *Challenge*, which washed ashore here in 1982—130 years after the ship was built. If you wish to stay the night, pitch a tent in the park campground; or, if you've registered long in advance (about 11 months or so), spend a night at the Teepee Campsite in, you guessed it, your very own teepee!

Continue north a short distance on South 12th Street, turn right on Panther Avenue, then left on South 9th Street to the **Sheboygan Indian Mound Park**. It was here, from AD 500–750, that mysterious effigy mound builders created 34 earthen mounds in various animal, conical, and linear shapes. Eighteen remain preserved in the park's 15 acres, and you can walk among them by following the path through surrounding woodland. And whatever you do, don't miss the Open Mound Exhibit!

Driving northwest now, you can find more insight into Native American culture inside the **Sheboygan County Historical Museum**, 3110 Erie Avenue, Sheboygan, Wisconsin 53081, (920) 458-1103, www.co.sheboygan.wi.us/html/d_museum.html. Learn about Native American lakeshore history, when people traversed Lake Michigan in dugout canoes. The canoe on display was discovered in the nearby Sheboygan Marsh—it had been sunk for safekeeping, and was never retrieved by the owner. Learn why canoes were crucial to survival. Peer into display cases to see the copper and bone fishhooks and harpoon points from the Old Copper Culture period of 5000–1000 BC. Also look for small displays on Great Lakes coal freighters and shipwrecks that have a connection to the Sheboygan area. Show up for the museum's **Fish Boil** in October—but don't ask them to fry a Sheboygan brat.

Can you see that gorgeous U.S. flag waving in the wind to the south off I-43? Its 7,200 square feet of red, white, and blue fly from America's tallest flagpole at 338 feet—and each star is three feet high! Drive east toward the center of town where you can get close to more amazing sites. The **John Michael Kohler Arts Center**, 608 New York Avenue, Sheboygan, Wisconsin 53081, (920) 458-6144, www.jmkac.org, captures creativity both outside and in. Behold the noble ruins of an Andrew Carnegie Library, a nineteenth-century Italianate home, and soaring glass-walled galleries representing the latest in architectural innovation. And that's just the exterior! Rotating exhibits located throughout the center (some tucked into surprising nooks and crannies), artwork that flows from past to present, and insight into Kohler Company history make a visit to the Kohler Arts Center a must. And even the restrooms are beautiful!

Walk or drive over to the **Wreck of the *Lottie Cooper***, Deland Park, 715 Broughton Drive (in front of the marina), (920) 458-2974, where you'll find the hull of an actual ship—not a replica. Built in Manitowoc, Wisconsin in 1876, the *Lottie Cooper* was a three-masted schooner that measured 131 feet long. She sank in 1894 just off the Sheboygan Harbor when gale-force winds whipped up on the lake.

Years later in 1992, the hull of the *Lottie Cooper* was hauled out of the water when the City of Sheboygan began the construction of a new marina. This massive relic is unique on all of the Great Lakes; it's a ship on land that you can touch and even climb aboard; a ship built by hand, without the use of power tools. Feel the scarred, old white oak beneath your hand and discover a tribute not only to boatbuilders and seamen of the past, but to the old forests of Wisconsin, as well.

Go deep to experience two late nineteenth-century shipwrecks that remain entombed near the Sheboygan shore: the schooner *Hetty Taylor* and the steamer *Seleh Chamberlain*. Located a few miles offshore, their positions are marked by buoys with anchor hooks, supplied courtesy of the Historical Society of Wisconsin with help from Sea Grant. Call (608) 272-2832 to take the dive.

Other points of interest by the water include **Fountain Park**, 100 Block, North 8th Street, where people of a century ago came for the mineral fountains' supposed healing properties; **Schwarz Fish Market**, 828 Riverfront Drive, (920) 452-0576, for perch, whitefish, smelt, and northern pike; and the **Riverfront Boardwalk (Fish Shanty Village)**, Riverfront Drive, (800) 457-9497, for a stroll through commercial fishermen's old stomping grounds. Today you can shop the shanties or hire one of the many charter fishing boats docked there.

You can also time your visit to Sheboygan to experience one of the city's water-centered events. The January **Polar Bear Swim** and the July **Great Cardboard Boat Regatta** may have you thinking that Sheboyganites are all wet, but just wait until September when they catch a wave during **Dairyland Surf Classic**. It's the largest freshwater surfing competition in the world, and you do not want to miss it. In fact, you do not want to miss any of what Port Washington or Sheboygan have to offer. But now, pop that last juicy bite of brat into your mouth and get ready for the next stop along the lakeshore: Manitowoc.

FROM THE GALLEYS

NewPort Shores, 407 East Jackson Street, Port Washington, Wisconsin 53074, (262) 284-6838, www.foodspot.com/newportshores. Great Lake Michigan views are just the beginning of a great meal. Feast on sandwiches of cod and lake perch, whitefish from Canada, orange roughy from New Zealand, steaks, chicken, or the nightly fish fry. Dinners include soup, salad, choice of potato or rice pilaf, and dinner rolls.

Port Hotel Restaurant & Inn, 101 East Main Street, Port Washington, Wisconsin 53074, (262) 284-9473, www.theporthotel.com. Prime rib is the specialty of the house, but don't overlook other great steak and seafood choices. Dinner begins with a relish tray of crisp vegetables with pasta salad, and includes warm, crusty bread. Entrées are served with choice of salad and potatoes. Come for dinner, but stay for the night in this Neoclassical Revival beauty that now offers 10 elegant guestrooms, just as it did when it was built in 1902. Décor transports guests to Colonial Williamsburg and the French and Italian countrysides, while harbor views work local magic. Enjoy fine accoutrements such as Kohler Water Haven showers, towel heaters, and 120-channel satellite TVs. Each morning, a freshly prepared breakfast is delivered to your door.

Whistling Straits Restaurant, N8501 County Road LS, Sheboygan, Wisconsin 53083, (800) 344-2838, (920) 457-8000. At this famous golf course along Lake Michigan, the clubhouse restaurant offers American cuisine with a taste of the Briish Isles. Lunch choices include the Sheboygan Double Brat and the Homemade Corned Beef Sandwich with smoked bacon. The Dublin Beef Stew is an especially hearty meal of braised beef tips with mushrooms and onions, roasted garlic whipped potatoes, and French beans. Start dinner with an appetizer of White Truffle Scallops and savor an entrée of Beef & Scallop, Duet of Duck and Quail, T-bone Steak, or one of many more delicious options.

TO THE DOCKS

Blue Harbor Resort, 725 Blue Harbor Drive, Sheboygan, Wisconsin 53081, (866) 701-BLUE, (920) 452-2900, www.blueharborresort.com. Life is good at this sweeping resort of classic seaside fashion. Settle into an Adirondack chair surrounded by beach grass; play in the sand and take a dip in the lake. Fly down waterslides that whip around the indoor waterpark, or make a splash outside in the pool. Grab a lakeside table at Seabird Restaurant, and eat "underwater" or "aboard ship" at the Rusty Anchor Buffet. Guest suites offer boatloads of variety, such as the cool Kidaquarium and the three-bedroom Presidential suite. Like other resorts that feature bigger-is-better water parks, this one is a kiddie heaven. Condos, which are separated from the water park and main building, are a good choice for guests who prefer a little less action. Find it all where the Sheboygan River meets Lake Michigan.

Holiday Inn Harborview, 135 East Grand Avenue, Port Washington, Wisconsin 53074, (262) 284-9461, www.holiday-inn.com/ptwashington. Harboring great views, this hotel is sparkling-clean with an indoor pool, spa and sauna, and The Rusty Anchor Saloon & Eatery.

Port Washington Inn, 308 West Washington Street, Port Washington, Wisconsin 53074, (877) 794-1903, (262) 284-5583, www.port-washington-inn.com. Up on Sweetcake Hill you will find this blend of sumptuous furnishings, respectful innkeepers, a lighthouse and lake views, and lovely organic soaps. Curl up with in-room TVs/VCRs, movies, cable, and hot and cold beverages. Dorothy's Room wraps you up in Victorian crimson and a carved four-poster bed. Or climb a spiral staircase to the new Top of the World Suite, from which you may never wish to emerge. But in the morning, crusty wheat bread—home-ground and baked on-site—supplies reason enough to come downstairs.

AIDS TO NAVIGATION

Port Washington Tourism Council, Pebble House, (800) 719-4881, www.portwashingtonchamber.com/tourism.html.

Sheboygan County Chamber of Commerce & Convention and Visitors Bureau, (920) 457-9491, www.sheboygan.org.

Manitowoc to Algoma

From the Guestbook of Westport Bed and Breakfast, Manitowoc:
"We so enjoyed the poached pears and eggs benedict for breakfast. A real treat for New Yorkers who do not take time to enjoy that meal!" —Janice & Bruce

"There are a lot of stories about tunnels that used to connect between this building and those buildings over there during the Prohibition era. It's just all stories, but all of a sudden, like here, you see a change in the stonework." —Kristine Ruehl, Hotel Stebbins, Algoma

DRIVING NORTH FROM Sheboygan, take Lake Shore Drive (County Road LS) rather than I-43 for some great lake views and a pleasant Sunday-drive experience. A little north of the Whistling Straits golf course, the road goes right by the lake. Enjoy the gentle, rural ease of Manitowoc County, where the fields of dairy farms roll down to the shore and happy Wisconsin cows graze near pretty homes that line the lake. Fortunately, not all of the precious lakefront land is in private hands; thanks to the Manitowoc County Parks, much of it is still free and open to everyone.

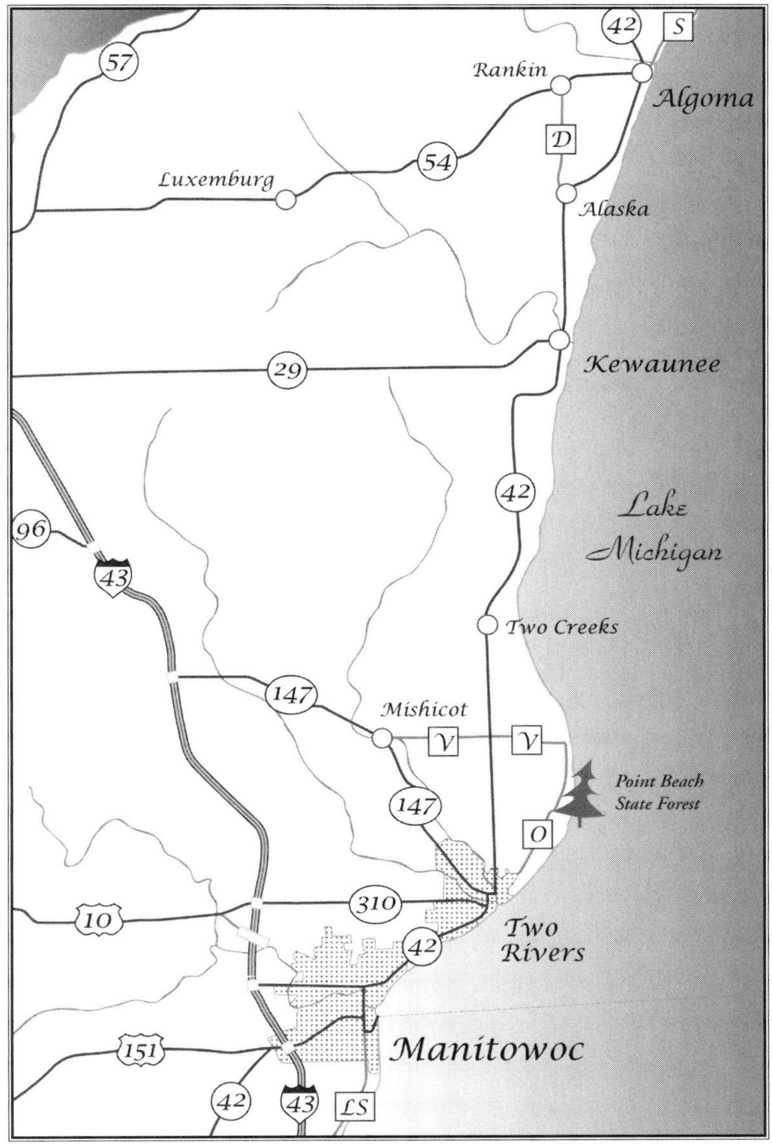

Manitowoc

Less than two breezy miles north of Cleveland, pull into the south parking lot of the 160-acre **Fischer Creek Conservation Area**, (920) 683-4185, www.co.manitowoc.wi.us/recreation/fischer.asp. Here you can grill out and hike an old Civil War trail that linked Milwaukee with Fort Howard in Green Bay. This trail does not bear a historical marker, but you will find it running parallel and a bit inland from the lakeshore. Spot wild strawberries and wildlife along the trail, catch a glimpse of the old boathouse by the shore, and hear echoes of both the past and your own voice within the cool concrete silos, the most obvious signs of the park's farming history.

Seagull nesting sites, Kewaunee, Wisconsin

Catch of the day, Good Tidings Nautical Gifts, Algoma, Wisconsin

After leaving the park, continue north about eight miles toward Manitowoc, a wonderfully walkable town. It's just plain fun to poke around the downtown shops. Don't even think about missing the **Wisconsin Maritime Museum**, 75 Maritime Drive, Manitowoc, Wisconsin 54220, (866) 724-2356, (920) 684-0218, www.wisconsinmaritime.org. One of the largest maritime museums in the Midwest, it sits on the site of the original Goodrich Transportation Company, which was founded in 1868 and went on to build and operate commercial vessels.

Allow half a day or more to thoroughly enjoy all of the exhibits and the guided **USS *Cobia Submarine*** tour. Moored in water, the battleship-gray World War II sub has a black teakwood deck, guns, and a conning tower with a broom mounted on it to signify a clean sweep of the enemy. Below deck, watch your head as you duck through hatches from a torpedo room, sit at the steel-sided green tables of the crew's mess hall, and imagine the heat and noise of the engine rooms where hand signals were often the best method of communication. Marvel at the cramped conditions and the mind-boggling array of controls and switches that the 80-member crew had to master, and cover your ears when the guide sounds the diving alarm. Explore the *Cobia's* history of six war patrols, marked by the sinking of 13 Japanese ships.

The Manitowoc Shipbuilding Company, which contributed a total of 28 subs to the war effort, was the only inland shipyard ever to build subs; and although *Cobia* was actually built in Connecticut, it got here following a transfer to the Naval Reserve Center in Milwaukee. Once decommissioned, it was transferred a second time to Manitowoc's port. Can't get enough of the sub? Offered only a few weekends every year, you and your family can bunk aboard the *Cobia* in the Overnight Education Program.

After your sub tour, resurface outdoors and walk back into the museum, where you can immerse yourself in Manitowoc's shipbuilding tradition. What began with wooden sailing ships became the largest single shipyard on the Great Lakes by 1950, and continues today with the Burger Boat Company's production of luxury yachts. See the early Mackinaw model fishing boat and the model ship gallery that displays big ships in small but detailed form. Explore the engine room's 1911 steam engine that once supplied power for icebreakers and passenger carriers. Study the wood-frame cutaway to learn about ship construction, and peer into the windows of a ship's chandlery. If you have kids along, they will be tugging at your sleeve to dive into the Children's Waterways Room where they can operate locks, build a dam, and interact with the underwater archeology video screen. Finally, step out onto the observation deck for a good look at the sub, and to read about the evolution of the Manitowoc waterfront.

Not far north of the museum and waterfront, you'll arrive at the magnificent **Rahr-West Art Museum**, 610 North 8th Street, Manitowoc, Wisconsin 54220, (920) 683-4501, www.rahrwestartmuseum.org. This 13-bedroom manse, which mixes the best of an art museum with a historical home tour, has a quirky connection with Sputnik IV: as legend has it, a piece of the Soviet spacecraft clattered back to Earth and landed in front of the museum, where it was found by two of Manitowoc's finest. Once identified by NASA and the Smithsonian Institution, the piece was eventually returned to its Soviet makers. View the replica here as you enter the museum's modern American art wing, which is a newer addition to the original 1891 home.

Enter the original home through the arched porte cochere that once received horse-drawn carriages and now leads visitors toward a grand staircase and bronze statue of the Roman god Mercury. Note the delicately carved ribbons and fleur-de-lis carvings on the woodwork. Compare the gallery art with the home's Victorian grandeur. Climb the stairs to the second floor, where displays range from Chinese ivories to an international doll collection. Among the permanent collection of American landscapes is a 1980 watercolor, *Cargo Sunrise*, by contemporary American artist

Patricia Norton, whose ghostly seascape could very well be a scene from the shore just a few blocks east of the museum.

The house has a maritime connection in that the West family, who generously contributed to the museum, co-founded the Manitowoc Shipbuilding Company in 1902. Today it is known as The Manitowoc Company, and has marine divisions in Marinette and Sturgeon Bay.

The seven-mile drive north from downtown Manitowoc to Two Rivers along State Highway 42 closely parallels the lakeshore and the **Mariners Trail**, www.marinerstrail.net. Paved and popular, the trail supplies the state's longest continuous views of Lake Michigan across six leisurely miles. On your way up from the north end of Manitowoc, pull into **West of the Lake Gardens**, 925 Memorial Drive, Manitowoc, Wisconsin 54220, (920) 684-6110. The name refers not only to the location, but also to the aforementioned West family. This six-acre paradise puts on splendid seasonal color shows, using the lake as a cool blue backdrop. Look for the sunken water lily pool and the kite-shaped reflecting pool.

Two Rivers

It's only a little over seven miles from Manitowoc to downtown Two Rivers. The **Rogers Street Fishing Village & Great Lakes Coast Guard Museum**, 2102 Jackson Street, Two Rivers, Wisconsin 54241, (920) 793-5905, www.rogersstreet.com, is the site of a former French-Canadian settlement on the river that beautifully preserves what remains of the settlers' scrappy shanties. Start your guided tour with a look at who the people were and how they lived; the period rooms, pocket violin, and rope bed with straw mattress all have stories to tell. Cross the ramp into the connected fishtug that was built entirely of wood in 1936. Follow your guide across the flower-flanked boardwalk to the 1800s LeClair Shed to learn about icing the catch and boiling the gill nets—and be sure to ask for the "Fish in the Guts" recipe!

Climb up Two Rivers' first lighthouse, which remains the only original wooden pierhead light of the Great Lakes. Here on the museum grounds, it is safe from wave damage. Learn about the most famous Christmas Tree Ship, the *Rouse Simmons*, which sank offshore of Two Rivers in 1912.

See what's coming out of the smoker today at **Susie-Q Fish Market**, 1810 East Street, Two Rivers, Wisconsin 54241, (920) 793-5240, and belly up to the bar like the sailing merchants once did at **Kurtz's Pub & Deli**, 1410 Washington Street, Two Rivers, Wisconsin 54241, (920) 793-1222. Poke around inside Two Rivers' three other museums, including the **Historic Washington House & Museum**, 1622 Jefferson Street, Two Rivers, Wisconsin 54241, (888) 857-3529, (920) 793-2490, where you can commemorate the founding of the ice cream sundae by ordering one at **Ed Berners' Ice Cream Parlor**.

Need more refreshment? Where the

Mariners Trail leaves off, the **Rawley Point Recreational Trail** begins. By car, take State Highway 42 to County Road O. Along the way, take a dip at **Neshotah Beach Park**, and continue north to the **Point Beach State Forest**, 9400 County Road O, Two Rivers, Wisconsin 54241, (920) 794-7480, www.wiparks.net. Explore 2,900 acres of evergreens and sands along six miles of lakeshore. Check out the 1894 **Rawley Point Lighthouse** that soars 113 impressive feet into the sky; and although you can neither tour nor touch it, you can photograph it from a variety of angles, including from the beach. Hike for 11 miles along the water and in the forest, and sunbathe and swim when the weather is warm.

Back on State Highway 42, electrify your journey by driving about 10 miles north of Point Beach State Forest to the newly re-opened **Point Beach Energy Center**, 6400 Nuclear Road, Two Rivers, Wisconsin 54241, (800) 880-8463, (920) 755-6400, www.nmcco.com. There you can tour a simulated nuclear reactor, generate your own electricity, and learn about renewable energy.

Kewaunee

From downtown Two Rivers, drive 23 miles north to Kewaunee. Back in 1892, the first cross-lake carferry service was launched between Kewaunee, Wisconsin and Frankfort, Michigan. Follow Hathaway Drive out to the historical marker that tells you about this event. The U.S. Navy's USS *Pueblo* was built and launched here for World War II service, and today you can tour a World War II-era tugboat, the ***Tug Ludington***, that was saved from the scrap heap by the people of Kewaunee. You can find this military craft docked at

Commercial fishtugs, Two Rivers, Wisconsin

Tug Ludington, Kewaunee, Wisconsin

the south wall of Kewaunee harbor, (920) 388-5000, www.cityofkewaunee.org/content/recreation/tug/index.shtml. A veteran of the D-Day Invasion that towed ammunition barges to Normandy, this 115-foot tug later assisted with construction and maintenance of Great Lakes harbors.

Board *Tug Ludington* on her aft deck and enter the galley where your guide will point out the clever features that prevented dishes and coffee cups from clattering to the floor in the event of wave action. Remarkably, the china is original, as are much of the tug's accoutrements. Check out the mess, the engine room, and the original engineer's chair; don't miss the brass gong, the telephone, the heads, the crew's quarters below water level, and the comparatively comfier captain's quarters. Give the pilothouse wheel a spin, or clang the bell on the forward deck.

While in town, add to your lighthouse collection or start a new one at **The Lighthouse Shop**, 705 North Main Street (State Highway 42), Kewaunee, Wisconsin 54216, (920) 388-3565, www.lighthousegiftshop.com.

As you head out of town, you may find that something's fishy at the DNR's outlying **C. D. "Buzz" Besadny Fish & Wildlife Area and Anadromous Fish Facility**, N3884 Ransom Moore Lane, Kewaunee, Wisconsin 54216, (920) 388-1025. Watch through an underwater window as trout and salmon fight their way up fish ladders into holding tanks for spawning and egg collection. Call ahead, though, because fish are not always present, and various species migrate according to their own seasonal schedules.

Algoma

It's a 12-mile drive from Kewaunee to Algoma. Walk the streets where dockside warehouses once stored lumber and farm crops for eventual shipment to Lake Michigan ports. Look up to see the hillside steeple of St. Mary's Catholic Church, which is listed on Lake Michigan navigational maps. Locate the mid-century Art Dettman Fish Shanty.

Follow the **Crescent Beach Boardwalk** to the marina for a look at **Christmas Tree Ship Point**. The marker explains that in the 1800s, 52 schooners bearing Christmas trees passed this point, and the captain of the most famous of these, the *Rouse Simmons*, was born in Algoma. Cast off for charter fishing adventures in this sportfishing capital. Afterward, haul your cooler over to **Bearcat's Fish House**, 295 4th Street, State High-way 42, Algoma, Wisconsin 54201, (920) 487-2372, for old-fashioned smoking of your catch. Visit **Good Tidings Nautical Gifts**, 304 Steele Street, Algoma, Wisconsin 54201, (920) 487-3353 to find sea-inspired gifts of every style and taste. Take the wines of **Von Stiehl Winery**, 115 Navarino Street, Algoma, Wisconsin 54201, (800) 955-5208, www.vonstiehl. com, for a taste-drive before choosing your favorites, including regional cherry varieties. Mosey on into **Hotel Stebbins**, 201 Steele Street, Algoma, Wisconsin 54201, (920) 487-5521, www.thehotelstebbins. com, for a meal and a peek into the past. Originally built in 1858 by 18-year-old Captain Charles Fellows, the country's longest-running business still thrives today. It even has a telephone booth with its original Bell System sign.

Or, in an offbeat version of the traditional shore lunch, let Tug Boat Willy deliver your meal at the **Port Side II Restaurant**, 709 North Water Street (State Highway 42 North), Algoma, Wisconsin 54201, (920) 487-9704. Work it all off on the **Ahnapee Trail**, www.ahnapeetrail.org, a former railroad bed that spans about 30 rural miles to Casco and to Sturgeon Bay.

Up next is Door County, unique among the Lake Michigan shoreline for classic coastal charm and a rural interior. Come along—you don't want to miss this.

FROM THE GALLEYS

Courthouse Pub, 1001 South 8th Street, Manitowoc, Wisconsin 54220, (920) 686-1166, www.courthousepub.com. People crowd this innovative eatery and micro-brewery because the fresh food is always creatively prepared. The grilled tenderloin with portabella mushroom is tender and flavorful. Entrées come with choice of soup or salad, and the rolls are satisfyingly dense with an old-fashioned yeast aroma and thin, crispy crust. Come Friday and indulge in lake perch that is lightly dusted and pan-fried in walnut oil.

Wallstreat Grill, 901 Buffalo Street, Manitowoc, Wisconsin 54220, (920) 682-2533. Sandwiches include a deep-fried, half-pound walleye with melted cheddar and red onions on a grilled hard roll, with choice of fries or tri-color tortilla chips with black bean salsa. Entrées include crab-stuffed tenderloin, pan-fried rainbow trout, chicken pecan, and plenty more. Vegetables are fresh, buttery, and tenderly crisp to perfection.

ONE LAST RUN

There have been many shipwrecks offshore from Two Rivers, but none have garnered quite as much fame and lore as the Christmas Tree Ship named *Rouse Simmons*. This Milwaukee-built three-masted schooner met her fate in 1912, while making the last run of the season from Manistique, Michigan to Chicago.

"Many captains, in order to supplement their annual income, would make one last run to get Christmas trees and sell them to Chicagoans," explained Sandra Zipperer, Executive Director of the Rogers Street Fishing Village.

But when a November storm blew up on Lake Michigan, waves poured over the deck and froze upon the heavy load of trees. At the U.S. Life-Saving Station in Kewaunee, they spotted the ship keeled over in the water.

"Her sails were torn; the booms were shattered, battered, and broken, and she was flying the distress flag," Zipperer continued. "Unfortunately, that day the station lifeboat was under repair. So they called the Two Rivers station."

Although the station captain went north in a lifeboat, the storm raged and darkness had fallen, and the ship was lost. Waterlogged evergreens surfaced near the site for years; but the wreckage remained undiscovered until 1971, when a scuba diver found it still filled with hundreds of trees.

Phil Rohrer's Lunch, 1303 22nd Street, Two Rivers, Wisconsin 54241, (920) 794-8500. Homemade "raw fries" and soups, and daily fresh lake perch specials with real mashed potatoes. Breakfast served all day.

Waterfront Bar & Grill, 215 North Main Street, Kewaunee, Wisconsin 54216, (920) 388-0505. Classic pub fare with a seaside spin: sandwiches, hamburgers, ostrich burgers, seaburgers, walleye or bluegill fingers and fries basket, and cheese curds.

TO THE DOCKS

Algoma Beach Motel, 1500 Lake Street, Algoma, Wisconsin 54201, (920) 487-2828, www.algomabeach.com. Roadside motel price; beach condo experience. Book a lakeside room and let the sights and sounds take you away. Stroll the beach to the red lighthouse, or stretch out on a deck chair and lounge the day away.

Best Western Inn on Maritime Bay, 101 Maritime Drive, Manitowoc, Wisconsin 54220, (800) 654-5353, (920) 682-7000, www.bestwestern.com. Renovated in 2006, the inn puts you within walking distance of the maritime museum and in earshot of foghorns. Watch boats in the harbor, including the great SS *Badger* passenger carferry. Enjoy the indoor pool and hot tub, on-site restaurant, and pleasant new décor that includes a boat in the lobby.

Lighthouse Inn on the Lake, 1515 Memorial Drive (State Highway 2), Two Rivers, Wisconsin 54241, (800) 228-6416, (920) 793-4524, www. lhinn.com. To get closer to the water, you would have to be in it, for this family-owned inn is built east of the highway and right on the beach.

Westport Bed & Breakfast, 635 North 8th Street, Manitowoc, Wisconsin 54220, (888) 686-0465, (920) 686-0465, www.thewestport.com. If, while wandering through the art museum, you thought it would be lovely to live in such splendor, consider a stay at this inn, located just up the street. Cream city brick encases the rich and classical décor, characterized by sumptuous fabrics, in-room fireplaces, lace curtains, and windows that stretch to the ceiling. The first-floor Serenity Suite features a double whirlpool tub and a private porch that overlooks the backyard garden. In-room amenities include snacks, mini-fridges stocked with soft drinks and bottled waters, and TV/DVDs with a selection of movies. Discover the secret in the dumbwaiter. Choose candlelit, full gourmet breakfast in the dining room (fresh fruit, egg hot dish, delicious sides, orange juice, and coffee), or continental breakfast in your room—at an hour that suits your schedule. Guests arriving on the SS *Badger* without their car enjoy pickup service.

AIDS TO NAVIGATION

Manitowoc Area Visitor & Convention Bureau and Visitor Information Center, (800) 627-4896, www.visit manitowoc.info.

Two Rivers Information Center, (888) 857-3529, www.two-rivers.org.

Kewaunee Chamber of Commerce, (920) 388-4833, www.kewaunee.org.

Algoma Chamber of Commerce & Visitor Center, (920) 487-2041, www.algoma.org.

Door County

From the Guestbook of Glidden Lodge Beach Resort, Sturgeon Bay:
"We love the new decorating. The colors seem to extend the lake right into the condo."

—Jeff & Paula, Maize, Kansas

"The harvest moon last night was an awesome sight from our window table at the [resort's] restaurant. A great blue heron strutted along the beach in the light of the moon, dunking his enormous beak into the lake to retrieve a treat now and then." —Dick & Pat, Sandwich, Illinois

"Two of the questions I get a lot are, 'Have you ever been burned?' and 'What do you do when it rains?' I tell them, 'No, not seriously,' and 'I get wet.'"

—Tom Christianson, Master Boiler, White Gull Inn, Fish Creek

THE DOOR COUNTY peninsula has always been tied to the water. Its 300 miles of rocky and sandy shoreline, over 200 shipwrecks, over 40 islands, 10 lighthouses, and five state parks attract visitors; and when a commercial fisherman has an accident on the job, an entire community holds its breath. There are three maritime museums, all originally founded by commercial fishermen at Gills Rock, and each with a unique focus. By the time you tour all three, you will be able to rattle off the differences between gill, trap, and pond nets. Enjoy narrated boat tours, sailing cruises, watercraft rentals, and sport fishing charters up and down the peninsula. To get to Door County from Algoma, take County Road S to County Road U north for the closest drive along the shoreline. Lake views are sporadic, but the agricultural countryside is scenic and a stop at the **Robert LaSalle County Park** gets you down to the water. While there, send the kids off for a search of the park's 1930s historical marker (hint: it is in the upper parking lot). When you hit State Highway 57, merge with the traffic zooming into downtown Sturgeon Bay, turning left on your way to the maritime museum.

Sturgeon Bay

Remember the days of catching whitefish from a birch bark canoe, of sailing a schooner by the wind, and of boarding a steamer bound for a classic lakeside resort? No? Then a visit to the 20,000 square-foot **Door County Maritime Museum & Lighthouse Preservation Society**, 120 North Madison Avenue (south of the Michigan Street Bridge, which is west of the State Highway 42/57 bridge), Sturgeon Bay, Wisconsin 54235, (920) 743-5958, www.dcmm.org, is your ticket to the peninsula's extraordinary maritime past.

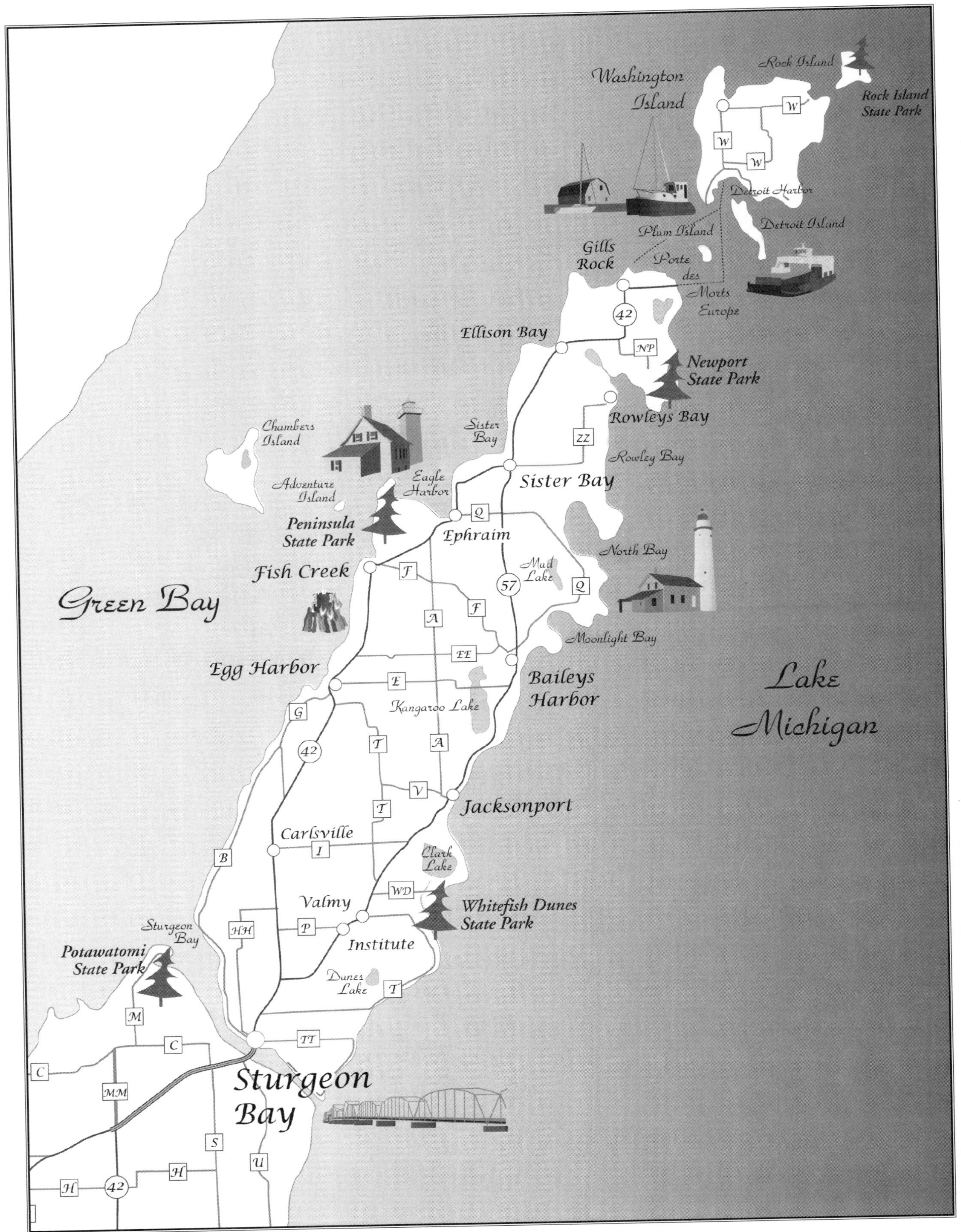

Rock Island
Washington Island
Rock Island State Park
W
Detroit Harbor
Detroit Island
Plum Island
Gills Rock
Porte des Morts
Europe
42
Ellison Bay
NP
Newport State Park
Rowleys Bay
Chambers Island
Sister Bay
ZZ
Rowley Bay
Sister Bay
Adventure Island
Eagle Harbor
Peninsula State Park
Q
Ephraim
Fish Creek
Mud Lake
North Bay
57
Green Bay
F
A
Moonlight Bay
EE
Egg Harbor
E
Baileys Harbor
Lake Michigan
G
Kangaroo Lake
T
V
Jacksonport
Carlsville
I
B
Clark Lake
WD
Valmy
Whitefish Dunes State Park
Sturgeon Bay
HH
P
Institute
Potawatomi State Park
Dunes Lake
M
TT
C
Sturgeon Bay
MM
S
H
U

Your journey through the museum begins in ancient times. Learn about the archeological digs at Whitefish Dunes State Park that unearthed 35,009 artifacts dated from 100 BC to the late nineteenth century. You may discover that the past life on the lakefront was not so different from that of the present.

For more recent maritime history, jump ahead to the period of 1835–1860, when schooners brought most of Door County's first settlers to shore. Later, when the canal linking Sturgeon Bay to Lake Michigan was cut and steamships began to replace schooners, commercial marine transportation flourished and businesses boomed. This was especially true of the Goodrich line. The line's steamships also carried passengers to and from Door County shoreline ports, which was the easiest way for early tourists to visit the pretty peninsula with its burgeoning resort hospitality. Moving on, you can learn about the young man who, against all Depression-era odds, dreamed of owning a boatyard and built Peterson Builders from the ground up—a successful company that went on to build U.S. Navy Minesweepers and other vessels. That's all in the past, but when the whine of power tools and the pounding of hammers shatter the calm museum air, then a boatbuilding class must be in session inside Jim's Boat Building Shop. Peek through the windows and Jim will probably invite you into this living museum exhibit where students spend hundreds of

Waves of Lake Michigan pound bluffs at Cave Point County Park, Jacksonport, Wisconsin

Peaceful waters of Baileys Harbor from pier of Blacksmith Inn on the Shore, Baileys Harbor, Wisconsin

Keeping watch at Cana Island Lighthouse, Baileys Harbor, Wisconsin

hours building small watercrafts that will eventually be launched by a lucky raffle winner.

The great shipbuilders of Sturgeon Bay have a rich tradition of serving commercial and military needs. Learn more about it as you step inside a ship's pilothouse and the world's first shipping container; look inside the confines of a diver's recompression chamber and press buttons to see where local maritime interests are located. Step outside of the museum to view the 1931 Michigan Street Drawbridge and a variety of old commercial vessels docked in the bay.

One of these is the red Chicago fireboat that takes passengers on a two-hour run up the bay to view the 1883 **Sherwood Point Lighthouse**, the bright red **Canal Station/Pier Head Light**, shipbuilding activity, and many points in between. For more information on this ex-citing cruise, contact **Door County Cruises**, Maritime Museum/City Dock, Sturgeon Bay, Wisconsin 54235, (920) 495-6454, www.doorcounty-cruises.com. Alternatively, you can drive out to the Canal Station/Pier Head Light and walk out along the breakwater, keeping in mind that this is a working light and the catwalk is strictly off limits. You could make the long drive out to **Sherwood Point Lighthouse**; but because it's used by the military as a retreat, it's off limits to the public. Better to take the cruise.

Soak up more history across the Michigan Street Bridge at the **Door County Historical Museum**, 18 North 4th Avenue, Sturgeon Bay, Wisconsin 54235, (920) 743-5809. This great little museum houses intriguing displays dedicated to wildlife, cherry growing and picking, classic summer resorts, and everything else that contributes to the county's timeless charm.

Drive westward to **Potawatomi State Park**, 3740 County PD, Sturgeon Bay, Wisconsin 54235, (920) 746-2890, www.dnr.state.wi.us, and get lost in the primeval northern forest. Climb the 75-foot tower, as people have done since 1932, for a 16-mile overview of islands and tiny cottages on the water's edge. Launch a boat for access to Sawyer Harbor, Sturgeon Bay, and Green Bay. Enjoy rocky shores in lieu of swimming beaches. In case of confusion, know that **Potawatomie Light** is not here but up at **Rock Island State Park**, www.dnr.state.wi.us, which is north of Washington Island. To get there, you will have to skip across the lake aboard two separate ferries (the Washington Island Ferry and then the ***Karfi***). It's well worth it, but best to plan ahead.

As you head deeper into Door County, take State Highway 57 to County Road WD and the Lake Michigan shore for an unforgettable beach experience at **Whitefish Dunes State Park**, 3275 Clark Lake Road, Sturgeon Bay, Wisconsin 54235, (920) 823-2400, www.dnr.state.wi.us. The park's 865 acres of wooded land and miles of sandy shoreline should be enough to get you close to nature. On nice summer days, this wide swath of sparkling sand fills up with happy people and their colorful toys. Off-season, thoughtful beach walkers remember warmer days and listen to the mournful cries of herring gulls.

But to get more out of this park than a tan, stop into the nature center where you can learn about the surrounding environment. Take a hike to see what lies beyond the foredunes, which are off-limits to conserve their fragile flora. The Red Trail leads to Old Baldy, a 93-foot dune with an observation tower at its summit. There you can catch a glimpse of Lake Michigan and Clark Lake. Close your eyes and listen for the calls of ovenbirds; and on clear days, savor the mix of hot sun and cool entrance.

Now drive the short distance north to **Cave Point County Park**, County Highway A, Jacksonport, Wisconsin. Here the

Birds' eye view from 75-foot Eagle Tower, Peninsula State Park, Fish Creek, Wisconsin

Spotted in woods of Peninsula State Park, Fish Creek, Wisconsin

breezes. As you come back down to Earth, head right on the Red Trail through an arid habitat. At the Green Trail crossing, turn right toward the water and enjoy an invigorating beach walk back to the park lake pounds and echoes off the ancient exposed rocks of the Niagara Escarpment. It is a hollow, mesmerizing sound that will stay in memory long after you have left the park. The area's stunning bluffs were formed over 400 million years ago in what geologists call the Silurian Period.

Gill nets and *Seediver*, Ken Koyen's working commercial fishtug, looking out toward Rock Island, Washington Island, Wisconsin

Inquisitive ostriches, Double K-W Ostrich/Exotic Animal Farm, Washington Island, Wisconsin

If you are traveling through Door County in August, make plans to be in Sturgeon Bay during the **Classic and Wooden Boat Show**, (920) 743-5958, or in Jacksonport for **Cherry Fest**, (920) 823-2288.

Baileys Harbor

Peace and quiet are yours in Baileys Harbor, which is 22 miles north of Sturgeon Bay. Enjoy the beautiful marina and refreshingly untouristy feel of the small town, and take time to see the unique aids to navigation. About a mile northeast of town, the **Baileys Harbor Range Lights**, which include the Upper and Lower Range Lights and residence, remain in the firm hands of the U.S. Coast Guard and offer neither tours nor entry. You are, however, quite welcome to walk around outside to observe these structures, and through the marshy areas down to water's edge. From there, catch a glimpse of the Cana Island Lighthouse to the north, as it is easily distinguishable by its causeway. We'll get there, but first, take a scenic hike along the adjacent **Ridges Sanctuary**, (920) 839-2802, www.ridgessanctuary.org. There is a small fee, but it goes toward preserving this delicate environment. Located on an island near town, the **Old Baileys Harbor Light** is uniquely known for its birdcage lantern room. During the annual Door County Lighthouse Walk, a boat cruise will take you there.

To get to **Cana Island Lighthouse**, 8800 Cana Island Road, www.dcmm.org, take County Highway Q at the northern edge of Baileys Harbor, and make a sharp right onto Cana Island Road. Park at the causeway and walk across its white, rocky surface, enjoying the wild, tranquil views along the way. During times of high water, many visitors wade across. Pay admission and continue past lilac bushes to the 1869 lighthouse. Clad in steel and painted white, it was automated in 1944 and is still active today.

Except during the annual **Door County Lighthouse Walk**, you cannot climb or even enter the tower. In the keeper's quarters, learn about offshore shipwrecks, storms and their effects, Lake Michigan water levels, and how the unique configuration of the bays and causeway generate waves. You are never too old to understand how a Fresnel lens bends light rays to focus them into one beam, so experiment with its magic for yourself inside the children's room. Back outside, stroll the grounds as the keepers would have done, past the stone fences to the rocky but eroded white stones and trapped pools. Commercial fishermen have been known to drop a gill net or two in these coastal waters.

Stavkirke, Norwegian church, Washington Island, Wisconsin

A sunset over Lake Michigan, Sunset Resort, Washington Island, Wisconsin

Glidden Lodge Beach Resort, Sturgeon Bay, Wisconsin

Ken Koyen, canine pals, and commercial fishtug *Welcome* out back of KK Fiske Restaurant & Granary Bar, Washington Island, Wisconsin

Fish Creek, Ephraim, Sister Bay

Take the 10-mile drive across Door County to Fish Creek. Drive through the **Peninsula State Park** to the 1868 **Eagle Bluff Lighthouse**, Peninsula State Park, 9462 Shore Road, Fish Creek, Wisconsin 54212, (920) 839-2377, www.dnr.state.wi.us. Your guide will explain that the light is solar powered with a back-up battery for cloudy days. Enter the handsome keeper's quarters' original winter kitchen where you can shop for gifts and view antique kitchenware. Study the period rooms, and hear the story of a piano that was hauled up the rugged cliffside but did not fit through the doorway. Upstairs, consider that the seven Duclon brothers slept in one of the two bedrooms. Climb spiral stairs to the tower. Back outside, learn about the Green Bay lakescape that sparkles out beyond the nineteenth-century stone wall. Your guide will point out Pirate, Strawberry, and Chambers islands, as well as the 1868 **Chambers Island Lighthouse** that is only accessible by boat. Squint to make out the Upper Peninsula of Michigan on the horizon.

You may just want to plan a whole day at the 3,700-acre **Peninsula State Park.** Go biking, hiking, or kayaking; explore the park's natural and cultural sites, including Blossomburg Cemetery, the Nature Center, and Eagle Tower for beautiful blue views of Green Bay. On summer evenings, the woods set the stage for performances of the **American Folklore Theatre**, office located at Green Gables, North Ephraim, Wisconsin 54212, (920) 854-6117, www.folkloretheatre.com. Regional stories are audience favorites, so join the line early for general admission tickets.

Tucked into the bay just beyond Peninsula State Park's northern entrance is Ephraim, a picturesque village with white frame buildings and church steeples. Enjoy lakeside dining or a sailing cruise, then join a historic walking tour of the **Ephraim Village Museums**, 3060 Anderson Lane, Ephraim, Wisconsin 54211, (920) 854-9688, www.ephraim.org. The small complex includes the Anderson Barn History Center, the Anderson Store, the Iverson House, the Pioneer Schoolhouse, and the Goodletson Cabin. The cozy Svalhus, a Norwegian-style home with an overhanging second story that doubles as a porch roof, is open by appointment only. After your museum visit, stroll along the Anderson Dock, where early tourists once disembarked from passenger steamers. Inside the graffiti-covered walls of the dock building, view the works of locally prominent artists.

As you continue north, your next stop is Sister Bay, a town that combines traditional Scandinavian hospitality and new mega-resorts that sprawl along State Highway 42. Get close to the water on a walk through the **Sister Bay Marina**, 817 North Bay Shore Drive, Sister Bay, Wisconsin 54234, (920) 854-4457, www.sisterbay.com/marina, which offers 35 slips for transient boaters. There's a waiting list system, so plan ahead. Book a narrated boat ride with **Shoreline Charters**, (920) 854-4707, www.shorelinecharters.net, or **Sail Door County**, (920) 495-7245, www.saildoorcounty.com. Attend **Marina Fest** the Saturday of Labor Day Weekend to enjoy a classic wooden boat show, Coast Guard displays, children's boat-building sessions, a water ski show, an evening decorated boat competition, and food such as breakfast pancakes, whitefish sandwiches, and corn on the cob. View the recently-acquired Viking Ship, representative of the area's Norwegian heritage.

WASHINGTON ISLAND FUN FACTS

The very first sailing vessel on the Great Lakes, the *Griffin*, sailed out of Washington Island in 1679 after picking up a load of beaver pelts. It was never heard from again.

After 1850, one of the new town board's first acts was to establish a school. Today, the Washington Island school district is the smallest K-12 public school in Wisconsin.

Washington Island is home to America's second-oldest and largest Icelandic settlement.

Every year, the Sievers School of Fiber Arts teaches homespun skills to 600 students.

Washington Island's permanent population is 680.

Egg Harbor

From Sister Bay, drive about 16 miles to Egg Harbor, where you can enjoy the small town charm of quaint shops and easy access to the lake. Stroll past the pretty foliage and picnic benches of **Harbor View Park**, and walk down to the quiet waterfront to watch the boats. Stop at the classic cherry orchard markets outside of town. Many of the markets, which are family operations that may go back to the midcentury, offer samples of their classic Door County products. So dip crackers and pretzels into the cherry salsas, cherry jams, and cherry mustards to discover your favorites. Stop into the **Wood Orchard Market**, 8112 State Highway 42, just north of Egg Harbor, Wisconsin 54209, (866) 763-2334, (920) 868-2334, www.woodorchard.com, for an exceptionally delicious chopped cherry jam.

Accordionist Lou Close entertains diners at Door County Fish Boil, White Gull Inn, Fish Creek, Wisconsin

Ellison Bay, Gills Rock, Northport, Washington Island

On the way to Gills Rock, take a detour through Ellison Bay to **Newport State Park**, 475 County Highway NP, Ellison Bay, Wisconsin 54210, (920) 854-2500, which has 11 miles of Lake Michigan shoreline and 2,373 acres of wilderness with trails and backpack campsites. For beauty and seclusion, this is the one; and it's only 21 miles from Egg Harbor.

At the top of the peninsula, be sure to visit the **Door County Maritime Museum**, 12724 Wisconsin Bay Road, Gills Rock, Wisconsin 54210, (920) 854-18444, www.dcmm.org, to explore shipwrecks, early lifesaving innovations, and commercial fishing. Ring the bell of the 1856 schooner *Sardinia*, and view actual shipwreck remains, including anchors, a dead-eye (a piece that held the rigging to keep masts vertical), a ship's rib, and more artifacts that divers brought to the surface before the practice was prohibited by law. Listen in on actual radio communications between the U.S. Coast Guard and the captain of the *Edmund Fitzgerald*, and find out about the *Fleetwing*, which is the closest visible wreck. View an early lifesaving device, the Lyle gun,

Lighting up the night at the Door County Fish Boil, White Gull Inn, Fish Creek, Wisconsin

which resembles a small cannon and was used to shoot a line of rope from shore out to disaster sites. Board the 1930 fishtug *Hope,* and watch footage of her last lift in 1992. Farther on, view an old sailsled, study boat engines, and learn the history of the Washington Island Ferry that began in 1940. **Wisconsin's Maritime Trails**, www.maritimetrails.org, says you don't have to be a diver to experience the wreck of the *Fleetwing.* Snorkelers and kayakers can get a good look, since the old schooner rests in 11–25 feet of water. Landlubbers can take it in with the assistance of the organization's historical marker, erected at the Garrett Bay Public Boat Ramp in nearby Liberty Grove.

LIGHTING UP THE NIGHT

It has been over a century since the U.S. Coast Guard stopped using kerosene to light its Great Lakes towers.

But at the dozen or so Door County restaurants that do fish boils, kerosene remains the fuel of choice. As skies darken over the courtyard of White Gull Inn, the firepit crackles. Seated at wrought iron tables with drinks in hand, the diners, who for now are the audience, sing along to *Eidelweiss.*

Hours ago when the diners were shopping or boating, Master Boiler Tom Christianson was back in the kitchen nicking redskin potatoes, counting whitefish, and bringing the water to boil. Now on stage, he dumps in two loads of the potatoes. "A pinch of salt," he cheekily announces while pouring in cupfuls of the white crystals.

"It's actually one pound of salt to every two gallons of water. Some of it is absorbed by the potatoes, some of it is picked up in the fish. But the real purpose of the salt is to change the specific gravity of the water. It's kind of like swimming in Lake Michigan or swimming in Great Salt Lake. No matter who you are, you're going to float more in the Great Salt Lake. So what happens is the salt makes the fats and oils from the fish come to the top. When you throw the kerosene on the fire, these boil out. When you take the fish and potatoes out, they don't taste fishy," he explains.

Later, with hair beginning to dampen, Christianson adds steak-cut whitefish and begins to get happy with the kerosene. He narrates as he goes, and fields questions with answers that are as liberally laced with humor as the kettle is with salt. Finally, right before the fish and potatoes are perfectly done (Christianson decides exactly when this is), he throws on more kerosene. This makes the fish oil boil over into the fire so flames lick the night sky and the branches of a nearby birch (Christianson swears the tree hasn't grown since he began doing this 10 years ago). Christianson and an assistant then push a long pole through the kettle, haul it off the fire, and disappear into the dining room. No one in the audience needs to be told to follow; and once inside, they line up as servers drop three potatoes and two chunks of fish on each plate. Diners help themselves to chunky tartar sauce and lemon wedges before moving to tables already set with sliced breads, pitchers of melted butter, and bowls of crunchy, creamy coleslaw *Roll out the Barrel* and other polka favorites, played by a strolling accordionist, make the buffet line go fast, but a request for the Macarena is turned down. Servers come around asking diners if they want seconds. Many do, agreeing that the fish, all locally caught, has a deliciously clean taste. Others cannot wait for the cherry pie à la mode, home-baked with sweetened tart cherries and a flaky crust sprinkled with sugar crystals.

For everyone here, the Door County Fish Boil will be one of their brightest Door County memories. For the Master Boiler, it's just another good night's work.

Ask for directions at the museum. The *Fleetwing* set sail from Menominee, Michigan and was headed for Chicago when she went down, only a year after her 1867 construction in Manitowoc. The ship was built by Henry B. Burger, whose small shipyard eventually became the Burger Boat Company, which still thrives today.

Islands are more about water than land, and the 680 people who call Washington Island home keep a close eye on the lake that surrounds them. On the western shore, you can catch the kind of sunsets over the lake that the folks in Michigan watch from their cars as if at a drive-in movie. Peak visitor season is July and August, but if you want true peace, come in June when the weather is warm, the shops, restaurants, and accommodations are open, and the tourists have yet to descend. If you don't have a boat, there are two ways to get there. Board the ***Island Clipper***, 12731 State Highway 42, Gills Rock, Wisconsin 54210, (920) 854-2972, www.islandclipper.com, for a narrated cruise. You can't bring your car, but a bicycle or moped is fine. Upon arrival at the island, you can board the **Viking Tour Train**, 12731 State Highway 42, Gills Rock, Wisconsin 54210, (920) 854-2972, www.islandclipper.com, for a narrated tour with stops along the way.

Or drive two miles northeast from Gills Rock along the frequently-photographed, "slow down!" road to Northport. There at the top of the peninsula, board the **Washington Island Ferry Line**, Northport Pier, State Highway 42 and Death's Door, Washington Island, Wisconsin 54246, (800) 223-2094, (920) 847-2546, www.wisferry.com, for a brief, breezy ride that is not narrated but allows you to bring your vehicle. Both the cruise boat and the ferry take you past the **Pilot Island Lighthouse** (established in 1858 and in dire need of repair) and **Plum Island Range Lights** (the rear tower is visible), and on to fabled Washington Island, which sits like a cherry atop the Door Peninsula. This is when you'll discover that the county's inviting name had a sinister origin. Today it could be considered a doorway to paradise, but so many vessels sank in these waters that early French explorers called it Porte des Morts: Door of Death. It is also said that Native Americans told of an evil spirit haunting the waters because they, too, met their share of trouble here.

Washington Island Cherry Train Tours, 1396 Airport Road, Washington Island, Wisconsin 54246, (920) 847-2039, www.cherrytraintours.com, has traversed the island since 1963, and it is priceless. A red station wagon pulls visitors along in open-air trams for a fully guided tour of attractions and island charms.

After a spin around the harbor, the Cherry Train delivers you in comfort—and with full doses of driver patter—to favorite island spots that you could also visit independently. Stops include the **Double K-W Ostrich/Exotic Animal Farm**, Old West Harbor Road, Washington Island, Wisconsin 54246, (920) 847-3202, where a Packers fan leads the group past livestock that is both useful to the farm and demonstrative of how some animals can be saved. Past pet projects have included raising a Bengal tiger that is now in a zoo, and raising a dwarf horse, a breed that cannot eat grain and only lives three years. A cinnamon bear sits teddy bear style as the group learns of her extraordinary diet—hand-fed pecans. Waving a cane, the guide warns visitors to keep a healthy distance from the male ostrich, which is extremely aggressive and can kick like a shotgun. Safely behind the fence, though, the big-bodied bird limits himself to a display of outstretched wings and head-pounding.

At tour's end, the farm sells sticks of ostrich meat that are perfect for munching during the rest of the Cherry Train ride. Stop next at the **Stavkirke**, east of Main Road on Town Line Road. The Stavkirke is a Norwegian church that island volunteers lovingly and slowly constructed near the end of the twentieth century. Employing Old World shipbuilding craftsmanship, they used white cedar, one white pine log, and wood dowels, but no nails, in the mainframe. Hear remarkable stories of the schooner and tool belt that hang inside. Another stop is **Schoolhouse Beach**, one of the island's public beaches, that, since 1999, has become fiercely protective of its white limestones. So many of these precious stones have disappeared into pockets and purses that the next one will cost $250. Just inland, the dark cedar forest contrasts with the Caribbean-blue of the beach.

Door County's northernmost maritime museum is the **Jackson Harbor Maritime Museum**, Jackson Harbor Road, Washington Island, Wisconsin 54246, (920) 847-2522. The commercial fishtug, retired U.S. Coast Guard boat, icehouses, and old fisherman's cottage paint a pretty picture of the stories told inside. If the museum reminds you of an old fishing village, it's because in the old days, two Scandinavian brothers operated a dock, rented net sheds to fellow fishermen, and salted herring for shipping right here on this site. Buy a copy of the *Island Fish Cookery* cookbook to try out some tasty seaside recipes at home. Learn about the boy who had an appendicitis attack and was whisked to safety aboard a U.S. Coast Guard boat. (Years later, when the boy grew up, he located the boat, bought it, and donated it to the museum.)

Have you noticed all the people waving at you on Washington Island? Have you stopped locking your car? And have you begun to think it normal for a chiropractor to have an office in a lumberyard, or for a student to be the only member of his graduating class? Are you sure you want to get back on that ferry?

FROM THE GALLEYS

Inn at Cedar Crossing, 336 Louisiana Street, Sturgeon Bay, Wisconsin 54235, (920) 743-4249, www.innatcedarcrossing.com. This charming cornerstone of old Sturgeon Bay serves whitefish only after 4:00

p.m., and a variety of salads, sandwiches, pastas, and entrées throughout the day. Wouldn't Brie Cheese Beignet, with its port wine reduction and fresh berries, whet your appetite for a Grilled Pork Chop with herbed mashed potatoes? After dinner, check into one of the gorgeous guestrooms upstairs.

KK Fiske Restaurant & Granary Bar, 1177 Main Road, Washington Island, Wisconsin 54246, (920) 847-2121. Island native and owner Ken Koyen says that when the tourists start snapping pictures of each other in front of the "Fresh Lawyers" sign, summer has once again come to Washington Island. (The "lawyers" are really a kind of fish called burbot; ask a local to explain the nickname.) Part of the building is a mainland granary that Koyen acquired in exchange for baling hay, then had shipped via the ferry and finally rebuilt. Note the square timbers, wooden pegs, and elevator. Got time? Koyen can tell you the origin of every bit of wood in the place, including stairs from an island school he once attended. Friday nights, try the Captain's Platter, a delicious serving of local whitefish and lawyers (fresh-caught by Koyen, using a weather-beaten fishtug and gill nets), perch, and pickled fish or whitefish livers, along with a glass of Island Wheat Ale. Koyen supplies island-grown wheat to the Capital Brewery near Madison.

The Washington Hotel, Restaurant & Culinary School, 354 Rangeline Road, Washington Island, Wisconsin 54246, (920) 847-2169, www.thewashingtonhotel.com. Slowly savor the island's premier gourmet dining experience. Weather permitting, do this out on the spacious front porch, where long shadows spread across the lawn like a blanket. The six-course, fixed-price dinner is always a seasonal affair. In early June, it may begin with hour-old mozzarella and intensely flavored morel mushroom soup. The mushrooms are locally harvested, as are the pasta wheat and the leeks that accompany tender leg of lamb. Asparagus spears, grilled and perfectly crisp, are sourced from a southern Wisconsin farm. Savor Wisconsin artisanal cheeses and desserts. But, oh, the breads! Baked from freshly ground whole wheat in the kitchen's brick oven, they are thick and chewy with a satisfying crust. Selected wines accompany each course. Stay in the hotel that a ship's captain built for his counterparts, where guestrooms are named for ships that bear significance to the island's Detroit Harbor.

White Gull Inn, 4225 Main Street, Fish Creek, Wisconsin 54212, (800) 624-1987, (920) 868-3517, www.whitegullinn.com. Convenient to the main highway but set off from it and close to the lake, this classic inn packs all the charm you expect of Door County into a single, perfect destination for comfort food and cozy lodging. Make advance reservations for the Door County Fish Boil, and arrive half an hour early to witness the preparations and famously fiery moment of the boilover.

Don't forget to try a freshly baked cherry pie. And dine from the menu that features entrées such as slow-roasted salmon fillet basted in lemon-herb butter sauce, or rosemary and garlic rubbed pork tenderloin.

TO THE DOCKS

Blacksmith Inn on the Shore, 8152 State Highway 57, Baileys Harbor, Wisconsin 54202, (800) 769-8619, (920) 839-9222, www.theblacksmithinn.com. Choose from two separate inns. Reminiscent of a preserved New England seaside inn, the Harbor House was built in the 1990s. Handrails polished as smooth as glass and Door County Cocoas welcome guests into luxurious rooms with private, lakeview balconies, mini refrigerators, and sumptuous beds. Sit in a cane chair just to hear the comforting creak of woven fibers. Light the gas fireplace and soak in the double whirlpool tub. At the adjacent 1912 Zahn House, discover the historic blacksmithing connection that offers similar amenities against a backdrop of stovewood construction and antique furnishings. Follow the boardwalk through the private, pristine wetland that redwing blackbirds patrol each spring, and that ends at the private pier. Launch a kayak into the calm harbor waters, and take your time getting to breakfast, because it is available across a two-hour window. Try homemade granola, muffins with yogurt, and a selection of fruit juices.

Glidden Lodge Beach Resort, 4676 Glidden Drive, Sturgeon Bay, Wisconsin 54235, (866) GLIDDEN, (920) 746-3900, www.gliddenlodge. com. Contemporary yet rustic condos arc along a private stretch of lakeshore with a sandy beach and lofty pines. With only 31 units, the resort retains a sense of peace. Enjoy double whirlpool tubs, gas fireplaces, and galley kitchens with a full-size refrigerator, microwave, sink, and dishwasher. Indoor pool and spa, gas BBQ grills on the lawn, volleyball net, swimming beach, and lounge chairs. The adjacent **Donny's Glidden Lodge Restaurant** is housed in the stone building of the original, 1939 Glidden Lodge. Walk off your delicious meal along the beach all the way to Whitefish Dunes State Park.

Sunset Resort, Old West Harbor Road, Washington Island, Wisconsin 54246, (920) 847-2531, www.sunsetresort washingtonisland.com. Before sleep, there are the sunsets. The sky and water tend to glow for hours, and the water, on which you may see a pair of swans, is never a single shade of blue. Scandinavian hosts maintain this rambling, fourth-generation Icelandic family resort, which has sat comfortably on the western shore since 1902. No one knows for sure how the tradition of placing personally inscribed, heart-shaped rocks on the fireplace mantel got started, but it is true that guests often seem to leave their hearts in this place. Guests can poke around inside the Antiquity Room, which is dedicated to nothing but family artifacts, including a spinning wheel once brought over from Iceland. Book a second-story lakeside room for the best views and seagull sounds, bring your boat (up to 24 feet) for complementary dockage, and begin to feel like family. Summer breakfasts feature Scandinavian specialties, notably a little something called Barkräm Pankaka—Icelandic pancakes filled with cream and yogurt and topped with warm cherry sauce.

AIDS TO NAVIGATION

Door County Chamber of Commerce Visitor Center, (800) 52-RELAX, www.doorcounty.com. Ask for the lighthouse map, which is a great aid to navigation.

Washington Island Chamber of Commerce, www.washingtonislandchamber.com.

Green Bay to Marinette

From the Guestbook of Rose of Sharon Bed and Breakfast, Oconto:
"You have outdone yourselves in making this a place for comfort and rest."
—Kyle & Phyllis, Hamilton, Ohio

THE WEST SHORE of Green Bay claims 120 miles of shoreline, all the way from its namesake city to the Michigan border. The city is most famous for its football team. When visiting the area, sports fans from other Midwestern cities know they have ventured deep into Packer Country, but for the most part they tend not to get hurt. That leaves them free to discover the city's remarkable range of other attractions, including a waterside wildlife sanctuary, zoo, railroad museum, and pioneer village. Join in the fun, and as you continue up the west shore, see for yourself what the smaller bay towns have to offer clear on up to the Michigan border. Locals like to call this the quiet side of the bay, but they are quick to point out that by boat, it's a short run across to Door County.

Green Bay

East of the mouth of Fox River, the acclaimed **Bay Beach Wildlife Sanctuary**, 1660 East Shore Drive, Green Bay, Wisconsin 54302, (920) 391-3671, www.baybeachwildlife.com, provides urban refuge on 700 acres. For visitors, there are three wildlife viewing areas: Nature Education Center, Wildlife Habi-Trek, and Observation Building/Resch Wing. Learn how the

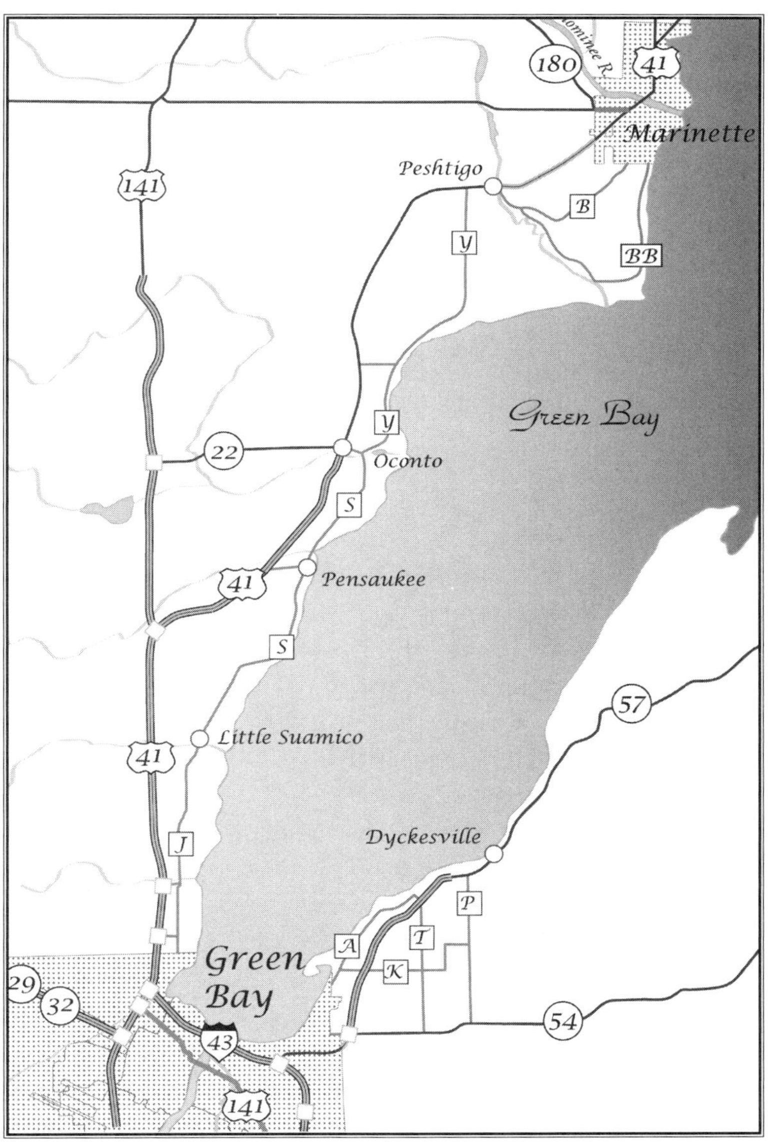

pros conduct their observations and studies of species such as the Blanding's turtle. To get there, follow the flocks of geese or take I-43 to Exit 185.

To visit **Heritage Hill State Historical Park**, 2640 South Webster Avenue, Green Bay, Wisconsin 54301, (920) 448-5150, www.heritagehillgb.org, jump back onto I-43 and merge onto State Highway 172. Across 61 tidy acres, explore 25 regionally historic buildings that represent four interpretive areas and time periods: A Growing Community, Ethnic Agricultural Area, Fort Howard, and La Baye.

477 Sport Sedan by Cruisers Yachts, Oconto, Wisconsin

Campground with easy access to Lake Michigan, North Bay Shore Recreation Area Oconto County Forest, Wisconsin

At this point, you are still east of the Fox River. Cross the State Highway 172 bridge and make tracks for the **National Railroad Museum**, 2285 South Broadway Avenue, Green Bay, Wisconsin 54304, (920) 437-7623, www.nationalrrmuseum.org. Sit in the world's largest steam locomotive, the Union Pacific Big Boy, and ride a full-size train; study the antique railroad equipment and journey through America's great railroading age.

Ground zero for Packer Country is only a couple of miles northwest. And, hey, there is real history here: Did you know that "Green Bay Packers" is the longest standing team name in NFL history? Or that the Packers have won more championships over the course of 80-plus years than any other pro football team? Even if you are from Chicago or Minneapolis, you may as well throw in the towel and experience the **Lambeau Field Atrium**, 1265 Lombardi Avenue, Green Bay, Wisconsin 54304, (920) 569-7500, www.packers.com, and board a London double-decker bus for the **Legends of Lombardi Avenue Tour**, 1901 South Oneida Street, Green Bay, Wisconsin 54304, (888) 867-3342, www.packercoun try.com.

Do you see a breathtaking cloud of sails on the horizon, puffed into the lake breeze? Then it must be late July, and you are in for a treat, because the **Tall Ship Festival**, (888) 867-3342, www.tallshipgreenbay.com, is once again sailing in to port.

About 12 miles northwest of downtown and not far off U.S. Highway 41, the **Northeastern Wisconsin Zoo (NEW Zoo)**, 4378 Reforestation Road, Green Bay, Wisconsin 54313, (920) 434-7841, www.newzoo.org, entertains your family with burrowing owls, macaws, snow leopards, and a whole assortment of wild ones. The 1,560 acres of the Brown County Reforestation Camp is like a bonus prize for zoo visitors; enjoy the trails and trout ponds there.

Now drive 27 easy miles from the zoo on U.S. Highway 41 to sleepy Oconto; and if you want to sound like a native when you get there, leave off the "t."

Oconto

Slow down in a town where fishing is a passion. It is also home to **Cruisers Yachts**, (866) 734-2770, www.cruisersyachts.com, which makes luxury vessels that get boatloads of attention on the lake. If one of these beauties is posed at the company dock at **Oconto Breakwater Park & Harbor**, which sits at the end of Harbor Road off County Trunk Y, it's bound to get your attention, too. Drop a line in the water and trade fish stories at this relaxed, refreshingly undeveloped waterfront. For boaters, there are city docks and two marinas that offer full boat service, transient docking, and a public launch.

Shadows lengthen across front lawn of stately Lauerman House Inn, Marinette, Wisconsin

Stroll the streets of old Oconto, where recent renovations have restored the original spit and polish. Indulge in fine chocolates at **Grandma's Candy, Cake & Confections**, 1022 Main Street, Oconto, Wisconsin 54153, (920) 835-4923. For local color, pop into the **Lumber Mill Gallery Framery**, 107 Smith Avenue (U.S. Highway 41 at the bridge), Oconto, Wisconsin 54153, (920) 834-4494. Owner-photographer Dick Doeren sells original photographs of the region as well as a wide selection of artworks. Farther along, the **Beyer Home Museum**, 917 Park Avenue, Oconto, Wisconsin 54153, (920) 834-6206, www.ocontoctyhistsoc.org, connects history with a house tour. Guided tours start in the annex with its main street shops and exhibits on fur trading, lumbering, commercial fishing, and the building of pleasure craft. Discover how the lumbering and fishing enterprises transformed these northern woods and waters into a bustling industrial center in the 1830s. View ancient artifacts of the Copper Culture, which flourished in this area from about 500 BC to 6000 BC. Tools and jewelry from that period represent the first known examples of hand-forged metal, and some of these pieces are on display.

Move along into the gorgeous red brick house that Cyrus Hart, who ran a shipping and ferry service on the lake, built in 1868. Fans of house tours will love this one with its lavish Victorian furnishings, abundance of woodwork, and elaborate ceiling lights. You have to admire the craftsmanship, if not the material, that went into the making of the Victorian genealogy project that hangs on one wall. It's called a hair wreath, for it was fashioned of human hair. Discover other Victorian peculiarities like the coffin corner built into the parlor staircase. The servants' staircase features a half window built below eye level; the purpose was to show passersby that the owners were wealthy enough to *have* servants.

Outside, old trees shade the grand, parklike grounds. Indeed, the grounds are spacious enough to stage Oconto's biggest bash each June. This is **Copperfest**, when music, a lumberjack show, a hamburger-eating contest, a trout pond, a copper penny find, and lots of other entertainment gives everyone something to celebrate.

Drive half a mile west of U.S. Highway 41 on Mill Street to a somewhat small but historically significant site called **Copper Culture State Park**, c/o N10008 Paust Lane, Crivitz, Wisconsin 54114, (715) 274-5123, www.dnr.state.wi.us. This is ground zero for all the local references to copper. Archeological excavations and later studies revealed that about 6000 years ago Copper Culture Indians, the earliest known people to inhabit Wisconsin, buried their dead at this site along with implements made of copper, stone, bone, and shell. It is believed that the copper originated from the Upper Peninsula of Michigan. The historical marker reads: "Ranking among the world's first metalsmiths, these people hammered native copper into tools and weapons." It concludes: "At the time of the discovery [1952] it was found to be the oldest manifestation of human beings in all northeastern North America east of the Mississippi River." Although it was determined that commercial gravel operations had disturbed much of the site during the 1920s, at least 45 skeletons were excavated along with 26 copper artifacts.

Peshtigo

A little inland but conveniently off U.S. Highway 41 and only 15 miles north of Oconto, there is a church where homage is paid to one of the most terrible tragedies that happened anywhere along Lake Michigan; one that still burns bright in local memory. On October 8, 1871, fire raged through this area and killed an estimated 1,200–1,600 people. Based on the 1,200 figure, the death toll was about five times greater than that of the Great Chicago Fire—on the same day. The summer-long drought, combined with the decimation of the forests, is said to have sparked the event during a storm. It is with a sense of reverence that visitors enter the **Peshtigo Fire Museum**, 400 Oconto Avenue, Peshtigo, Wisconsin 54157, (715) 582-3244, www.peshtigofire.info/museum.htm. In the adjacent **Peshtigo Fire Cemetery**, a mass grave is the final resting place of 350 people. Additional markers tell the heart-wrenching stories of individuals who either died or survived. One man kept wetting the heads of two children in the Peshtigo River. Unfortunately, his heroic efforts at saving their lives resulted in disaster when they later died of hypothermia. It is said that more than 800 Peshtigo residents died before it was all over.

On a lighter note, the church basement is loaded with neat old stuff. Antique boat aficionados will recognize the Thompson name. They can drool over the 1914 15-footer that was built of cedar and white oak and offered for sale in the company catalog for $45. Today, early Thompson boats are collectibles. Who says boats are not an investment?

Marinette

Another seven miles gets you from Peshtigo to Marinette. The lumber barons of the late nineteenth century took the trees but left their legacy in the grand Riverside Avenue homes along the Me-nominee River, which was, from 1865–1895, one of the most important lumbering rivers in the Upper Great Lakes. Pre-settlement, the Menominee people harvested the river's wild rice. In a nod to this legacy, images of wild rice are etched into the U.S. Highway 41 bridge. Cross a footbridge to Stephenson Island where green grass is smattered with

CRUISERS YACHTS

Bank fishermen fumble with monofilament line as the yacht, all dressed in white, glides swanlike down the length of the harbor. Her beauty is there to admire, but not necessarily to have.

She does, after all, cost over half a million dollars.

She is Cruisers Yachts' dream-come-true 477 Sport Sedan, a showboat splashed inside and out with necessary luxuries. Someone carefully thought about every inch of her, not just to add more comforts, but to make each the best it could be.

Reaching Green Bay, the 477 roars up to cruising speed. Oconto disappears in her wake, and she dances with the open water. The height and angle of the cockpit make it look as if a seabird has just landed on the lake, balancing there with wings still outstretched.

Those on board recline amid buttery leather seating, cherry cabinetry, a home theater system, stainless steel refrigerator and freezer units, and a master stateroom with a queen-sized island berth. The 477 is a new chapter in a long story that began in the 1890s when boatbuilder Peter Thompson went to work at the Racine Boat Company. In 1904, he and four brothers founded the Thompson Bros. Boat Manufacturing Co. on the site of an old lumber mill in Peshtigo. In 1953, in response to a labor strike, the younger Thompsons started Cruisers Inc. in Oconto, which is still headquarters for this American manufacturer today

Later that afternoon, the 477 arrives back in the harbor. The fishermen are still there, and one sends a wave, with a look of pride in his eyes. This beautiful boat was, after all, built in Oconto.

trees as well as grills, picnic tables, benches, and a life-size bronze of two boys standing on a river boulder. About to dive into the water, one of the boys remains caught in a moment of summer that we would all wish would last forever.

Hitched to a wagon piled high with fresh-cut lumber, a pair of horses draws visitors into the **Marinette County Historical Society Logging Museum**, Stephenson Island, Marinette, Wisconsin 54143, (715) 732-0831, www.marinettecounty.com/museums.htm. Admire the artistry of beaded accessories and tools that were made long ago by Menominee and Chippewa artisans. Learn about life in a snowy lumber camp through the remarkable detail of a miniaturized scene that is a highlight of the museum. Peering into the winter camp scene, you can almost see steam rising from the muscles of horses straining to pull another load of lumber, and you can almost smell the bacon frying in the cook's shanty. Mounted above the scene are actual lumbermen's paychecks from the 1890s. Look for the apothecary jar that is filled with sawdust from an old Menominee River sawmill. The man who had the inclination to collect these fragments also crafted the miniature scene. Farther on, discover the connection between lumbering, the river, and the lake. Find out who Isaac Stephenson was, and why his name can still be found on buildings and businesses around town, and on the island as well.

For boaters, Stephenson Island is a short stroll upriver from the slips at **Nestegg Marine**, 300 Wells Street, Marinette, Wisconsin 54143, (888) 563-7834, (715) 732-4466, www.nesteggmarine.com. Join the family at this full-service facility that offers a ship's shop packed with everything from name brand deck shoes to anchors. In the market for a new sailing yacht? The showroom gleams with sleek, shiny toys that cannot wait to make some waves. Just downriver from Nestegg is **Marinette Marine**, a division of The Manitowoc Company that builds technologically advanced vessels including U.S. Coast Guard cutters and Staten Island ferries. Tours are not available, but you may be able to see some of the shipyard activity from the river.

Finally, take a dip at Marinette's **Red Arrow Park** and soak up the sun on its clean, sandy beach. Join the bird watchers who flock to the adjacent **Seagull Bar State Natural Area**, which is a sandspit and marsh at the mouth of the Menominee River.

This ends the Wisconsin tour, but Michigan is in sight across the bridge. And since Michigan has the longest shoreline of the four states that border Lake Michigan, you have a lot to look forward to. What are you waiting for? Cross that bridge!

FROM THE GALLEYS

Brothers Three, 106 Superior Avenue, Oconto, Wisconsin 54153, (920) 834-3471. Offering pizza, Mexican, and Italian fare inside the only commercial building that remains in Oconto from the logging heyday.

The Dockside, 1302 Harbor Road, Oconto, Wisconsin 54153, (920) 835-5555. Locals love this newer hotspot that overlooks parkland and the water and thoughtfully offers burgers and entrees in more than one portion size. Dinner entrées come with a soup and salad bar (sample the thick house raspberry dressing). Try a crock of chili with sour cream, extra cheese, and chopped onions. On Fridays, they start frying up the fish at noon and offer a quality selection: choose perch, walleye, bluegill, haddock, or Alaskan pollack.

Enjoy waterfront patio dining and boat dock at sister restaurants located at **The Harbor Village**, 1330 and 1350 Marine Street, Green Bay, Wisconsin 54301. For casual fun and a muscle car-themed menu, try **Jimmy Seas Pub Grill & Fenders**, (920) 438-7640, www.jimmyseas.com. For fine dining, try **Marco's Seafood Club**, (920) 884-6779, www.marcosseafood.com. Marco's menu features fresh, creative fare such as smoked salmon salad with dried cherries, goat cheese, candied pecans, and a raspberry-balsamic vinaigrette. The wild mushroom strudel appetizer is encased in puff pastry, and the lavender honey duck breast is served with parmesan polenta cake

.

TO THE DOCKS

Holiday Inn City Centre, 200 Main Street, Green Bay, Wisconsin 54301, (800) 457-2929, (920) 437-5900, www.holiday-inn.com/greenbay-city. Downtown on the Fox River, find Packers and UW-Green Bay Phoenix–themed guestrooms, live entertainment Friday and Saturday nights, riverfront dining, and Foxy Lady River Cruises, (920) 432-FOXY.

Lauerman House Inn, 1975 Riverside Avenue, Marinette, Wisconsin 54143, (715) 732-7800, www.lauermanhouse.com. This magnificently columned Colonial Revival on the river was built in 1910 for a local department store magnate whose descendants remain local business owners and civic leaders today. Guestroom décor is a stylish departure from traditional Victorian B&B design. Relish the high ceilings, vivid colors, sumptuous fabrics, and feathered pillows mixed with carved antique furniture and contemporary conveniences. The second-story front porch overlooks the river. In the morning, you will have difficulty parting company with the Egyptian cotton sheets and goose down duvet, but the breakfast chef will encourage you with a hot, fresh entrée, homemade pastries, fresh fruit, and Starbucks coffee.

Rose of Sharon Bed & Breakfast, 1109 Superior Avenue, Oconto, Wisconsin 54153, (920) 834-9885, www.roseofsharonbnb.net. The Lingelbach Room is historically furnished with photos of the home's original brewing family and elaborate Victorian style. The sunny yellow and garden-flower stenciling of Amri's Garden room are as fresh as a spring day, and honeymooners especially love the richly appointed Hearts & Lace Room. Enjoy the suite-sized rooms (two with double whirlpools), the innkeepers' relaxed hospitality and genuine warmth, and the enormous wrap-around porch. In the morning, rise to freshly whipped orange froth in a stemmed glass, fruit-stuffed French toast, maple sausage links, fresh fruit, and breakfast blend coffee.

AIDS TO NAVIGATION

Packer Country Regional Tourism Office, (888) 867-3342, www.packercountry.com.

Oconto County Tourism, (888) 626-6862, www.ocontocounty.org.

Marinette Area Chamber of Commerce, (800) 236-6681, www.marinettechamber.com.

MICHIGAN

"Michigan's all about water."

—Roger P. Scharmer, Landscape Designer, Muskegon

AS A MARITIME destination, Michigan shines bright. More lighthouses were built here than in any other state; many have been restored and opened to the public, and others are coming along nicely. This is largely a volunteer effort, a demonstration of how close the shoreline residents are to their lake.

But perhaps the most dramatic evidence of that closeness is the residents' devotion to their sunsets. On the west coast of Michigan, the watching of sunsets is a most popular spectator sport. It has specific start times, prime viewing spots, and an unpredictable outcome. But if they all seem a little obsessed with sunsets, you can forgive them knowing that at 10:00 p.m. on a June evening, the land is dark as night but the sky over the water is just changing from pink to orange to blue. In Michigan, summer lingers in the evenings as if the sun itself cannot stop looking.

Residents will often say that they have dunes while Wisconsin has rocks. Perhaps they can be forgiven the boast, since Michigan has more sand dunes than any other state in the country. As a visitor, you can enjoy these formations on many levels.

But spectacular sights await in the lake as well, for Michigan has designated 11 underwater preserves, three of which are covered in the book: Manitou Passage Underwater Preserve, Southwest Michigan Underwater Preserve, and Straits of Mackinac Shipwreck Preserve. Most of the preserves' popular dive sites are marked by buoys in the summer, and can be accessed from shore.

Culturally, Michigan has an increasing number of grand old vessels serving as marine museums and, in some cases, steaming their way through the water again to thrill a whole new generation of mariners. Discover how the cold, fresh, Great Lakes waters preserve American history far below the level of the land. It is a testament to the power of the lake and to maritime life, and a world well worth exploring today.

Upper Peninsula: West

From the Guestbook of Celibeth House Bed and Breakfast, Blaney Park:
"Lovely home, lovely hosts! Those delicious breakfasts—cookies and cakes were very special. Loved spending time on the deck and chatting and watching the hummingbirds. Hope to be back soon—the northern lights were an extra special treat!" —Tom & Nancy

THE FABLED UPPER Peninsula crests like a wave over the top of Lake Michigan. From Menominee to Manistique, it stretches along some 100 miles of shoreline—and that's only halfway to the Straits of Mackinac, where Lake Michigan mixes waters with Lake Huron. You'll get there, but not before discovering the long, lonely lakeshore of the UP. As you drive along past the cottage lots that bear-hug the lakeshore, take time to pull into county and state parks, as well as a national forest, for direct lake access. Enjoy the beautiful bay views around Escanaba and Gladstone, and absolutely do not miss a little ghost town by the name of Fayette.

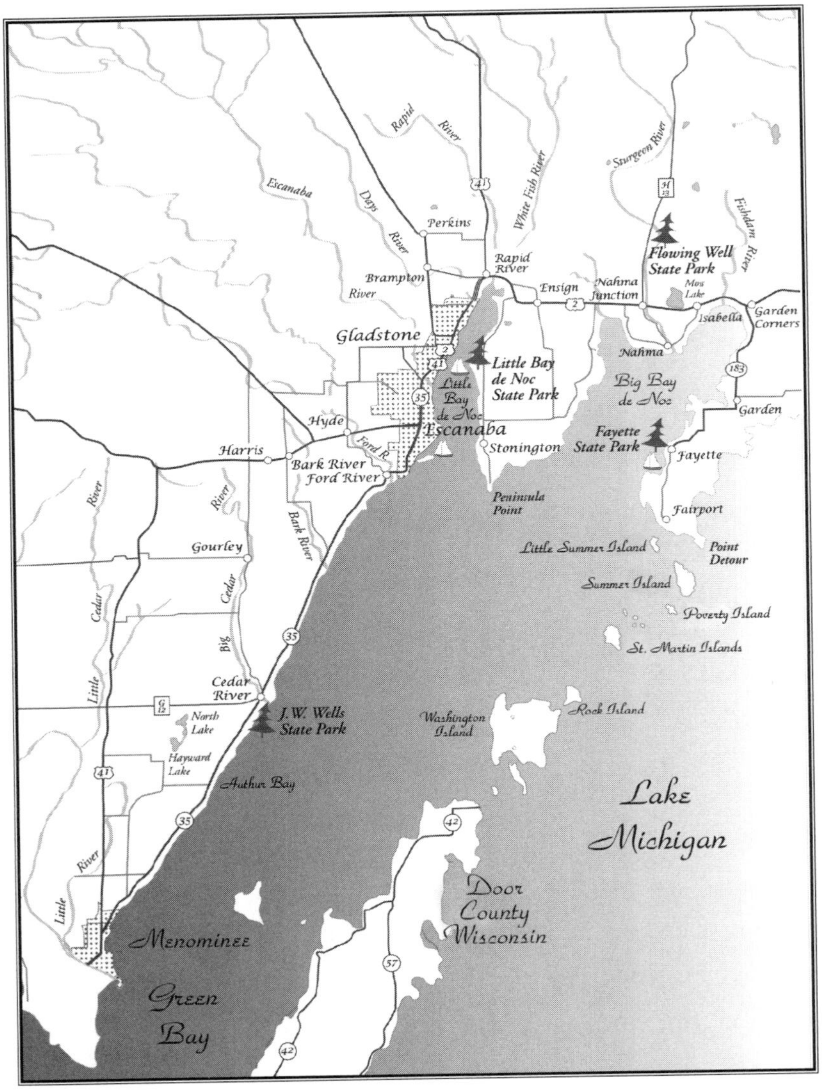

Menominee

Let's start in Menominee. The **Great Lakes Memorial Marina Park**, off 10th Avenue and on Green Bay, is a summer hotspot with its busy marina, sandy beach, 1930s breakwater and band shell, fishing pier, and August **Waterfront Festival**. It is conveniently close to downtown shops. Nearby, the **Heritage Museum**, 904 11th Avenue, Menominee, Michigan 49858, (906) 863-9000, exhibits artifacts and stories of the UP's legendary fur trading, commercial fishing, and lumbering eras, all in a big red church.

Menominee is a busy town, but its buildings and streets soon give way to the northern forests. Drive east on State Highway 35 for 15 miles to the **West Shore Fishing Museum**, Bailey Park, Highway 35, Menominee, Michigan 49858, (906) 863-3347. If you miss the first sign, turn off on the second and drive through the forest a short distance. See the restored net house, fisherman's home, and boathouse. Discover the fishing history of Green Bay's west shore. Enjoy the peaceful, secluded setting along the lake.

Next, head to the 678-acre **J. W. Wells State Park**, N7670 State Highway 35, Cedar River, Michigan 49887, (906) 863-9747, www.michigan.gov/dnr. At this point you are about 25 miles northeast of Menominee, on land once owned by a pioneer lumberman and later improved by the Civilian Conservation Corps. Sunbathe and swim on the sandy beach, bring some food to throw on the grills, and send the kids to the play equipment. Consider renting a rustic cabin for an overnight adventure, and ask about early spring brown trout fishing.

Somewhere between the state park and Ford River, turn your watch back one hour to be on Eastern Time. Being on the western boundary of Eastern Time gives Michigan an edge when it comes to spectacular sunsets—you can still see light in the sky and upon the water when other Great Lakes states have gone dark.

Bays de Noc

Logging trucks whiz along State Highway 35 in an ongoing harvest of the region's legendary timber. 30 miles northeast of the state park, you'll arrive at Escanaba's stretch of shops, but veer off the strip to get close to Little Bay de Noc and its special attractions. Having two bays means there are two peninsulas, which of course means more water views and a fine fishery. Watch freighters at the ore dock, and visit the **Sand Point Lighthouse and Historical Complex**, Ludington Park (north end), 16 Water Plant Road, Escanaba, Michigan 49829, (906) 786-3763. First lit in 1867

Weathered pilings and Furnace Complex, Fayette Historic State Park, Garden, Michigan

and decommissioned in 1939, the lighthouse is a maritime museum with a fourth order Fresnel lens and late nineteenth-century furnishings. Learn the story of the lady keeper and the remarkable restoration that required adding a missing 10 feet to the tower. Interestingly, and for reasons that remain unclear, the tower element was built on the side away from the lake. The complex's **Delta County Historical Museum** sheds light on the past through county logging, shipping, and railroad industry artifacts. Also on display are an antique boat, U.S. Coast Guard history, uniforms, flags, and period rooms.

Crumbly ruins of the Company Store, Fayette, Michigan

Pleasure boats dock at Snail Shell Harbor in front of Superintendents' House, Fayette, Michigan

On the way to Gladstone, sit back and take in sweeping views of Little Bay de Noc. Drive the Stonington Peninsula down to its southern tip where the **Peninsula Point Lighthouse**, (906) 474-6442, stands 40 feet tall and provides panoramic views of Lake Michigan, as it has since 1866. But back then, its real purpose was to guide wooden sailing ships past channel shoals so they could call at the busy northern ports.

Continue on to Big Bay de Noc. This area is developed, but it is also part of the Western Region of the **Hiawatha National Forest**, (906) 786-4062, www.fs.fed.us/r9/forests/hiawatha. From Garden Corners, it is 17 miles south on State Highway 183 down the Garden Peninsula (which is not part of the national forest) to **Fayette Historic State Park**, 13700 13.25 Lane, Garden, Michigan 49835, (906) 644-2603, www.michigan.gov/dnr. Don't miss the ghost town here where nearly 500 people once toiled at one of the UP's most productive iron smelting sites. Now it is idyllic; but in its heyday, it was a noisy, dirty town owned by the Jackson Iron Company and kept well-oiled by the laborers. Today it took you about an hour from Escanaba to get here; but back then, it would have taken two days by stagecoach. Or you could have arrived as some residents did, by tying themselves together with rope and walking across the frozen Little Bay de Noc.

You'll get a fabulous view of Fayette from the **Visitor Center.** It is tempting to rush right down and explore everything that lies before you, but take a few minutes to push the button on the diorama for an excellent introduction to the history and the lay of the land. From 1867–1891, the town of Fayette functioned within four sections: the industrial area on Snail Shell Harbor; the centrally located commercial buildings; the Middle Class Neighborhood around the peninsula and by the lake; and the Lower Class Neighborhood up on the hill. This classic ghost town is filled with well-preserved buildings and crumbled ruins alike, all of which you can walk inside. And the whole entrancing place is surrounded by water. Ready to explore?

Start your self-guided tour at the silent, hulking **Furnace Complex** that, for 24 years, emitted noise, odors, and heat in the production of nearly 230,000 tons of pig iron for the steel industry. Walk around inside the massive casting rooms and by the blast ovens of this early American foundry. Walk over to the limestone bluff, a rocky outcropping that once filled the town with chalky limestone.

Retrace your steps to the dramatic ruins of the **Company Store**. This favorite photo opportunity was once a bustling mercantile center that sold dry goods, hardware, and groceries at high prices. The store burned in the 1920s, leaving behind the romantic ruins you see today.

Behind the store is the **Hotel** that operated until World War II. For a short time in the 1880s, the Hotel was reopened by the captain of a passenger ship.

After the closing of the smelting operation, the workers who remained in Fayette turned to commercial fishing and farming, and the area became a summer resort. The **Post Office** stayed open until the 1950s, and the entire place became a state park in 1959.

Follow the trail down to the end of the peninsula that spirals around **Snail Shell Harbor** in the way its name suggests. Where ships once docked to transport Fayette's finished pig iron to market, only the soaked and softening remnants of pilings remain.

Learn about the **Boarding House Site** as you make your way toward the white house that served as the superintendents' residence, which was considerably removed from the rest of the town. Spacious enough by today's standards, it is said that to the laborers, the house represented an unattainable comfort. Enjoy a picnic lunch nearby. Boaters are in for a treat, as they can dock at this amazing site that is as scenic as it is historic.

Finally, feel like an archeologist as you pick your way among the pebbles to locate the rough, shiny, and colorful artifacts of **Slag Beach**. Called slag, these bits and pieces were by-products of the industrial operation and dumped here as waste. Here they remain, twinkling in the sun and helping to tell the Fayette story.

Fayette is more than just a ghost town: you can camp in semi-modern sites; boat camp; fish for perch, smallmouth bass, northern pike, and walleye; scuba dive in Snail Shell Harbor; swim; and hike five miles of trails through the beech-maple forest and the town.

Retrace your route back to U.S. Highway 2 at sleepy Garden Corners and continue east on Highway 2 to Thompson. Look toward the lake to see the last port of call of the **Christmas Tree Ship**, the ***Rouse Simmons***, which sank off Two Rivers, Wisconsin. Hard as it is to believe today, Thompson once had four lumber companies, four saloons, three churches, and three doctors. You may wish to detour north on State Highway 149 to the **Thompson State Fish Hatchery**, 944 South State Highway 149, Manistique, Michigan 49854, (906) 341-5587, which raises brook, brown, and rainbow trout, Coho salmon, musky, northern, walleye, and suckers for sport fishermen. Continue on Highway 149 to **Palms Book State Park**, northern terminus of Highway 149, (906) 341-2355. Here at Michigan's largest spring, 10,000 gallons of 45-degree water gush out from underlying limestone fissures—every minute. Board the self-operated raft to see brook trout and the boiling sands where the spring water erupts. The Indian legends that once swirled around the spring were debunked when the park's original champion admitted to having fabricated them to attract the tourists. That will give you something to talk about on the way to Manistique, which roughly marks the halfway point across the U.P.

FROM THE GALLEYS

Log Cabin Grille & Bistro, 7531 U.S. Highway 2, Gladstone, Michigan 49837, (906) 786-5621 www.logcabingrilleandbistro.com. Enjoy satisfying steaks and seafood with an emphasis on freshness, creative presentations, and generous portions. Dine-in or take-out to suit your schedule.

Schloegel's Bayview Restaurant & Gift Shoppe, 2720 10th Street (U.S. Highway 41), Menominee, Michigan 49858, (906) 863-7888, www.tastefullydifferent.com. Scandinavian and regional influences at this lakeside restaurant, including signature Swedish meatballs; German potato pancakes with choice of chilled applesauce, sour cream, or maple syrup; and UP pasties. Also serving American fare from burgers, bacon, or liver n' onions to steaks and fresh local fish. Table settings include bird guides for instant identification of species that flock to the waters of Green Bay. After your meal, pick up locally made chocolates, maple syrup, and bakery bites, and stroll outside to the shore.

Stonehouse Restaurant & Carport Lounge, 2223 Ludington Street (corner of U.S. Highway 2, State Highway 35, and U.S. Highway 41), Escanaba, Michigan 49829, (906) 786-5003, www.stonehouse escanaba.com. Savor fine dining in a casual atmosphere. The Great Lakes Platter offers broiled whitefish, broiled walleye, and beer-battered perch. Entrée choices also include Walleye Meuniere, Chicken Grand Traverse with dried cherries in cherry wine cream, and Maytag Mignon that is wrapped in bacon and stuffed with king crab.

Swedish Pantry Restaurant, 819 Ludington Street, Escanaba, Michigan 49829, (906) 786-9606, www.swedish pantry.com. Your Swedish grandmother could be in the kitchen whipping up pancakes, meatballs, and ham-stuffed potato dumplings. American fare includes homemade soups and pot roast. Try the Swedish pancakes with imported lingonberries.

TO THE DOCKS

Celibeth House Bed & Breakfast, 4446 North State Highway 77, Blaney Park, Michigan 49836, (906) 283-3409, www.bnbfinder.com/bedandbreakfast/ level3/17053. This charming 1895 home, once a lumbering company headquarters, offers 71 private acres for roaming, a small private lake with fishing opportunities, and seven spacious guestrooms with private baths. Full breakfast and evening snacks enhance your stay.

Lindberg's Cove Resort, 1407 North Lakeshore Drive, Gladstone, Michigan 49837, (906) 428-4913, www.baydenoc. com/lindbergs. Relax in tree-shaded cottages on the shores of Little Bay de Noc. A 14-foot aluminum rowboat is included with each cottage, and you can bring your own motor (up to 15hp) if you wish. Fish the bay for walleye, bass, and northern pike. Weeklong rentals are available, and nightly reservations are taken if a cottage has not been rented up to two weeks prior.

The Cottage, Fayette Historic State Park, (906) 644-2603, www.michigan.gov /dnr. This 1970s-style ranch is a former manager's residence, now available for year-round rentals—right in Fayette Historic State Park. Functional, not fancy, it's all about location. Since it is not a big lodge, you have the place to yourself, including a backyard fire ring for those evenings under the stars. You have to clean up after yourself down to the vacuuming; but, hey, it will give the kids something to do.

The Summer House Bed & Breakfast Inn, nine miles south of U.S. Highway 2 on State Highway 183 South, Garden, Michigan 49835, (906) 644-2457. Stay in this 1880 Colonial Revival offering two guestrooms with king-size beds and private baths, and others with shared baths. Full breakfast included; kayak and bike rental; gift shop on premises. Convenient to Fayette Historic State Park.

AIDS TO NAVIGATION

Bays de Noc Convention & Visitors Bureau, (800) 533-4FUN, www.travelbaysdenoc.com.

Marinette Area Chamber of Commerce, (800) 236-6681, www.marinettechamber.com. Note: serves Menominee, Michigan as well.

Upper Peninsula Travel & Recreation Association, www.uptravel.com.

Upper Peninsula: East

"...the Upper Peninsula is like another world, its so hard to believe that there could ever be a place so beautiful and flawless..."

—From the Guestbook of www.uptravel.com

U.S. HIGHWAY 2 TAKES YOU across the eastern half of the UP's Lake Michigan shore to the town of St. Ignace, which is covered in the next chapter. Expect no major attractions along this route beyond the Seul Choix Point Lighthouse and before St. Ignace, so take the opportunity to relax and explore on your own. Who knows what wildlife you may encounter, or what northern trees you may identify, along an empty back road that disappears into a wild and remote forest?

Manistique

But first let's start in Manistique, which is 55 miles from Escanaba. Upriver from the U.S. Highway 2 bridge, what looks like a lighthouse tower and keeper's quarters is really the **Historic Manistique Water Tower and Schoolcraft County Museum**, www.manistique.org/oldtower.html. The tower, a red-brick beauty, soars almost 140

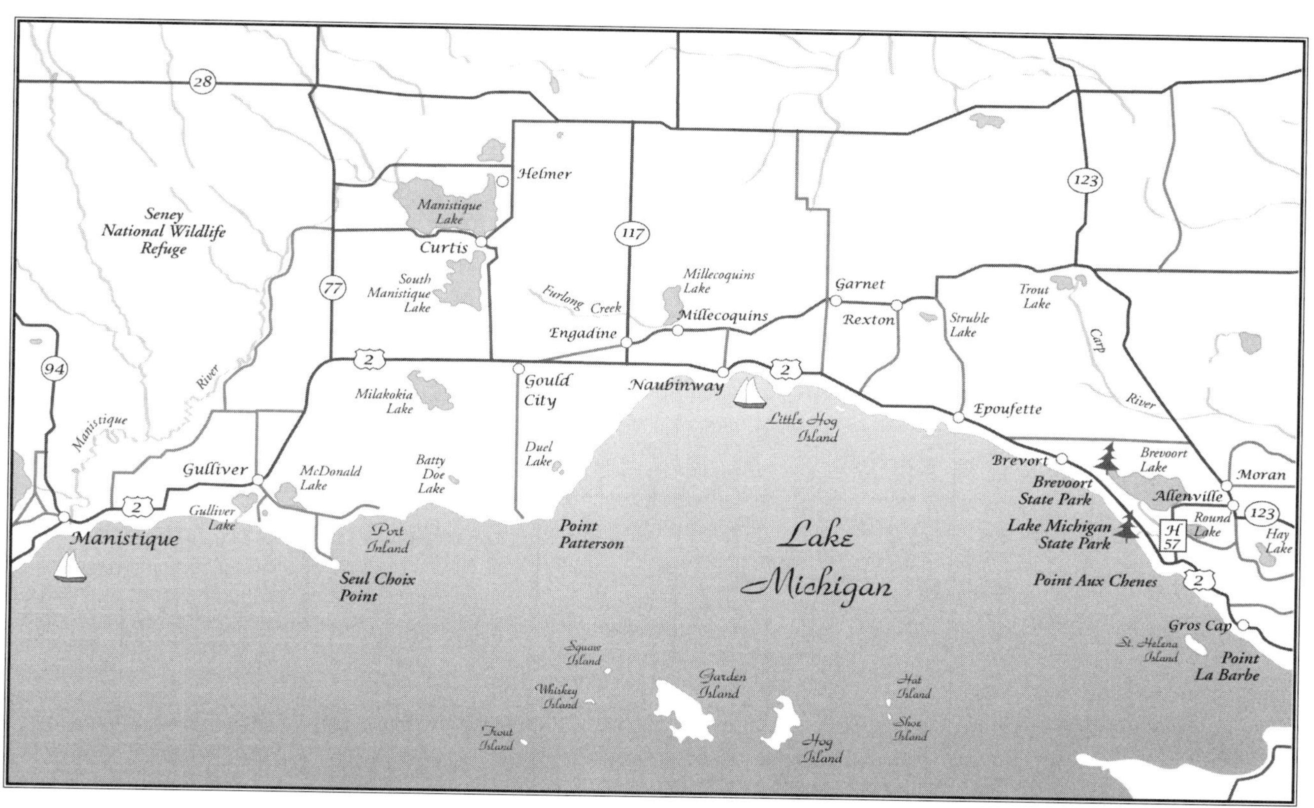

Handsome (and haunted?) Seul Choix Point Lighthouse, Gulliver, Michigan

At the Siphon Bridge, Manistique, Michigan

feet into the air and has a capacity of 200,000 gallons of water. Built in 1922, it features gently arched windows, Bedford limestone trim, and a concrete cornice.

When *Ripley's Believe It or Not* got ahold of the nearby **Siphon Bridge**, at old U.S. Highway 2 and the Manistique River, it put the concrete contortion on the tourist map. Built in 1919 to channel water to a paper mill without flooding the city, the bridge spans both the river and its unusual flume. Ripley challenged you to believe that the bridge was actually below the water level of the flume. It was, indeed, and partially supported by the water. This is no longer the case, as restoration efforts are underway.

Starting at the East Breakwater Light at the harbor, the **Manistique Boardwalk** meanders along almost two miles of shoreline that birds and butterflies love. Enjoy a pleasant, scenic walk that is somewhat removed from the highway. Signage says the shoreline zone contains a rich range of wetland habitats, from swales to beach flats. If you are staying at one of the clean, comfortable, and reasonably priced motels on the eastern end, consider having someone from your party drive you to the lighthouse so you can walk the entire linear route without backtracking.

As you leave Manistique behind, you will come to a large log building billed The Largest Gift Shop in the North. A fun roadside stop, this is **Treasure City**, 5711 West U.S. Highway 2, Manistique, Michigan 49854, (906) 341-2364. Here you can load up on northern-inspired gifts and trinkets, everything from stuffed toys to a snack called Bear Poop.

The **Seul Choix Point Lighthouse**, 3183 County Road 431, Gulliver, Michigan 49840, (906) 283-3183, www.greatlakelighthouse.com, keeps watch just east of Manistique and southeast of Gulliver. To reach this fully operational lighthouse from U.S. Highway 2, turn southeast onto County Road 432 (Port Inland Road) then right onto County Road 431 (Seul Choix Road). If you are wondering how to pronounce it, say "Sis-Shwa" and you will fit in well enough. If you are wondering how it got this name, early French sailors will tell you: caught in a fierce storm, this point of land became their only chance for refuge—their Seul Choix, or "Only Choice."

Enjoy a free tour of the museum inside the beautifully restored keeper's quarters, and note the copper doorframe molding of the 1925 addition that afforded privacy to the assistant keeper. Artifacts on hand include an antique organ, a box camera, and a wedding dress. Pay the nominal fee to climb the white tower, but listen for the sound of ghostly footsteps. Afterward, browse in the great gift shop, and see additional museum exhibits in the Steam Fog Horn Building. If Seul Choix seems like a lonely outpost, consider that in the 1800s, there was a fishing village not far away. The remaining village buildings are in private hands and unmarked.

Back on U.S. Highway 2 at Gulliver, continue east through Schoolcraft County. Somewhere before Gould City, you'll

MAKING THE "ONLY CHOICE"

Sometimes it takes a while for history to be brought to light.

As president of the Gulliver Historical Society, Marilyn Fischer has written a 353-page history of the Seul Choix Point Lighthouse. Included in the book are reprints of the old keepers' logs.

"We were very fortunate to have one of our Coasties [U.S. Coast Guardsman], come back. He asked to have a tour of the lighthouse, where he had been stationed not long before the time when it would be unmanned. He started crying when he saw one of the back bedrooms. He said, 'I'm so ashamed. Can I meet you somewhere for dinner? I want to confess something,'" Fischer explained.

That evening, the man brought his family to Fischer's nearby restaurant.

"I said, 'now what's this true confession?'" Fischer began. "He said, 'when I left in 1972, there was a wooden crib of books up in the attic of the boathouse, and I helped myself to some of them. I would like to return them.'"

The man offered to throw in his old uniform and photos by way of restitution.

The books, it turned out, were the original keepers' logbooks from the period 1895–1930. To Fischer, they were pure gold. She had been wondering about them for 20 years.

"The names of the early keepers weren't documented anywhere, and here this man gives me these books. And there's all the names of all our early lightkeepers—where they came from, where they went, plus their signatures," Fischer said, adding that it was not unusual for such items to be taken as souvenirs.

Fischer said it turned out for the best. "Had he not taken the logs, they would have been lost forever—just like the later-dated logs left behind!"

Fortunately, for both Fischer and the history of the Seul Choix lighthouse, the former Coast Guardsman made, it seems, the "only choice."

You can buy Ms. Fischer's book at the lighthouse gift shop.

arrive in Mackinac County. You may as well learn how to pronounce it now, before thoroughly embarrassing yourself on the island, so, here it is: the "ac" is pronounced "aw." You may see it spelled both ways, as in "Mackinaw City;" but don't let that confuse you. It's always "aw."

Pull into the Roadside Park just east of Naubinway, where a sign explains why the northernmost point of Lake Michigan, which you passed about a mile back, is significant to American history. Now continue on to the **Garlyn Zoological Park**, W9104 U.S. Highway 2, Naubinway, Michigan 49762, (906) 477-1085, www.garlynzoo.com. On these 40 acres, stroll the cedar mulch trails to enjoy a variety of wildlife native to northern forests. Here is your chance to boast of close encounters with UP cougars, wolves, black bears, and river otters. Buy grain to feed the deer, goats, and llamas.

Before arriving in Epoufette's tiny downtown, pull into the **Scenic Overlook** both for the view and to learn that Epoufette has been a fishing village since 1859. Stop for regional delicacies, especially pasties and smoked fish.

Four miles west of Brevort, which was an 1875 Swedish settlement and is now a crossroads town, the **Cut River Bridge** spans 641 feet across a limestone gorge that plummets 147 feet. Get a good look at the viewing platform, have a picnic at the eastern end, and take the stairs all the way down to the river.

The Eastern Region of the **Hiawatha National Forest**, (906) 786-4062, www.fs.fed.us/r9/forests/hiawatha, begins just east of Brevort. As you continue through the forest along U.S. Highway 2, you will quickly reach the easternmost point of the UP's Lake Michigan shore. Next up is St. Ignace. To explore St. Ignace, you can opt out of crossing the Mackinac Bridge to avoid paying a toll each way and driving 10 miles round-trip. Then again, it may be worth it just for the experience, because, as you will soon discover, this bridge is worthy of its nickname, the Mighty Mac.

FROM THE GALLEYS

Beaudoin's Café & Marathon Service, W11599 U.S. Highway 2, Naubinway, Michigan 49762, (906) 477-6292. Broasted chicken, steaks, chops, fish, and bison; homemade pies and muffins; and fixin's for your car, too.

The Upper Crust Bakery & Deli, 375 Traders' Point Drive, Traders' Point at the Dock, Manistique, Michigan 49854, (906) 341-2253. Out on the harborfront at the Manistique River, this cute café offers indoor or deck seating. Enjoy fresh, gourmet sandwiches loaded up with corned beef, roast beef, pastrami, chicken, smoked turkey, or honey baked ham. The Goodwillie is hot pastrami and scallion cream cheese; the Glorified Grill Cheese melts cheddar, Swiss, and provolone with Canadian bacon, red onions, and mushrooms. On Sundays, don't miss the delicious Wisconsin cheese soup.

TO THE DOCKS

Colonial Motel, 1111 East Lakeshore Drive (U.S. Highway 2), Manistique, Michigan 49854, (906) 341-6656, www.visitmanistique.com/colonial/motel.html. For cleanliness, comfort, reasonable rates, and proximity to the lakefront Manistique Boardwalk, this one is an excellent choice among a string of motels. In-room microwave for your popcorn, and a refrigerator for all your other snacks.

King's Motel & Cabins, W1655 U.S. Highway 2, Naubinway, Michigan 49762, (906) 477-6271, exploringthenorth.com/kingsmotel/kings.html. Clean rooms and cabins with continental breakfast and nearby beaches.

Northshore Motor Inn, 801 East Lakeshore Drive (U.S. Highway 2), Manistique, Michigan 49854, (906) 341-2420, www.visitmanistique.com/northshore/motel.html. With no road between you and the lakeshore, this location is very convenient.

AIDS TO NAVIGATION

Manistique Area Tourism Council, www.onlynorth.com.

Schoolcraft County Chamber of Commerce, www.manistique.com.

Upper Peninsula Travel & Recreation Association, www.uptravel.com.

St. Ignace, Mackinaw City, Mackinac Island

Wife: *"Well, if we rent bikes for an hour and a half, we're not going to have time to shop."*
Husband: *"Okay."*
Wife: *"Because we have to shop."*
Husband: *"Okay."* —At the Mackinac Island State Park Visitor's Center, Mackinac Island

"We've got the t-shirts and the goofy hats, but it's one of the thinnest veneers of tourism I've ever seen— the carriage trade goes back 150 years; the architecture is historic. I fell in love with living this whole part of history." —Bob Tagatz, Grand Hotel, Mackinac Island

SPANNING THE FABLED Straits of Mackinac, the Mighty Mac bridge connects St. Ignace to Mackinaw City, thus unifying the two pieces of Michigan. Sure, northern Yoopers (folks from the UP) have been known to refer to the good folks of Mackinaw City—who live below the bridge—as trolls; but what do the people of the Lower Peninsula care? After all, they've got those great bridge views to boast about. And when evening settles on the Straits and the lights of the bridge sparkle like diamonds, any little rivalries float away like freighters on the horizon.

St. Ignace

Before you do anything, try saying St. Ignace with the accent on the first syllable, so that it sounds like *ig*-nis. That and the earlier "Mackinaw" lesson should get you through this part of Michigan with no taking it all in, continue on to **Bridge View Park**, then cross I-75 (not the bridge), and pull into America's third-oldest city, St. Ignace.

Learn more about native history and early European settlement at the **Museum of Ojibwa Culture and Marquette Mission Park**, 500–566 North State Street, St. Ignace, Michigan 49781, (906) 643-9161. At the **Fort De Buade Indian Museum**, 334 North State Street, St. Ignace, Michigan 49781, (906) 643-6622, view the movie *Black Robe* and study the collection of military and Indian weapons.

Launching your own boat? The **St. Ignace City Marina and Boat Launch**, (800) 447-2757 for DNR Marina reservations, or (906) 643-8131 for Harbor Master, offers new facilities, including 136 slips, four boat ramps, a fish-cleaning station, and additional comforts and conve-

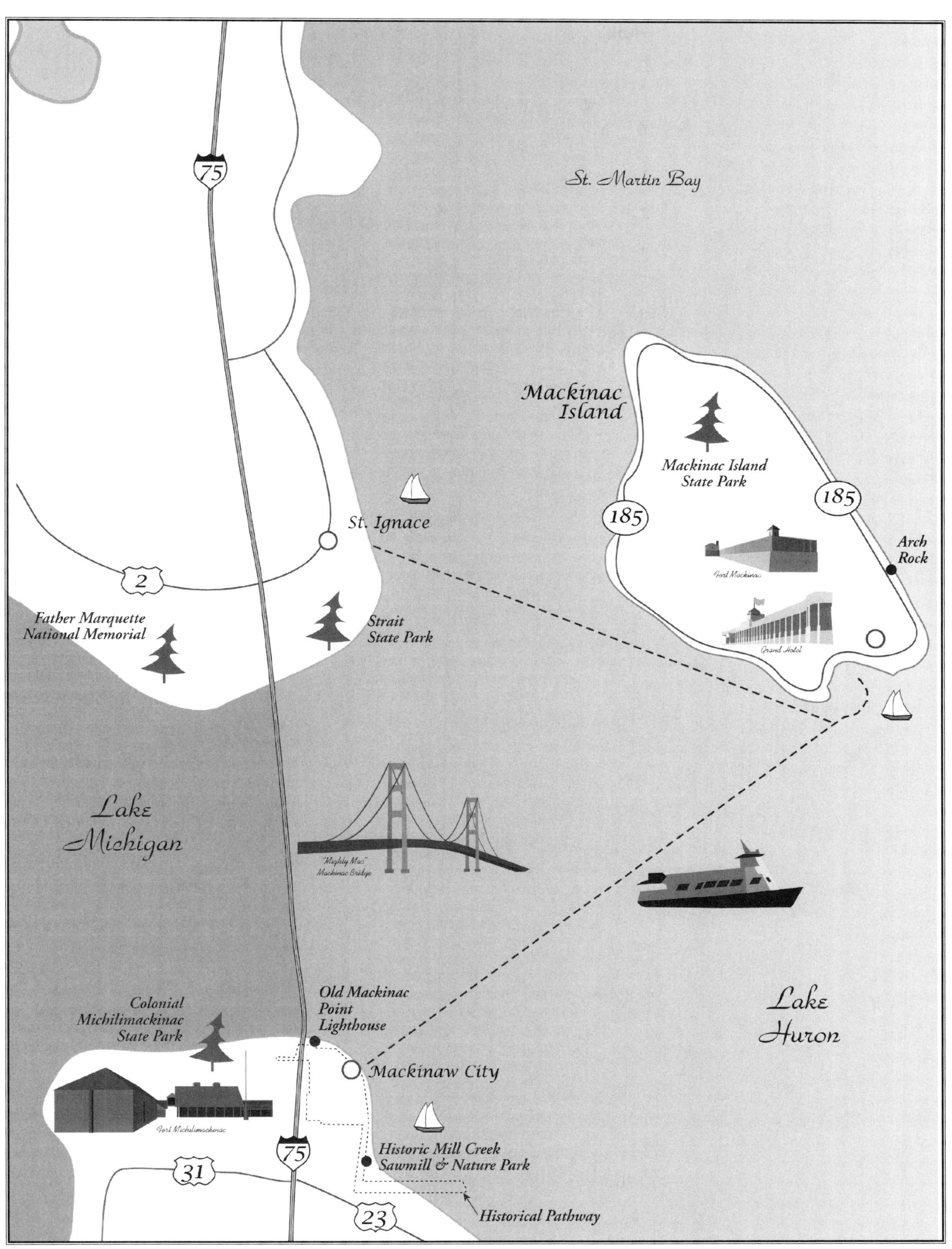
75
St. Martin Bay
Mackinac Island
Mackinac Island State Park
185
185
St. Ignace
Arch Rock
Fort Mackinac
2
Father Marquette National Memorial
Strait State Park
Grand Hotel
Lake Michigan
"Mighty Mac" Mackinac Bridge
Colonial Michilimackinac State Park
Old Mackinac Point Lighthouse
Lake Huron
Mackinaw City
Fort Michilimackinac
75
Historic Mill Creek Sawmill & Nature Park
31
23
Historical Pathway

niences. For fresh and smoked fish, sausages, and spreads, pop into the **Mackinac Straits Fish Co.**, 109 West Elliott Street, St. Ignace, Michigan 49781, (906) 643-7535, www.msfishcompany.com.

You can catch a ferry from St. Ignace to Mackinac Island, or cross the bridge and board one in Mackinaw City.

Lilacs bloom at Public Boating Facility in gesture of welcome to ferries arriving at Mackinac Island, Michigan

Horses of summer bound for Mission Point Resort, Mackinac Island, Michigan

Mackinac Bridge

Even with 466,300 cubic yards of concrete, 11,840 tons of cable, and a total weight of 1,024,500 tons, the Mighty Mac manages to look elegant, with cables that cascade down like window valances. Spanning five miles from the Upper to the Lower Peninsula, the roadbed slopes gradually climbs upward to achieve a height of 199 feet above water at its halfway point. Far below, the water plunges 295 feet to the bottom of the Sraits. As you begin to cross, tune in to Radio 1610-AM for a handy and pleasant narration about the bridge. For any drivers who secretly harbor a fear of crossing an expanse so vast, know that the maximum speed is 45 mph, and no stopping is allowed on the bridge. Also, should you find yourself traveling in the wrong direction, be aware that U-turns are also prohibited.

Construction began in 1954, and the bridge was first opened to traffic in 1957. Dogs, deer, and even a skunk have been found making the crossing.

As you drive south, you'll find Lake Michigan to your right, Lake Huron to your left, and the Straits of Mackinac below. Historically, the Straits have been both an important resource for the natives and a strategic point of control for settlers, as well as the site of shipwrecks. Today the **Straits of Mackinac Shipwreck Preserve**, www.michiganpreserves.org/straits.htm, maps out 148 square miles of sunken treasure in the form of 15 known wrecks.

And for those a bit faint of heart or stomach, know that the bridge may bow eastward or westward as much as 20 feet on windy days.

Mackinaw City

Once you cross the bridge going south, you'll arrive in Mackinaw City. Kitschy and fun, the clutter of shops along Central Avenue sells all the essentials, from fresh fudge to collectible lighthouses. Get an ice cream cone before following the **Historical Pathway**. This collection of some 40 markers reveals the colorful history of the area's Native Americans, fur traders, French and British soldiers, and commercial fishermen. Many of the signs have a maritime focus. Standing across the street from **Bell's Fishery**, 229 South Huron Avenue, Mackinaw City, Michigan 49701, (231) 436-7821, you can read about the area's first large fishery, built on that site in 1892. It shipped five to seven tons of fresh or salted fish to market each week, including lake trout, whitefish, herring, and perch. Bell's, by the way, is an enterprise of the Little Traverse Bay Band of Odawa Indians.

Not far from where the Historical Pathway snakes past the reconstructed fort (we'll get there), you can actually stand under the Mackinac Bridge. Take a moment to enjoy this unique view of its raw underbelly. Further along the Historical Pathway, you'll come to **Alexander Henry Park**, a prime spot for watching the slow advance of bridge traffic and freighters, and admiring the grace of the Old Mackinac Point Lighthouse. If you don't feel like walking, let the folks at **Mackinaw Trolley Company**, 706 South Huron Avenue, Mackinaw City, Michigan 49701, (877) 858-0357, (231) 436-7812, www.mackinawtrolley.com, whisk you about town as they show you the sights. But in order to see the lights, why not book a three-hour **Shepler's Lighthouse Cruise**, (231) 436-5023, for close-up views of at least four lighthouses with expert narration by the Great Lakes Lighthouse Keepers Association.

The multi-site pass is a great value and gets you into three of four great sites, one of which is on Mackinac Island. Starting in Mackinaw City, visit the reconstructed fort and village of **Colonial Michilimackinac**, at the bridge, just west of I-75, Mackinaw City, Michigan, (231) 436-4100, www.mackinacparks.com. Originally built in 1715 by the French, the fort was later abandoned and occupied by the British, and then, in 1763, captured by the Indians. During the American Revolution, the British decided they needed a more strategic vantage point, so they built a new fort on Mackinac Island (which we'll see later). Michilimackinac faded into history; but raised eyebrows.

History runs deep here. Read the first chapters of the story at the 15-station **Father Marquette Memorial**, 720 Church Street (one block west of I-75 and off U.S. Highway 2), St. Ignace, Michigan 49781, (906) 643-8620, www.michigan.gov/marquettememorial. Father Jacques Marquette, a French missionary, established the European settlement of St. Ignace in 1671, just 51 years after the Pilgrims landed in the New World. Learn about Marquette's experiences, along with those of the Native Americans whose lives he influenced, here at the memorial. After because archeological digs have unearthed so many artifacts, the abandoned fort and fur-trading village have been effectively reconstructed. Today, costumed soldiers, French voyageurs, and villagers pull visitors into the excitement of an Indian attack and British Redcoat musket fire, the elegance of a French wedding, and the aromas of baking pies and simmering stews. Tour the reconstructed barracks, guardhouse, and other period settings and exhibits. View the excavated artifacts in the Treasures from the Sand exhibit.

Visit the handsome **Old Mackinac Point Lighthouse**, Mackinaw City, Michigan, (231) 436-4100, www.mackinacparks.com, which was founded in 1889 and re-opened for tours in 2004 after a 14-year interior restoration. In 1957, the Mackinac Bridge replaced the lighthouse's beacon as the primary aid to navigation through the Straits, but visitors can travel back in time to the days when a lighthouse keeper helped to ensure safe passage. Try your hand at activating fog signals and piloting a freighter through the dark. Study period rooms and climb the spiral tower stairs to view the original Fresnel lens. Having toured many of Lake Michigan's old lighthouses by now, you know how rare it is to find an original Fresnel lens in place, so this is a sight you do not want to miss.

Drive three easy miles south on U.S. Highway 23 to the 625-acre **Historic Mill Creek Sawmill & Nature Park**, Mack-

IT HAPPENED AT THE GRAND

All those somber faces and straight backs that characterize old photos would have us believe that our ancestors lived life more seriously than we do today. Silly us. We did not invent fun. They did.

Take Mackinac Island, for example. Back in the 1890s, there was horseracing—and betting—at the center of the island. But the folks who ran the Grand Hotel at the time were not about to lose guests' entertainment dollar to that sort of thing. So they began to advertise dog races before they had even begun to organize any.

"They advertised this on the Day Sheet before they actually had it," chuckled Bob Tagatz of the Grand Hotel, "including a wager sheet that indicated to people it was all right to bet—without actually saying so."

So when guests began showing up to see the races, the hotel owners had to get some dogs; and as Tagatz tells it, they did so on the mainland. But, of course, not having been trained, the dogs would not race.

Later, the story goes, someone found inspiration in the water that surrounded the island.

"They took the dogs out to the lake, and, what do you know? They all swam back—so they had a race."

And what did the guests think of the new water sport?

"This lasted for the next 13 years," said Tagatz, quickly adding that today's management does not go for such a thing.

But even though swimming dogs have faded into memory, racing still remains a popular island sport. Today, though, it is the people who do the competing—on land, by foot.

inaw City, Michigan, (231) 436-4100, www.mackinacparks.com. Powered by water, this working reconstruction buzzes and whines to the sound of saws splitting timber. Find yourself in 1790, fueling construction of the original Mackinac Island settlement. Visit the British Workshop and the American Millwright's House, attend a "Creatures of the Forest" naturalist program, and stretch your legs across 3.5 miles of woodland trails.

Crossing Over

Though you're technically touring Lake Michigan, there's one very important exception for venturing away to another of the Great Lakes. Connected to Lake Michigan by the Straits of Mackinac, Lake Huron is home to the state's most famous island—and one adventure that cannot be missed.

From either St. Ignace or Mackinaw City, the easiest way to get to Mackinac Island is via one of three privately-owned ferries: **Arnold Transit Company**, (800) 542-8528, www.arnoldline.com, **Shepler's Mackinac Island Ferry**, (800) 828-6157, www.sheplersferry.com, and **Star Line Hydro-Jet Ferry**, (800) 638-9892, www.mackinacferry.com. All offer service to the island at the same reasonable price, but with different types of boats and service. No cars are allowed on the island, so check the ferry schedules, make your arrangements, and get ready to travel back in time to the magical days of horse-drawn car-

View from front porch of Grand Hotel, Mackinac Island, Michigan

Fort Mackinac still stands guard, Mackinac Island, Michigan

riages and gracious hospitality. Make reservations early if you plan to stay overnight on the island, for the best rooms fill up fast during the short summer season.

Mackinac Island

The ferries let you off in the bustling downtown. Get your bearings at the fine **Mackinac Island State Park Visitor's Center**, Main Street across from Fort Mackinac, (231) 436-4100, www.michigan.gov, www.mackinacparks.com. Staff will happily answer questions, even if you are the 500th person that day to ask where the restrooms are. Study the displays, watch the video, and shop for island-related books and other goodies. Since you are downtown, why not get in a little shopping? Kids flock to the low-priced souvenir shops (where they'll find those funny hats you cannot help but notice), but visitors of all ages will love the fudge shops. Buying famous island fudge makes you a "fudgie," which is island-speak for "tourist." Let the islanders snicker all they want—what comes out of the kitchens of the shops is creamy and delicious. Positioned right in the windows of the shops, fudge-makers pour thick, creamy masses of the stuff onto marble slabs. Watch, drool, and inevitably break down as they work their chocolaty magic. One to try is **Murdick's Fudge**, www.murdicks.com, which was established way back in 1887. **The Balsam Shop**, www.balsamshop.com, offers maple syrup treats, cedar boxes, lighthouse collectibles, and handcrafted lilac glassware. **Freshwater Foods**, www.freshwaterfoods.com, specializes in packaged foods that are uniquely influenced by the Great Lakes and the Midwest. Try **Michigan Peddler**, www.michiganpeddler.com, for Michigan-made products (excluding automobiles). At **Scrimshanders**, www.scrimshanders.com, shop for fine nautical pieces including jewelry, much of it inspired by the whalers' ancient art of scrimshaw.

For a great overview of Mackinac Island that includes a lovely horse-drawn ride, sign up with **Mackinac Island Carriage Tours**, (906) 847-3307, www.mict.com. Your journey starts downtown, as the cheerful driver points out the Governor's Mansion, the only mall without a fudge

HORSES ON HOLIDAY

Mackinac Island Carriage Tours employs about 400 draft horses that live on Mackinac Island for about half the year. But what do they do when tourism shuts down for the winter? Some horses remain to serve island residents and businesses, but the bulk of them hightail it north to an Upper Peninsula farm. How do you move hundreds of horses? You hire the Arnold Transit Company, the only ferry line equipped to carry them.

"We use an enclosed boat (the Huron, which is our off-season boat as well) that is cleared of seats on the main deck," said Tony Frazier, Computer Systems Manager. "It smells like a barn when they arrive at their destination."

Every spring, Arnold helps to ferry nearly 700 horses that hold summer jobs on the island. Come late fall, Arnold takes them back, about 30 at a time, to St. Ignace. From there, the horses go to their winter home in Pickford, south of Sault Ste. Marie.

What is life like for them on the mainland?

"Lazy. All they need to do is relax and eat. The horses that have done this a few times remember and can be very excited to be making the trip," said Frazier.

shop, and the lilac tree that is over 200 years old. Arriving at the **Grand Hotel** and resting the horses at the top of the hill, the driver tells of the legendary hotel's mystique—the superlative length of its front porch, the tradition of dressing for dinner. The horses resume their pleasant clip-clop and take you to the first stop, **Surrey Hills Museum** and **Wings of Mackinac Butterfly Conservatory**. You'll then switch to a three-horse hitch that takes you past serene cemeteries and through part of the 1,780-acre **Mackinac Island State Park**, which covers a whopping 80 percent of the island and is mostly boreal forest. Enjoy the beauty of wildflowers in spring and towering trees all season long. Enjoy the patter of the driver who points out peculiarities such as State Highway 185 (Lake Shore Road/Main Street). The shortest state highway in the United States, Highway 185 has no recorded automobile accidents and no beginning or end. The carriage stops briefly at **Arch Rock**, which rises 150 feet above Lake Huron, then heads on to **Fort Mackinac**.

High on a hill, **Fort Mackinac**, Mackinac Island, Michigan, (231) 436-4100, www.mackinacparks.com, has a past as colorful as its yellow tearoom umbrellas. In the eighteenth century, though, the preferred color was red, as it was the British who built Fort Mackinac in 1780 to aid their fight in the American Revolution. Americans won the conflict and the fort, only to lose it to the British again during the War of 1812. Three years later, though, America got it back for good, and have since put the matter to rest by turning it into a visitor attraction. Fourteen original fort buildings stand today, and they are the oldest such structures in Michigan.

So what do you do in an old military fort? You clap hands over your ears and thrill to the boom of cannon and musket fire from the safety of the twenty-first century. You listen to a military music concert, play Victorian games, and kick up your heels in an English Rose Dance. You snap pictures as your children dress up in nineteenth-century clothing and practice the Manual of Arms before an interactive video display.

After exploring the fort, walk down the hill back downtown, or catch the next carriage to the **Grand Hotel**. Not staying at the hotel? For a small fee, you can still absorb its opulence on a self-guided tour and perhaps enjoy a spot of tea.

Another favorite way to get around Mackinac Island is to rent a bicycle. Adults and kids alike can gleefully explore the 4.4-square-mile island with the wind in their hair and silver spokes flashing in the sunlight. Before strapping on a helmet and setting off, though, all riders should be aware that bicycle collisions and fatalities do occur on the island. But with a reasonable amount of care, the estimated two-hour journey around is exhilarating, and side trips through the interior reward every explorer.

But if you really miss driving, then

hire your own horse and buggy at **Jack's Livery Stable**, Mahoney Avenue, Mackinac Island, Michigan 49757, (906) 847-3391, www.jacksliverstable.com. And if you want to get out on the water, take a sailboat ride aboard the ***Mackinaw Breeze***, Chippewa Hotel waterfront, reservations (906) 847-8669, boat (906) 430-0413, www.macbreeze.com.

Everyone adapts surprisingly well to the island's public transportation options that include even horse-drawn taxis. Who doesn't wonder, perhaps over a delicious dinner of fish from the local waters, whether they could get along this way on the mainland?

FROM THE GALLEYS

Galley Restaurant & Bar, 241 North State Street, St. Ignace, (906) 643-7960, www.galley-rest.com. Try Great Lakes broiled whitefish and trout, deep-fried lake perch, and whitefish livers.

Scalawag's Whitefish & Chips, 226 East Central Avenue, Mackinaw City, Michigan 49701, (231) 436-7777, www.scalawagswhitefish.com. Enjoy the nautical décor and casual atmosphere as you munch on their lightly breaded, moist, and flavorful fresh fish sandwiches. Homemade whitefish chowder comes in a cup or bread bowl.

The Yankee Rebel Tavern, 101 Astor Street, Mackinac Island, Michigan 49757, (906) 847-6249, www.yankeerebeltavern.com. Casual, creative fare with attention to ingredients. Walnut Summer Salad is a blend of mesclun greens with caramelized walnuts, dried cherries, blue cheese, pears, and champagne herb vinaigrette. Pot Roast on Wheat gets comfy beneath its blanket of melted cheddar. Grilled Yellowfin Tuna arrives encrusted in fennel with roasted shallot and pine nut risotto, smoked yellow pepper coulis, and seasonal vegetables.

1852 Grill Room at Island House Hotel, Mackinac Island, Michigan 49757, (800) 626-6304, (906) 847-3347, www.theislandhouse.com. Aged prime steaks, fresh fish, chops, and gourmet desserts featuring Ryba's fudge.

Harbor View Dining Room, Chippewa Hotel, 250 Main Street, Mackinac Island, Michigan 49757, (800) 241-3341, (906) 847-3341, www.chippewahotel.com. American regional fare with marina and Straits views. Kick back with the yachters inside the adjacent **Pink Pony Bar & Grill**.

Village Inn, Hoban Road, Mackinac Island, Michigan 49757, (906) 847-3542, www.viofmackinac.com. Certified Angus steaks, chops, ribs, and house special Planked Whitefish.

TO THE DOCKS

Grand Hotel, Mackinac Island, Michigan 49757, (800) 33-GRAND for reservations, (906) 847-3331, www.grandhotel.com. How do you top the style of horse-drawn carriages pulling up to the signature porch, harpists and orchestras accompanying diners and dancers, croquet on the lawn, and a refreshing dip in the pool? Enjoy it all as guests have since Victorian times. Consult the Daily Schedule each morning as you head down to the full breakfast where you might find Scottish salmon or Irish oatmeal. During the evenings, don your finery and savor the lavish, five-course dinner. Both meals are managed by the renowned Jamaican wait-staff and included in your stay.

Hotel Iroquois, www.iroquoishotel.com. Spectacular lakefront setting with family hospitality honed to perfection for over half a century.

Mission Point Resort, One Lakeshore Drive, Mackinac Island, Michigan 49757, Reservations (800) 833-7711, (906) 847-3312, www.missionpoint.com. Nothing between you and Lake Huron except a rolling carpet of lawn and chairs from which you may never want to get up. On-site restaurant options, salon with spa services, outdoor heated pool and hot tub, and a kids' activity center will keep you happy. The resort's Tower Museum teaches about local maritime shipping history, shipwrecks of the Straits, and Michigan lighthouses. The Great Lakes Suite features Straits views, three bedrooms, and four bathrooms; other rooms are tastefully appointed with inspiration from northern Michigan.

Sunrise Beach Motel, 11416 West U.S. High-way 23, Mackinaw City, Michigan 49701, (800) 334-7239, (231) 436-5461, www.sunrisebeachmotel.com. Located on the mainland's sunrise (Lake Huron) side and refreshingly removed from the clutter of downtown, this motel features an indoor/outdoor pool, continental breakfast, balconies over Lake Huron, and a generous stretch of sand. In the evenings, join the beach people around the fire pit, and watch a family of geese cruise like a freighter toward the lighted bridge.

AIDS TO NAVIGATION

St. Ignace Visitors Bureau, (800) 338-6660, www.stignace.com.

Mackinaw City Chamber of Commerce, (888) 455-8100, www.mackinawchamber.com.

Mackinaw Area Visitors Bureau, (800) 666-0160, www.mackinawcity.com.

Mackinac Island Tourism Bureau, (800) 454-5227, www.mackinacisland.org.

Cross Village to Charlevoix

From the Guestbook of The Bridge Street Inn, Charlevoix:
"The food & conversation were excellent – we could not have had a more restful stay. We can't wait to tell our friends what awaits them in Charlevoix and the Bridge Street Inn."

"A wonderful stay - such charm & beauty."

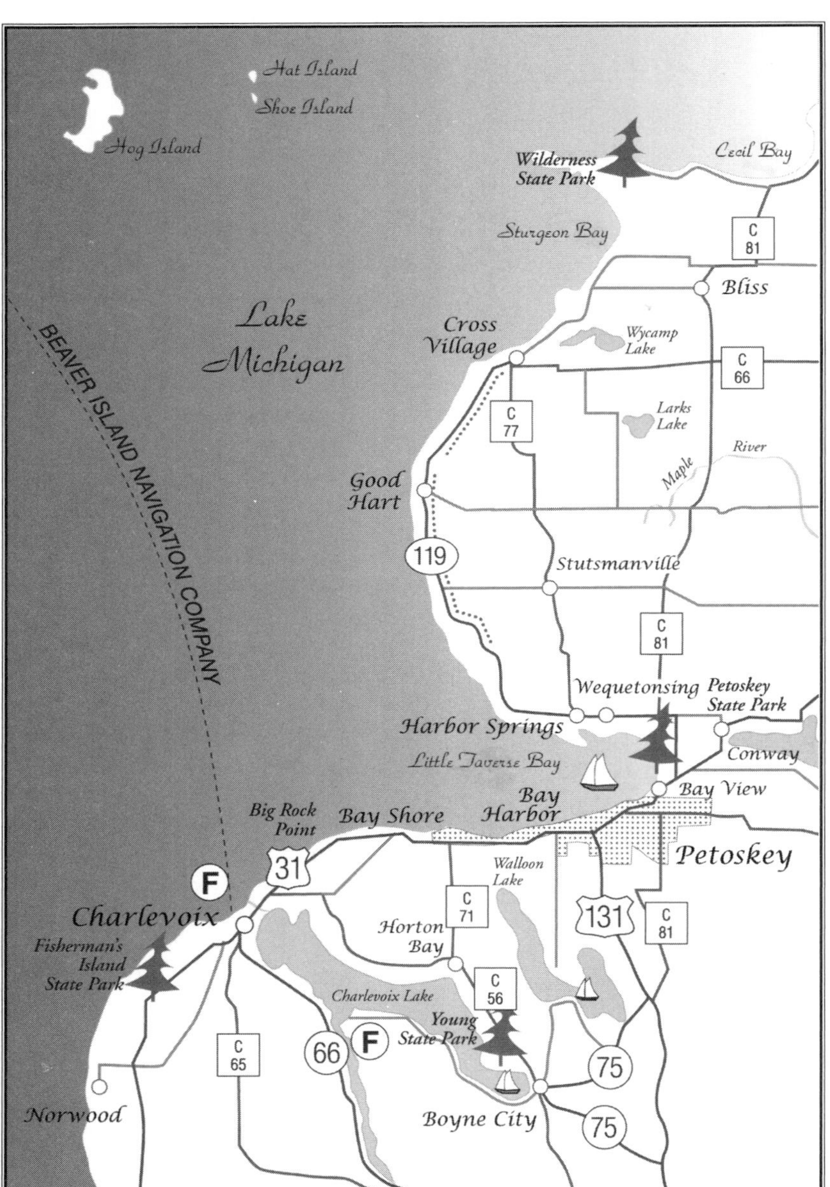

SCENERY IN BLUE and green, classic summer resort towns, sails puffed into the wind—get ready for a long, slow stretch of lakeshore where the priority of the day is making memories to last a lifetime.

Tunnel of Trees

Head south from Mackinaw City on County Road 81, which skirts Cecil Bay on the Lake Michigan side and leads to **Wilderness State Park**, (616) 436-5381, (800) 44PARKS for camping reservations. Lose yourself among 8,286 forested acres and along 26 miles of Lake Michigan shoreline. A hike to the far western edge rewards you with a look at the crumbling **Waugoshance Point Lighthouse** that Navy fighters used for gunnery practice during World War II. Restoration efforts are underway. Hike, launch a boat, fish for dinner, stay overnight in a rustic cabin, and see the stars as if for the first time in this beautiful state park.

Backtrack to County Road 81 and turn right on County Road 66 to Cross Village, a former fishing and lumber town.

Cross Village is on the tourist circuit for one reason: **Legs Inn**. At its heart, Legs Inn is a restaurant that serves regional and Polish specialties, including local wines and Polish beer. But its soul lies in its amazing architecture of pebbles on the outside and richly carved and varnished wood on the inside.

From Cross Village to Harbor Springs and beyond, State Highway 119 parallels the lakeshore; but it's not the water that makes this stretch of highway so famous. Nicknamed the **Tunnel of Trees**, the road along this route is so narrow that the surrounding trees grow right up and over it, creating a tunnel-like appearance. You can tell by all the mailboxes lining the road that there are plenty of cottages buried deep within the trees, but they are hidden like mushrooms and so do not tarnish the view. Largely northern hardwoods, the trees include red oak, sugar maple, American beech, white ash, eastern hemlock, and American basswood. The long way to Harbor Springs or Petoskey, this route is loaded with twists and turns. Take a quiet, secluded ride in autumn and witness the beautiful colors that seem to catch fire. In spring, see a doe cross the road with her fawn wobbling behind, or a litter of baby raccoons snuffling among the wildflowers.

The farther south you go along State Highway 119, the wilderness begins to recede and eventually gives way to the golf course mansions of Birchwood, and the restored Victorian homes of Harbor Springs.

M-119, the Tunnel of Trees, northwest Michigan

Harbor Springs

Permanently docked at the top of Little Traverse Bay, Harbor Springs puts on quite a display, with a picture-perfect harbor, upscale boutiques, and a well-dressed history. The town got its start as a summer resort destination that catered to the wealthy in need of escape not only from their cities, but also from their hay fever. They came by steamship and, starting in 1882, overland by train. By the 1920s, there were 11 Harbor Springs hotels to accommodate them.

Today, you can enjoy the same things

that attracted those early visitors. Spend afternoons on the beach or peruse the shops; maybe grab an old-fashioned ice cream soda. Just north of town, you can enjoy a guided trail ride at the handsome **Birchwood Farm Equestrian Center**, 518 West Townline Road (just off State Highway 119), Harbor Springs, Michigan 49740, (231) 626-2868. You may also choose to sail the balmy bay breezes with the fun-loving folks at **Windsurf Harbor Springs**, 5200 West Lake Road, Harbor Springs, Michigan 49740, (231) 330-1001, www.windsurfharborsprings.com.

As it has been for over a century, spending a summer weekend in Harbor Springs is like living in grace, but with your toes wiggling in the sand.

Whitecaps and rocky shores of a northwestern Michigan Roadside Park, Michigan

Bay View, Petoskey

North of Bay View, pull into **Petoskey State Park**, 2475 State Highway 119, Petoskey, Michigan 49770, (231) 347-2311, www.michigan.gov/dnr. Low dunes frame a sandy beach that is famous for its stones. Take a break from the pebble hunt, though, to read colorful signage that tells about the endangered Piping Plover. These birds migrate from the Gulf shore every spring to breed and build their own version of lakefront property. You can help the birds by being careful not to disturb their nests, which are little more than collections of pebbles on the sand.

Enjoy lovely bay views from the park; and once you have had your fill, get back on State Highway 119, merge onto Highway BR-31, and follow it the short distance down to Bay View.

Perched eight miles south of Harbor Springs and one mile north of Petoskey, Bay View is a unique resort town. As you admire the hilltop cottages, turn off busy Highway BR-31 at the Bay View Association sign. Pick up a **Bay View Association Walking Tour** booklet, (231) 347-6225, www.bayviewassoc.com, at the Terrace Inn, and embark upon a fascinating journey into a privileged past. Founded as a religious campsite in 1875, the association soon branched out from its spiritual anchor to address cultural and recreational needs. Today, musicians, lecturers, and speakers continue to make this summer place special and welcoming amid shaded, sloping lawns and hunter-green rocker-swings.

On to Petoskey, where you'll find a great lineup of shops, art galleries, and handsome Victorian architecture in the **Gaslight District**. At **American Spoon Foods**, 315 Bridge Street, Petoskey, Michigan 49770, (231) 547-5222, www.spoon.com, summer is preserved in jars. Try orchard-grown and wild-foraged jams in flavors ranging from sour cherry to brandied wild blackberry. Enhance a fish dinner with American Spoon Foods' Great Lakes Seafood Sauce, a delicious blend of capers, dill, onion, lemons, and parsley; or go all out with their Great Lakes birch bark basket. The district is packed with great little shops like this. Over at **Symons General Store**, 401 East Lake Street, Petoskey, Michigan 49770, (231) 347-2438, www.symonsgeneralstore.com, they stock the shelves to groaning beneath a bumper crop of gourmet goods. Have a field day harvesting locally gathered morels, locally baked organic breads made with well water and delivered fresh daily, international cheeses, and deli meats. Buy guest soaps made by Wildflower Soapworks of nearby Torch Lake. Finally, discover more regional treasures like Native American porcupine quill boxes and Petoskey stone jewelry at **Grandpa Shorter's**, 301 East Lake Street, Petoskey, Michigan 49770, (231) 347-2603.

Just a short distance inland from the

Dunes and trees, Petoskey State Park, Petoskey, Michigan

Evelyn House, a community building of historic Bay View Association, Bay View, Michigan

From the Kitchens of Stafford's Bay View Inn, Petoskey:

WHITEFISH MOREL

Brimming with Victorian sophistication, this 1886 landmark inn overlooks Little Traverse Bay and pleases guests with dishes such as . . .

4 fillets of fresh Lake Superior Whitefish
Cooking oil, flour, salt, white pepper, garlic powder, paprika, and onion powder for dredging

Mix the flour to taste with paprika, garlic powder, onion powder, salt, and white pepper. Dredge the whitefish in this mixture. Heat just enough oil to cover the bottom of a sauté pan and sauté the whitefish on both sides to a light golden brown. Place in 300-degree oven until ready to assemble dish. Make the Morel Mushroom Sauce.

MOREL MUSHROOM SAUCE
1 tablespoon olive oil
3 tablespoons butter
2 tablespoons shallots, minced
2 cups fresh morel mushrooms or reconstituted dried morels*
1 cup fresh Shitake mushrooms
2 tablespoons white wine
2 cups rich veal or beef stock
1 cup heavy cream
1 tablespoon brandy
salt and pepper to taste
roux to thicken if necessary

Combine oil and 1 tablespoon of the butter in a heavy-bottomed saucepan. Add shallots and mushrooms and cook until almost done. De-glaze with white wine. Simmer stock and thicken with roux to a medium consistency.** Strain sauce through a fine sieve and add the mushrooms to the mixture. Add heavy cream and brandy. Season with salt and pepper. Slowly whip in remaining 2 tablespoons butter.

Yields 4 servings.

*If using dried morels, place mushrooms in a saucepan and reconstitute with simmering white wine. Place juice and wine into the sauce.
** You may omit the roux if you prefer a thinner sauce.

marina, discover supposed healing waters and an unexpectedly decorative bridge at **Mineral Well Park**. Drive west along West Lake Street to the **Magnus Park** beach to hunt for Petoskey stones, which are generally rough and dull-gray with pockmarks of fossilized colony coral. You need to have these ancient treasures polished in order to see that their beauty lies not in their color, but in their pattern.

No luck finding your own Petoskey stones, or not sure of what to look for? Head back toward Bayfront Park to the **Little Traverse History Museum**, 100 Depot Court, Petoskey, Michigan 49770, (231) 347-2620, www.petoskeymuseum.org. Right there at the reception desk are unpolished and polished examples that you can study and touch. Move on through the museum to find out how Petoskey came to be a desirable resort community, and how the museum building itself had a hand in that. Did you know that Ernest Hemingway spent boyhood summers in the Petoskey area? Discover which of his works reflect those idyllic times, and where he came when first moving out of his family's Oak Park, Illinois home. Appreciate the artistry of Native American porcupine quill and birch bark artifacts, and recall the tragedy of a famous passenger pigeon that once called Michigan home.

Don't leave town yet. There is plenty more to do. **Historic Trolley Tours**, (231) 347-4000, www.staffords.com/historic-trolley-tours-68/, depart from Stafford's Perry Hotel, which is itself historic, for 90-minute narrated jaunts about town. In mid-August, Petoskey pulls out all the stops during **Festival on the Bay**, (231) 347-4150, www.petoskeyfestival.com. The bay is always hopping, and, de-pending on availability, you may have a chance to take a cruise on Shepler's Ferry Boat, cheer the winner of the canoe race, swim in the triathlon, marvel at the sandcastle demonstration, and savor local delicacies at Taste of Bay Harbor.

Driving south from Petoskey, pull into massive **Bay Harbor**, (888) BAY-HAR BOR, www.bayharbor.com, which is a big, bold resort and residential development on Lake Michigan. Because it sits in an old quarry, the views are stunning. At Highway BR-31, you'll stumble upon a vast collection of Victorian-style homes on a sprawling white resort at the water's edge. As you drive down into what was once the bottom of the quarry, catch a glimpse of the craggy bluff behind you. With lakefront mansions, townhouses, condos, shops, docks, a yacht club, an equestrian center, and golf courses, Bay Harbor is huge; but its extraordinary elevations make it unique among large developments. It even has its own museum, the **Bay Harbor History Museum**, (231) 439-2620.

By the time you arrive in Bay Shore, the views of Lake Michigan will keep tearing your eyes off the road. Fortunately, a sweeping **Roadside Park** will be coming up on your right. Here you can walk down to the water, watch the wind whip up the whitecaps, grill a Michigan whitefish sausage, take pictures, and relax. You can also take a bike ride or run along the paved, 29-mile **Little Traverse Wheelway**, www.topofmichigantrails.org, all the way to Charlevoix, if the views don't take your breath away first.

Yellow horse on the beach, Depot Beach, Charlevoix, Michigan

Charlevoix

It is 17 miles from downtown Petoskey to downtown Charlevoix. Charlevoix is a pretty town, with water on both sides. From east to west, the waterways are: Lake Charlevoix, Round Lake, Pine Channel, and Lake Michigan. To access Lake Michigan, hop a boat through Round Lake and the narrow Pine Channel, out past the pierhead light and into the open water. Amid the various pleasure crafts zipping about, you might see commercial fishtugs that supply **John Cross Fisheries**, 209 Belvedere Avenue (south of the channel and Bridge Street bridge), Charlevoix, Michigan 49720, (231) 547-253. Stop in for their addictive whitefish sausage and dip. Got a boat and want to shop? Tie up at a complementary shoppers' dock. Need a gift idea? The nautical candles of **Bullfrog Light Co.**, 05996 State Highway 66, Charlevoix, Michigan 49720, (231) 547-4407, www.bullfrogcandles.com, shine bright with understated images of lighthouses and sailboats.

Want to find a beach? Charlevoix has several sprinkled about town, each with its own style. A short drive north of the channel and on Lake Michigan, **Mount McSauba**, at North Point off Mount McSauba Road, is a favorite among boaters and beachgoers who want to get away from the crowds. North of the channel and on Lake Charlevoix, **Depot Beach**, off Dixon Avenue, is great for little kids with big sand castle dreams. For a dose of education in between lake dips and sunbaths, check out the nearby Charlevoix Historical Society Depot Museum, which overlooks the beach. Stay in town or escape to a secluded beach campsite at **Fisherman's Island State Park**, 16480 Bells Bay Road, Charlevoix, Michigan 49720, (231) 547-6641, www.michigan.gov/dnr. Though it's not on an island, there is a little island that you can gaze upon; and you can pull your car right up to your sandy, tree-shaded site.

Operated on a regular schedule by the **Beaver Island Boat Company**, 103 Bridge Park Drive, Charlevoix, Michigan 49720, (888) 446-4095, www.bibco.com, the ***Emerald Isle*** transports passengers for two hours to America's only former monarchy. James Strang, who began the Mormon sect still known today as the Church of Jesus Christ of Latter Day Saints, settled his colony on Beaver Island in 1848 and was proclaimed "king" of his church. After Strang's assassination, his followers were run off the island by an aggrieved party from Mackinac Island who arrived aboard *Welcome*, a sloop whose replica can be seen today. Learn about Beaver Island's commercial fishing, shipbuilding, and diving traditions inside an authentic 1906 net shed that has become the **Marine Museum**, 38105 Michigan Avenue, Beaver Island, Michigan 49782, (231) 448-2479.

FROM THE GALLEYS

The Fish Restaurant, 2983 South State Road, Harbor Springs, Michigan 49740, (231) 526-3969, www.thefishrestaurant.com. Specializing in fresh fish flown in from both coasts, this casual and fun eatery offers entrées such as wild mushroom walleye with morel bread pudding, and sides of garlic sautéed or creamed spinach, as well as roasted garlic mashed potatoes.

Juilleret's, 1418 Bridge Street, Charlevoix, Michigan 49720, (231) 547-9212.

Cinnamon French toast, homemade soups, whitefish sandwiches, and the decadent Thundercloud fountain (vanilla ice cream sundae drenched with bittersweet chocolate sauce and topped with a cloud of marshmallow fluff).

Legs Inn, 6425 Lake Shore Drive, Cross Village, Michigan 49723, (231) 526-2281, www.legsinn. com. Weird, wonderful décor makes Legs Inn a popular dining destination. Built in the 1920s by an immigrant from Poland, this is a stunning vision of wood and stone. The name refers not to a menu item but to the row of inverted stove legs on the roof. Start or finish your meal with drinks on the bluff overlooking Lake Michigan. Enjoy Polish specialties and American fare paired with Polish pivo (beer) and regional Michigan wines. The house specialty, a Polish-American dish called Whitefish Polonaise, features whitefish that is broiled and served with sautéed mushrooms and onions. Live music, a gift shop with Polish and Native American artworks, and housekeeping cottages.

Whitecaps, 215 East Lake Street, Petoskey, Michigan 49770, (231) 348-7092, www.whitecapsrestaurant.com. Offering fresh seafood and a raw bar in summer. Whitefish preparations include Whitefish Grenoble sautéed in olive oil and finished with white wine, lemon, butter, capers, and garlic. The Dry Aged New York strip is a 12-ounce grilled center cut. The Chicken Morel is oven-baked in a delicious morel cream sauce.

TO THE DOCKS

Beaver Island Lodge, 38210 Beaver Lodge Drive, Beaver Island, Michigan 49782, (231) 448-2396, www.beaverislandlodge.com. Savor American cuisine featuring regional specialties at on-site **Nina's Restaurant**, including brie with cherry pesto, and roast duck with tart cherry sauce. Feast your eyes on views of the surrounding island archipelago.

Birchwood Inn, 7077 Lake Shore Drive, Harbor Springs, Michigan 49740, (800) 530-9955, (231) 526-2151, www.birchwoodinn.com. Lodge décor, 10 acres, fireside gathering room, game room, outdoor pool, continental breakfast.

Bridge Street Inn, 113 Michigan Avenue, Charlevoix, Michigan 49720, (231) 547-6606, www.bridgestreetinn-chx.com. A three-story Colonial revival home from 1895, this cozy bed and breakfast is just a short walk from sandy beaches. It offers delicious breakfasts, a wrap-around porch with stunning views of Lake Michigan, and seven rooms adorned with beautiful antiques.

Stafford's Perry Hotel, Bay and Lewis Streets, 100 Lewis Street, Petoskey, Michigan 49770, (800) 737-1899, www.staffords.com. This pretty yellow hotel has overlooked Little Traverse Bay since 1899. In fact, it is the only original resort hotel still operating from that gracious era. Enjoy proximity to shops and on-site dining.

Terrace Inn, 1549 Glendale Avenue, Bay View, Michigan 49770, (800) 530-9898, (231) 347-2410, www.theterrace

inn.com. Built in 1911 as the lake lodge for the Bay View Association, this sprawling, three-story inn retains original antiques. The front steps lead to a park that sits along the beautiful waters of Little Traverse Bay. Relax at a terrace table or lounge inside the welcoming lobby, its doors thrown open to catch the bay's renowned lake breezes. Wander the halls to see photos of summers gone by. Upstairs, one guestroom boasts a pink taffeta bedspread, reminiscent of an evening gown, and mosaic accent tiles that shimmer like carnival glass. Is the inn haunted? Spend a night, and decide for yourself. In the morning, enjoy deluxe continental breakfasts in the dining room: fresh fruit and juices, granola, make-your-own waffles, pastries. Enjoy Bay View Association luxuries, such as musical performances, cultural programs inside historic buildings, and a sandy swimming beach.

AIDS TO NAVIGATION

Beaver Island Chamber of Commerce, (231) 448-2505, www.beaverisland.org.

Harbor Springs Chamber of Commerce, (231) 526-7999, www.harborspringschamber.com.

Petoskey-Harbor Springs-Boyne Country Visitors Bureau, (800) 845-2828, www.boynecountry.com.

Charlevoix Area Chamber of Commerce, (800) 951-2101, www.charlevoix.org.

Torch Lake to Traverse City

"Sunrise— 7:40. Colors orange-pinkish, blue water, and, toward the beach, grayish; 9:00 a.m.— colors flickering silver on the water."

—Stella Gadomski

AROUND HERE, calling the waters blue is like pointing to a rainbow and seeing one color. To describe it, you need words like aquamarine and sapphire and turquoise. Seemingly reflective of everything—purity, depth, weather, and maybe even mood—the waters of Grand Traverse Bay, the inland lakes, and the Manitou Passage never fail to astonish.

Torch Lake, Elk Rapids, Acme

Just east of Highway BR-31, Torch Lake glistens with Caribbean-blue clarity; so pull into any number of public access points to drink in the beauty and maybe drop a line in the water. Torch Lake's northern tip is at Eastport, which is 17 miles south of Charlevoix. Here you'll cross the **45th Parallel**, which means you are halfway to the Equator (or, if you prefer, halfway to the North Pole). Just south of here you'll find Elk Lake and the picturesque Grand Traverse Bay harborfront, known as Elk Rapids. Take your time traveling through these towns, for there is no hurry. A half mile north of downtown Acme on Highway 31, you'll find the **Music House Museum**, 7377 Highway 31 North, Williamsburg, Michigan 49690, (231) 938-9300, which delights visitors with guided tours of automatic music-making machines

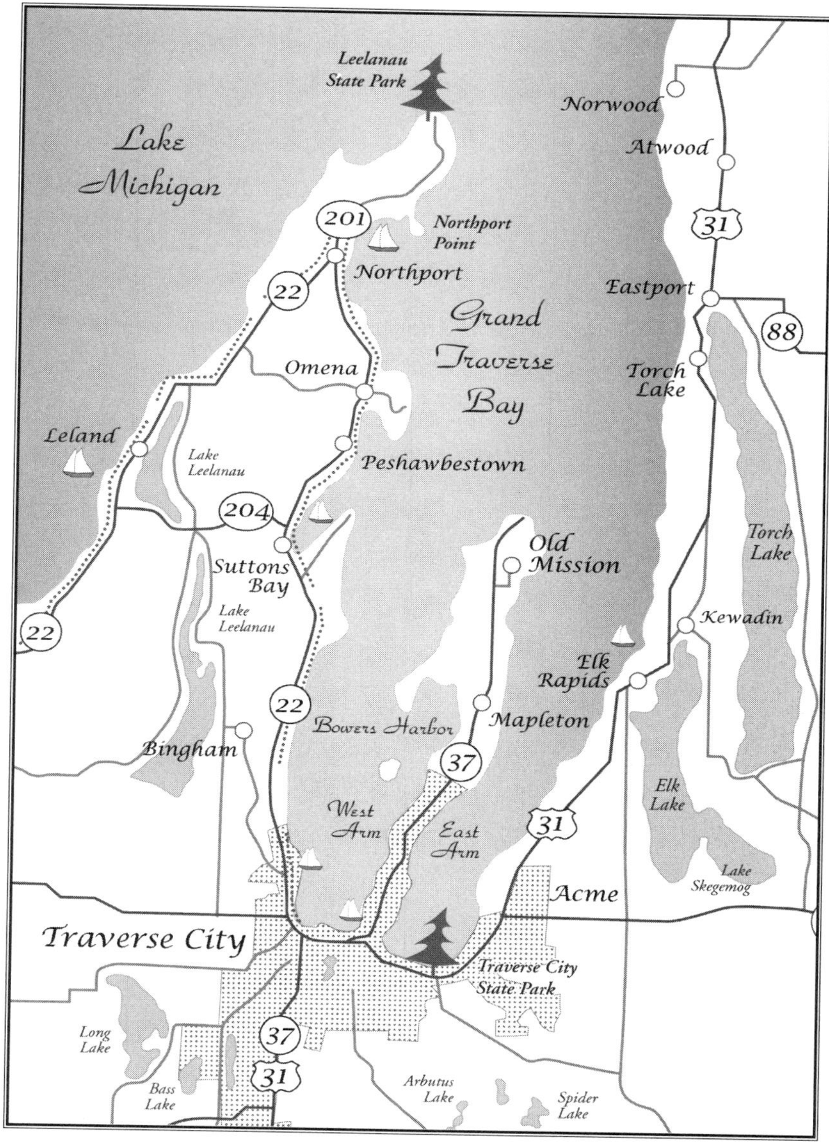

from 1870– 1930. As you continue south toward Acme, cherry trees begin marching up and down the well-drained hillsides in their green and red uniforms, preparing as they do every year for the **National Cherry Festival**, (231) 947-4230, www.cherryfestival.org.

Visitors drop anchor to shop the shanties, ice houses, and smoke houses of old Fishtown, Leland, Michigan

Two-masted schooner replica *Madeline*, replica sloop *Welcome*, and fishing boat, Traverse City, Michigan

Old Mission Peninsula

Long and narrow, the Old Mission Peninsula divides Grand Traverse Bay into the West Arm and the East Arm. Drive it for bay views and tastes of some of the state's finest wines. Because of the peninsula's micro-climate (a prime combination of lake and latitude), the grapes grown here produce award-winning wines. Varieties include Chardonnay, Riesling, Pinot Grigio, Pinot Noir, Merlot, and Gewürztraminer. Some of the vineyards have re-placed old cherry orchards, but they also continue to produce cherry wines. Consult www.wineriesofoldmission.com to plan your visit.

The lighthouse atop Old Mission Peninsula is a private residence, but you are welcome to picnic, sunbathe, and hike in the surrounding park.

Traverse City

Traverse City curls around the bowl of Grand Traverse Bay like a lazy cat, but it sure loves the water. You will, too, and here are some ideas to get you started. The folks at **Grand Traverse Balloons**, (231) 947-7433, www.grandtraverseballoons.com, will show you the whole thing from the air. Let the experts at **Uncommon Adventures**,

(866) 882-5525, www.uncommonadv.com, lead you on specialized, guided kayak trips tailored to varying skill levels. The **Traverse City State Park**, 1132 Highway BR-31 North, Traverse City, Michigan 49686, www.michigan.gov/dnr, is an urban park with nary a dune or hiking trail. But it is a fine place to toss whitefish sausage on the grill and watch for freighters on the horizon. West of downtown Traverse City, gaze at dairy cows and get your licks at **Moomers Homemade Ice Cream**, 7263 North Long Lake Road, Traverse City, Michigan 49684, (231) 941-4122, www. moomers.com.

Back downtown, the **Grand Traverse Heritage Center**, 322 Sixth Street, Traverse City, Michigan 49684, (231) 995-0313, www.gtheritagecenter.org, preserves the regional cultural heritage within the halls of a renovated Carnegie Library. The **Maritime Heritage Alliance**, www.mhatc.net, covers the maritime side of things, featuring two replica vessels, the schooner ***Madeline*** and the sloop ***Welcome***. The two-masted *Madeline* was an 1840s commercial vessel that once served as the first schoolhouse in the region. The original *Welcome* was built in 1775 at what is now Colonial Michilimackinac in Mackinaw City. To see the replica sailing ships, follow State Highway 22 a short distance up the West Arm of Grand Traverse Bay to Heritage Harbor, which is undergoing restoration.

Backtrack a short distance along State Highway 22 to the office of the ***Tall Ship Manitou*****, Traverse Tall Ship Company**, 13390 Southwest Bay Shore Drive, Dockside Plaza, Traverse City, Michigan 49684, (800) 968-8800, (231) 941-2000, www. tallshipsailing.com, and set off on a two-hour adventure beneath 3,000 square feet of billowing sail. The noon and evening sails include meals, while the overnight B&B experience will leave you starry-eyed.

Your kids already know how much fun water is; now, it is also educational. The new and improved **Great Lakes Children's Museum**, 13240 South, West Bayshore Drive, Greilickville, Michigan 49685, (231) 932-4526, www.greatlakes kids.org, shares the maritime story with kids in a new building with great bay views. At the new Water Table exhibit, they can channel and redirect water in hundreds of ways to observe its flowing properties. In the new Lighthouse Keeper's Quarters, they'll learn all about the role of keepers and their families in a playhouse type of environment. At Toddler Beach, the littlest ones bask in the joy of soft surfaces and colorful shapes. Teenagers help create the "Listening to the River" exhibits through summertime expeditions. Check out www.listeningtotheriver.org for the latest on this amazing project.

Leelanau Peninsula

The Leelanau Peninsula offers a variety of diversions, none of which are ever far from water. Topping the tip of the peninsula like an exclamation point is the

Grand Traverse Lighthouse, Leelanau State Park, 15390 North Lighthouse Point Road, Northport, Michigan 49670, (231) 386-5422, www.grandtraverselighthouse.com. It shines a bright welcome to visitors, as it has to mariners since 1850, making it one of the oldest lighthouses on the Great Lakes. Enjoy the on-site nautical museum, the 1920s and 1930s period furnishings, and a climb to the top. Outside, explore the restored Fog Signal Building and go for a walk on the beach.

Hate to leave? Keep the light in your sights for at least for a week or two by signing up to be a volunteer lighthouse keeper. Drive a little south to see the remainder of **Leelanau State Park**, (231) 386-7195, www.michigan.gov/dnr. These 1,350 acres include almost nine miles of hiking trails with spurs to Cathead Bay, and coastal dunes on the lakeshore.

If you drive back down the Leelanau Peninsula's western edge, you will arrive at sleepy Leland and its weather-beaten but celebrated **Fishtown**, www.leelanau.com/leland/. Fishtown is a historic fishing village located within the community of Leland, where commercial fishing was the mainstay for over one hundred years. Business peaked during the first three decades of the twentieth century, and declined to a single commercial fishery by the twenty-first century. Fishtown's charm is derived not from the ambition of a developer but from the fact that it is a genuine old fishing village. It's rare to find an authentic commercial fishing complex around the Great Lakes, let alone one that retains its maritime culture. Quaint fishtugs, charter fishing trawlers, and purely-for-pleasure boats gather at the docks. Below the dam, people dine on decks that hang over the water. Shop the **Village Cheese Shanty**, 199 West River Street, Leland, Michigan 49654, (231) 256-9141, and buy tickets for a boat ride out to the Manitou Islands through **Man-**

END OF THE ROAD

The road can take you all the way around Lake Michigan, but not beyond the water's edge. For that you need a boat. In Grand Traverse Bay, that boat should be the *Madeline*. Built by volunteers between 1985 to 1990, the *Madeline* authentically replicates a two-masted schooner that plied these northern waters from about 1845 to 1860—and served as the region's first private school.

It's all hands on deck when you sign up for a Heritage Sail aboard the *Madeline*. Everyone helps with the sails and steering, and gets a history lesson from the captain and crew.

Why should you do this much work?

"On a day with a good wind, the experience is breathtaking and you get a true understanding of why the sailors of the past fell in love with their jobs despite the dangers and hardships," says Kelly Curtis of the Maritime Heritage Alliance, which owns and operates a growing fleet of amazing vessels, including the *Madeline*.

Members of the Maritime Heritage Alliance, which is a non-profit organization based in Traverse City, harbor a not-so-secret love of boats; they restore old ones or build new ones from scratch before sending them out onto local waters. Visitors can sail, study maritime history, and enjoy an open house event that is fast becoming a local tradition with reenactments, food, games, vessel tours, and evening sails. To chart your course for adventure, visit www.mhatc.net.

Why is the work of the Maritime Heritage Alliance so important today?

"Before we had good roads or a railroad in the remote parts of our states, the most efficient way to move goods and people was on these beautiful schooners and sloops. Seeing them sailing on the Grand Traverse Bay gives us a taste of what life was like as our area was settled," explains Curtis.

Beyond historical accuracy, however, lies something deeper. Curtis explains it this way: "There is certainly a romance surrounding the water, especially when it takes a person back in time."

itou Island Transit, Fishtown Dock, Leland, Michigan 49654, (231) 256-9061, www.leelanau.com/manitou.

Scattered among the Leelanau Peninsula's cherry orchards, gourmet farms, and secret morel hunting grounds are lovely, leafy vineyards. About a dozen vintners take pride in their internationally award-winning wines, windswept water views, and uniquely individual legacies. Some names and labels are delightfully inspired by the marine location. Plan your visit at www.lpwines.com. Be in Leland in early June for the wildly popular **Leelanau Wine & Food Festival**, (231) 256-7747, www.lelandmi.com.

The Leelanau Peninsula's brightest star is the **Sleeping Bear Dunes National Lakeshore**, which includes the two baby-bear islands of North Manitou and South Manitou, and also dips down into Benzie County. All of this is covered in the next chapter. In the meantime, wouldn't a good dinner and a spectacular sunset be a perfect ending to your experiences in this elegant north coast region?

FROM THE GALLEYS

Foghorn Pub & Grille, 12930 West Bayshore Drive, Traverse City, Michigan 49684, (231) 932-8993. Savor seafood, Boone's air-dried aged beef, and other delicacies in this nautical-themed restaurant.

The Riverside Inn, 302 River Street, Leland, Michigan 49654, (231) 256-9971, www.theriverside-inn.com. Try creative northern Michigan cuisine such as pan-seared ostrich with trumpet mushrooms. Sit back and enjoy Leland River views from the dining room and the deck.

Trattoria Stella, 1200 West 11th Street, Traverse City, Michigan 49684, (231) 929-8989. This Italian menu changes daily and is based on fresh local ingredients and seafood from both coasts.

TO THE DOCKS

Bayshore Resort, 833 East Front Street, Traverse City, Michigan 49686, (800) 634-4401, (231) 935-4400, www.bayshore-resort.com. For the finest views and most intimate experience on the water, choose an upper-story bayfront room. From your private balcony, you can see the immaculately-groomed beach and small fleet of rentable watercraft. But step back into the room so the sliding glass doors frame only sea and sky. It is from this vantage point that the waves seem to roll right outside your window, as if you were on a cruise ship. Come nightfall, the lights from training vessels of the nearby Great Lakes Maritime Academy are enchanting. In the morning, take your place at the deluxe breakfast buffet: eggs, sausages, waffles, house-baked sweet rolls, fresh fruit, juices, coffee, and more.

Chateau Chantal, 15900 Rue de Vin, Old Mission Peninsula, Traverse City, Michigan 49686, (800) 969-4009, (231) 223-4110, www.chateauchantal.com. Views and vines. Enjoy a late Sunday morning brunch at The Boathouse Restaurant on the bay. Don't miss the renowned vineyard and tasting rooms.

Grand Traverse Resort and Spa, 100 Grand Traverse Village Boulevard, Acme, Michigan 49610, (800) 748-0303, (231) 534-6000, www.grandtraverseresort.com. Recent two-year, multi-million dollar renovation with more on the way at this lavish, 900-acre golf and spa property owned by the Grand Traverse Band of Ottawa and Chippewa Indians.

AIDS TO NAVIGATION

Leelanau Peninsula Chamber of Commerce, (231) 271-9895, www.leelanauchamber.com.

Traverse City Convention & Visitors Bureau, (800) TRAVERSE, www.mytraversecity.com.

Sleeping Bear Dunes National Lakeshore

"...outstanding natural features, including forests, beaches, dune formations and ancient glacial phenomena, exist along the mainland shore of Lake Michigan and on certain nearby islands...such features ought to be preserved in their natural setting and protected from developments and uses which would destroy the scenic beauty and natural character of the area."

—Senator Philip A. Hart of Michigan, who was instrumental in the establishment and protection of Sleeping Bear Dunes

LONG AGO, THE CHIPPEWA told of a mother bear that swam across the Lake Michigan to escape fire on the Wisconsin side. She reached land, but her two cubs couldn't make the swim and drowned offshore. To mark their passing, two islands rose up from beneath the water, and these are the North Manitou and South Manitou islands. The mother bear, meanwhile, forever waits on the land, her sleeping form marked at Sleeping Bear Point.

Such was the ancient origin of **Sleeping Bear Dunes National Lakeshore**, 9922 Front Street, Empire, Michigan 49630, (231) 326-5134, www.nps.gov/slbe. The scientific explanation has more to do with forces of wind and water, but it is the Chippewa legend that captures our hearts. One of only two national lakeshores on Lake Michigan, Sleeping Bear is the only place where you can get an aerial view of water without leaving land, and where you can look down upon seagulls floating over the water like pillow feathers.

No one who visits the Leelanau Peninsula should miss the opportunity to visit Sleeping Bear. Photographers love the barren, windswept wall of sand that slopes steeply down to Lake Michigan. It is the park's signature scene, but it's only part of the experience.

Make tracks from Traverse City by zipping westward across the Leelanau Peninsula on State Highway 72. Stop at the **Philip A. Hart Visitor Center**, (231) 326-5134 x328, to pick up a park brochure and trail maps (buy the inclusive booklet or ask for the ones you want), ask questions, and pay admission (the price is based upon how long you stay). Your Michigan state park sticker will not help you here, but your money will help the park. For example, the "plover patrol" program has been so successful that in recent years, this endangered beach bird, which alights on shore each spring and scrapes together a fragile nest of stones, has hatched more eggs in the park than anywhere else on the Great Lakes.

The Visitor Center's excellent exhibits teach you all about the Sleeping Bear environment. Walk through the exhibit area to learn that the dunes of Sleeping Bear cover a narrow band just a mile inland from Lake Michigan, and that the lake winds that created them also keep them active, a lifecycle that sometimes involves the sands sliding right into the water.

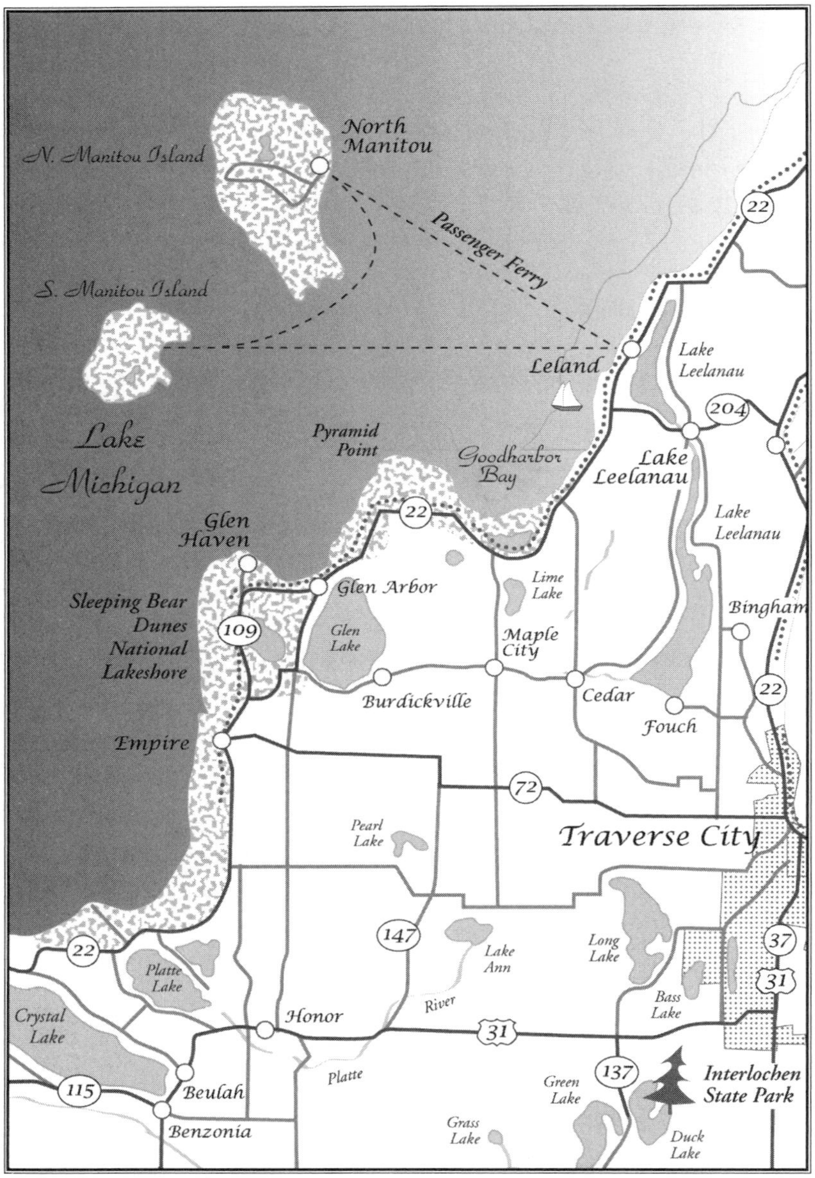

Sleeping Bear's landmark attractions and two lake-related museums lie to the north of the Visitor Center, so let's head off in that direction. The entire area, which is mostly in federal hands, covers 71,187 acres. The lakeshore is certainly a national treasure, but it's also a lot of fun. Dramatic beauty is coupled with plenty of room to explore, so take the kids and dash from point to point. Climb the dunes, but be cautious of steep drop-offs and the unpredictable nature of sandslides. Once you get a sense of what awaits you at Sleeping Bear, you can plan to return to particular points of interest and stay for a week—or an entire summer.

From the Visitor Center, drive to Empire for ice cream and continue north on State Highway 22 to State Highway 109, which is the main road through the park. The **Pierce Stocking Scenic Drive** off Highway 109 is 7.4 miles of twists and turns that loop around and take you conveniently back to its starting point. The points of interest and trailheads along the way are well worth the drive. At the Lake Michigan Overlook, look down—way down—upon the lake. From this 450-foot vantage point, it's not about detail, like the crunch of zebra mussel shells or the slap-slap of waves. It's about vastness, color, and calm, and the 1,600 miles of shoreline that, 11,800 years ago, the last of the Great Lakes glaciers left behind.

Back on State Highway 109, you come to the town of Leelanau and the famous **Dune Climb**. There they are, tiny people moving as if in a dream, slowly up and quickly down the staircase of shifting sands. And while it's not exactly the Chilkoot Pass of Alaskan Gold Rush days, this climb is definitely a challenge. You'll see people of all ages making the sandy scale, but it seems to be the kids who have the most fun, especially as they run and tumble back down.

Jump back onto State Highway 109 to the **Glen Haven Historic Village**, which is now part of the national lakeshore but was once a busy port and noisy lumber town where steamship captains stopped to buy cordwood. Today you can buy old-fashioned candies, toy U.S. Coast Guard helicopters, and maybe a farm stand puzzle at **D. H. Day's General Store**. See if sparks are flying inside the **Blacksmith Shop**, and drop anchor for a while in the bright red **Cannery Boat Museum**, the first of the park's two water-related cultural sites. What was once a fruit cannery is now home to a display of small Great Lakes boats. Wander around from lifeboat to fishtug, and read stories of scrappy vessels that now rest in comfort for all to admire. Over by the north window, the revolving cube-shaped lens hails from the offshore **North Manitou Shoal Light**, where keepers actually lived until automation in 1980. Out on the lake, the structure still sits atop a shoal, or sandbar, warning lake-goers of its dangerous presence under the water. The keepers, a crew of three, lived there for two weeks at a time, their home completely and immedi-

Lake Michigan Overlook, Sleeping Bear Dunes National Lakeshore, Michigan

Canoe couple, Bass Lake, Sleeping Bear Dunes National Lakeshore, Michigan

ately surrounded by water.

A quarter-mile up the road from the Cannery Boat Museum at Sleeping Bear Point, the **Sleeping Bear Point Coast Guard Station Maritime Museum** offers a peek into two boat sheds. The first of the two sheds houses the restrooms; the second is where you'll learn all about the rigors and bravery of the U.S. Life-Saving Service, which was established in 1871 and became the U.S. Coast Guard in 1915. Find out how the Lyle gun and breeches buoy could reach sinking ships from the safety of the shore, and how overturned surfboats were righted. Check out the little, if claustrophobic, life car; catch a live demonstration of the pioneering equipment; walk a historic beach patrol in the evening, and return in August for the **U.S. Life-Saving Service Festival**. After exploring the boat sheds, walk over to the keeper's quarters. This historic building houses two levels of exhibits on shipwrecks and station-life, which required daily practice sessions. Such vigilance was the hallmark of the U.S. Life-Saving Service, which, in the aggregate, rescued over 178,000 people.

Glen Arbor and Points North

Back on State Highway 109, drive east to the charming town of Glen Arbor. Growing like a cherry tree, **Cherry Republic**, 6026 South Lake Street, Glen Arbor, Michigan 49636, (231) 334-3150, www.cherryrupublic.com, now features lush gardens and a winery. Taste-test your way through the shop, and take home your favorite cherry salsas, sauces, and sweets. Even if the chocolate-covered dried cherries disappear before you can say, "Life, Liberty, Beaches & Pie," the condiments transport well and make tasteful gifts.

Re-enter the park and turn off onto the Port Oneida Road to see 18 old farmsteads spread across 3,400 acres. This is the **Port Oneida Rural Historic District**, which was, from 1860 through World War II, a subsistence farming community. In recent years, the community faced the threat of teardown, but people's fervent objections saved it. In the **Historic Olsen House**, you can learn how maritime history gave way to farming on these northern slopes. The surrounding buildings and rusting farm equipment stand as silent testimony to American agriculture. Even in their crumbling but protected state, the structures—farmhouses, barns, corn cribs, and sugar shacks—are beautiful. Join a guided tour in July or August, and stick around for the **Port Oneida Fair**.

Next, head off on the **Pyramid Point Trail**, a breathy upward hike past big-eyed paper birch trees to an impressive view atop a sandy dune. The roundtrip trek is only 1.2 miles, but an additional loop brings the total mileage to 2.7. Heed the warning signs, for it was here in 1996 that a dangerous landslide occurred.

Manitou Islands

Remember Leland and its weather-worn Fishtown from the last chapter? Drive there now to catch the boat ride out to the intriguing bear cub islands of Sleeping Bear Dunes National Lakeshore. From Empire, Leland is 27 miles to the north. **Manitou Island Transit**, Fishtown Dock, Leland, Michigan 49654, (231) 256-9061, www.leelanau.com/manitou, runs a pretty tight ship when it comes to schedules, so be sure to plan and reserve in advance. Which island you visit depends on what you want to do—North Manitou is a wilderness experience requiring at least one night of camping. You can camp on South Manitou, but you can also day-trip with the option of a guided motorized tour in an open-air vehicle; all other traffic is on foot.

On **North Manitou Island**, it's just you, your tent, your sense of adventure, and no services. Having waited only long enough to pick up last night's campers, the boat returns to Leland, and you're left to set up camp almost anywhere on these wooded 15,000 acres (the national park service does impose restrictions or a fee). This is true backcountry wilderness camping, and certainly closer than a typical campground to the experiences of early explorers; but if the backwoods are a bit too thick for your liking, you can also choose one of eight campsites at the **Village**. For most of its existence, this was the only village on the island, and was never named. One of the cottages on Cottage Row, which belonged to four Chicagoans, is thought to be the work of Frank Lloyd

Sand, sky, and stamina at Dune Climb, Sleeping Bear Dunes National Lakeshore, Michigan

Where the pier ends, summer begins, Otter Lake, Sleeping Bear Dunes National Lakeshore, Michigan

It's a long way down from Empire Bluff Trail Overlook, Sleeping Bear Dunes National Lakeshore, Michigan

Pioneer farm buildings, Port Oneida Historic District, Sleeping Bear Dunes National Lakeshore, Michigan

Wright. Other cottages were built with parts from the 1893 World's Columbian Exposition (known today as The Chicago World's Fair). The Village was part of the subsistence farming community and an enterprise that financed a private hunting preserve until the 1950s.

A trip to **South Manitou Island** is quite a different experience. For one thing, you can do it as a day trip. But plan on three hours round-trip, and pack a lunch, as there are no restaurants. Once depositing you on the island, the boat will linger nearby so you can re-board and be back in Leland the same day. The island's **Visitor Center** will set you up with information on hiking trails, shipwrecks, and the surrounding forest. Highlights include the **South Manitou Island Light**, which from 1871–1958 actively marked the lake's only natural harbor from here to Chicago. The Manitou Passage between the islands and the mainland saved schooners and steamships travel time but increased risk (more than 80 wrecked vessels can attest to that). Today, the lighthouse that helped guide ships through is open for tours and tower climbs. The **Manitou Passage Underwater Preserve**, www.michiganpreserves.org, is considered an excellent dive site for all levels of experience. Beginners can enjoy the easily accessible, shallow-water wreck of the ***Francisco Morazan***—which ran aground in 1960 and rests in only 15 feet of water. Above water, the freighter serves as a nesting site for shorebirds.

Southern Trails

South of Empire, the Sleeping Bear Dunes National Lakeshore arcs around Lake Michigan's Platte Bay. Turn off State Highway 22 at Wilco Road to hike the **Empire Bluff Trail** for fabulous views of the lake, the islands, and the famous windswept dune far to the north. If it's Sunday, you'll hear church bells ringing from Empire as you study the points of interest along the 1.5 miles to the boardwalk bluff. It may be hard to picture, but a fruit orchard once stretched from here to Empire, taking advantage of Lake Michigan's climate effects. Empire, by the way, is named for a schooner that was icebound here during a storm.

Farther south along State Highway 22, the Trails End turnoff leads to two small, pristine lakes: Otter and Bass. Here nature lovers glide across still waters on silent canoes, and chipmunks rustle through the woods as hikers quietly pass. Part of the 14.7 mile **Platte Plains Trail** circles the stunningly beautiful Bass Lake and leads you to a forest of pines and ferns through which the blue waters sometimes peek. For solitude and untouched nature, this is the place to be.

There are so many ways to experience the Sleeping Bear Dunes National Lakeshore. Tailor a visit to your own interests, whether that means sailing on the Manitou Passage or diving into the maritime past. Whatever you choose to do at Sleeping Bear, you will never forget it—just as one mama bear never forgot her two cubs.

FROM THE GALLEYS

Art's Tavern, 6847 Western Avenue, Glen Arbor, Michigan 49636, www.artsglenarbor.com. Hang with the locals as you eat, drink, and be merry over breakfast, lunch, and dinner.

Good Harbor Grill, 6584 Western Avenue, Glen Arbor, Michigan 49636, (231) 334-3555, www.glenarborwest.com. Breakfast, lunch, and dinner. Fresh seafood is a dinner specialty, some creations incorporating Michigan ingredients, including Cherry Pecan Whitefish and Cherry Apricot Chicken. Other dishes are infused with Italian or Indian flavors. And for something bold, try the Hearty Beef Chili: it's a complex blend of over 40 ingredients, including sirloin steak, ground beef, vegetables, and five chilies beneath a blanket of melted cheese.

Windows at Le Bear, 5705 Lake Street, Glen Arbor, Michigan 49636, (231) 334-2530. Here on the water, the menu changes daily so that the freshest seasonal ingredients find their way to your plate.

TO THE DOCKS

Glen Craft Marina & Resort, 6391 South Lake Street, Glen Arbor, Michigan 49636, (231) 334-4556, www.glencraftmarina.com. Luxurious beachfront suites on beautiful Glen Lake. Stay in the lodge or choose a rustic cottage. Rent boats or dock your own on-site.

The Homestead, America's Freshwater Resort, Wood Ridge Road, Glen Arbor, Michigan 49636, (231) 334-5100, www.thehomesteadresort.com. Whatever accommodations you select at The Homestead, you will be surrounded by water and woods. Get to know Lake Michigan's many moods firsthand, from serene to stormy. Enjoy all the lavish amenities, from fireplaces to steam showers, in this carefully crafted rustic setting.

Sleeping Bear Bed and Breakfast, 11977 Gilbert Road, Empire, Michigan 49630, (231) 326-5375, www.sleepingbearbb.com. In the morning, pull your chair up to the antique farm table for a gourmet breakfast based on delicious seasonal ingredients. How does baked French toast with bacon or cherry pecan sausage sound? How about an onion-cheese frittata or a red pepper-herbed cheese omelet? The menu changes to please guests as well as the chef, and seasonal juice blends keep everyone bright-eyed. Ask about the caterer's cookies.

AIDS TO NAVIGATION

Empire Chamber of Commerce, www.empirechamber.com.

Glen Lake Area Chamber of Commerce, (231) 334-3238, www.sleepingbeararea.com.

Leelanau Peninsula Chamber of Commerce, (231) 271-9895, www.leelanauchamber.com.

Sleeping Bear Dunes National Lakeshore, (231) 326-5134, www.nps.gov/slbe.

Point Betsie to Manistee

"I love the stairs. The way they're worn speaks so much to the history of the ship."
—Linda Spencer, SS *City of Milwaukee*

SOUTH OF THE Leelanau Peninsula, things begin to settle down as the glamour of the more northerly shores recedes. Here local colors and flavors come to the forefront with less fanfare but equal fascination. Here you'll find a lighthouse with quite the loyal following, and a carferry that may still have a ghostly captain on board. And that strange place the locals call Gravity Hill? You'll just have to see for yourself.

Frankfort

Not far north of Frankfort, turn off from State Highway 22 onto Point Betsie Road, which runs a short distance out to **Point Betsie Lighthouse**,

Frankfort, Michigan, (231) 352-4915, www.pointbetsie.org. Easy to get to, this picturesque, 1858 beacon comes complete with a sandy beach, devoted docents, and tower access. Buy a ticket in the gift shop, then start your tour in the keeper's quarters where very recent transformations feature exhibits and furnishings that transform the interior to the 1940s. And as for the name, Point Betsie is the Americanization of the French name for the point—Point Aux Bec Scies. As you climb the spiral stairs to the lantern room, you will be advised to watch your head in two places and to not touch the light, which is still operated by the U.S. Coast Guard. It marks the southern entrance to the treach-

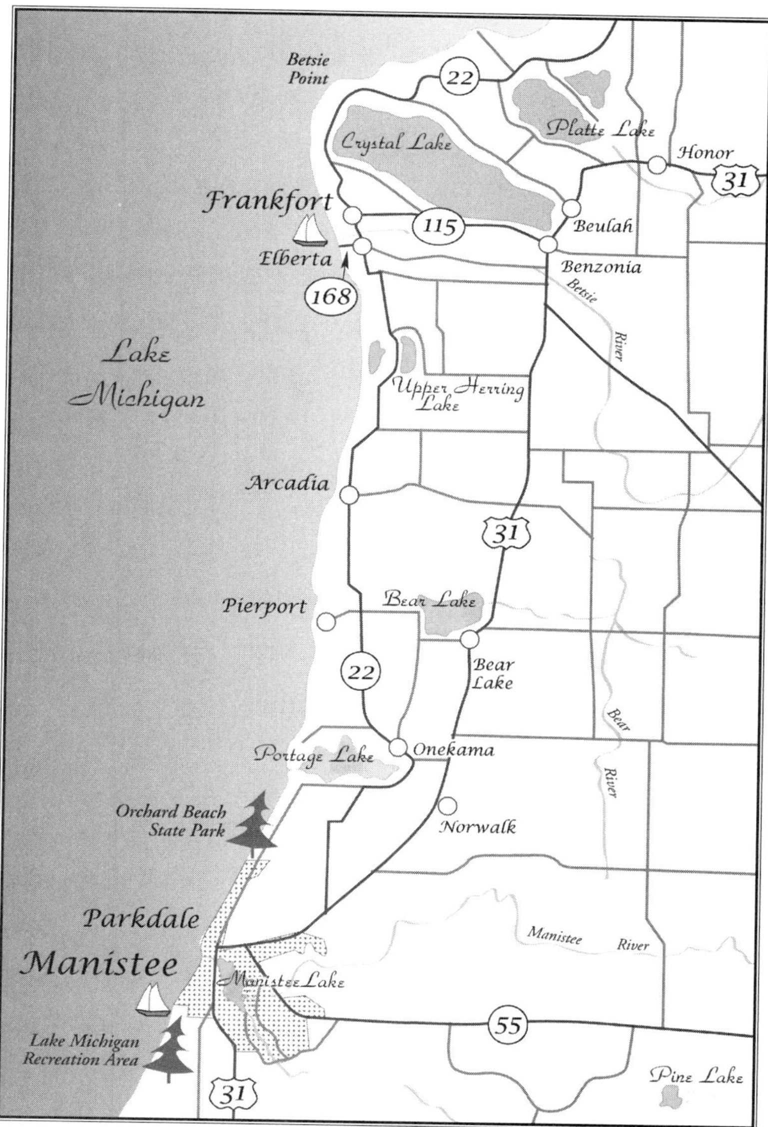

erous Manitou Passage that lies to the north at Sleeping Bear Dunes National Lakeshore. Point Betsie continues to be a viable navigational aid, shining its light across 27 miles. With its modern, fully automated Fresnel lens, today's light goes the distance with a mere 36-watt lightbulb and five back-ups. As your guide might point out, if a boater's GPS unit goes overboard in a sudden storm, the old tower light can be as helpful as it was to late nineteenth-century mariners. The tower is built very close to the lake, but the concrete apron that fans out from it ensures that it stays put.

Less visible today but of significance to the Lake Michigan maritime story is the role that Frankfort played at the dawn of the Great Lakes carferry age. It was in 1892 that a ship arriving here from Kewaunee, Wisconsin made the first successful transport of railroad cars across a body of water the size of Lake Michigan.

Here in Benzie County you can also tube, canoe, or kayak down the Betsie or Platte Rivers. In town, Frankfort offers boat docks, parkland, a historic mineral well, grills, and playground equipment, all on Crystal Lake.

South of Arcadia, you'll pass Bear Lake just off Highway BR-31. You'll soon reach Portage Lake off State Highway 22, at the town of Onekama. In a park overlooking Portage Lake, a faded sign tells of early settlers taking matters into their own hands against a sawmill operator. Look for the old steamship propeller that sits in the park like a sculpture. Drive over to the Portage Point Inn even if you are not planning an overnight stay, for this classic Lake Michigan resort is one of only a few remaining from its time. Once a summer playground for the wealthy, the inn eventually faded into decrepit memory. It was not until the 1990s that an avid sailor saw through the boarded-up windows and knew that those old glory days deserved a second chance. Because of his vision, you, too, can relish the resort's early twentieth-century charm.

Manistee

Five miles north of Manistee, pull into the Manistee County Blacker Airport and sign up with **Orchard Beach Aviation**, 2323 Airport Road, Manistee, Michigan 49660, (231) 723-8095, www.jackpine.com/~orcbchav, for a short, scenic flight over Lake Michigan. Come back down to Earth at **Orchard Beach State Park**, 2064 Lakeshore Road, Manistee, Michigan 49660, (231) 723-7422, www.michigan.gov/dnr, which was named for the apple orchard that once thrived on this lakeside site. Walk the stairs to the beach and play in a picnic area pleasantly sheltered with sassafras trees.

Around here, if you ask a local, "Where is the City of Milwaukee?" they are less likely to point across the lake than to U.S. Highway 31. Around here, Milwaukee refers to the **SS *City of Milwau-***

kee, 111 Highway 31 North, Manistee, Michigan 49660, (231) 723-3587, www.carferry.com. The vessel is moored on Manistee Lake, which connects to Lake Michigan via the Manistee River. The Manitowoc Shipbuilding Company built this 360-foot steel-hulled vessel in 1930, and she was operable until 1981. She is a tough old lady, but her passengers' hall, observation room, and staterooms are all elegantly varnished oak and brass. You can almost see ladies wearing white gloves and men smoking cigars inside these stylish surroundings. Your tour guide will show it all, from the engine room to the pilothouse and quarters of the captain and crew. The crewmen are long gone, but cuts and scrapes in the aft flicker table and worn treads on the pilothouse stairs remain. You may hear the story of Captain Jack, whose expectations for a full-size bed and personal head were not met, causing him to walk. Later, though, he did serve as relief captain, and drew his last breath on the ship. Some say he is still aboard.

Although moored in water, the SS *City of Milwaukee* does not go anywhere. But there are big plans in her future. In the meantime, check out the new Shipboard Bed & Breakfast option. Come autumn, don't go onboard alone, because, as legend has it, the carferry becomes a Ghost Ship. The galley, they say, has one ingredient with which to work—troublesome guests. As for Captain Jack, he is likely to put in an appearance as well.

Ready to explore old Manistee? Nicknamed the **Victorian Port City**, Manistee treats visitors to a romantic downtown scene with arches and turrets. Painted deep

Watching the water since 1858, Point Betsie Lighthouse, Frankfort, Michigan

Rock on at the porch of Portage Point Inn, Onekama, Michigan

gray and white, the **Manistee County Historical Museum**, 425 River Street, Manistee, Michigan 49660, (231) 723-5531, www.manisteecvb.com, houses an intriguing collection of Victoriana beneath a wraparound mezzanine and tin ceiling. Upstairs, a Philco radio plays oldies as you duck into a room that harbors the local lumber shipping history.

From pilothouse, *SS City of Milwaukee* carferry, Manistee, Michigan

Sun goes down over the Victorian Port City, Manistee, Michigan

Half a mile to the west, the society's other museum, **The Waterworks Building**, 540 First Street, invites you to poke around among its logging, railroad, and maritime collections. Afterward, head down to the Manistee River and walk along the 1.75 mile **Riverwalk**. From this point, you can walk west toward Lake Michigan and the Manistee North Pier Lighthouse, then back upriver to the Highway BR-31 bridge, reading interpretive signs and relaxing to the sights and sounds of the waterway. Pause at the net shed to learn that early commercial fishermen used Mackinac boats to set and tend their gill nets on Lake Michigan, and find out how they kept their catch from spoiling before shipment to market. If the timing is right, you can walk next to a freighter as it slowly squeezes through the river channel.

You might also see one of the Great Lakes cruise ships, including the *Niagara Prince*, the *Grande Mariner*, the *MV Columbus*, and *Le Levant*. Don't overlook those 50-odd charter fishing boats docked in the river, for they can net you big salmon and trout. Consider tossing your line in the water for the annual **Lake Michigan Tournament Trail**, www.tournamenttrail.net. The competition heats up every year, with various events featured up and down the lakeshore. **Water Bug Boat Tours**, Riverwalk east of the Elks Club on River Street, Manistee, Michigan, (231) 398-0919, www.manistee.com, offers a refreshing small-boat tour experience with no crowds and proximity to the water.

By the way, the western chunk of the million-acre **Huron-Manistee National Forest** sprawls all around here. For information on this vast natural resource where they will even let you cut your own Christmas tree, call the U.S. Forest Service Ranger Station at (231) 723-2211. Around the Fourth of July, you can party in the woods during the **National Forest Festival**, www.manisteecountychamber.com/mnff.html. Highlights of this event include the forest lunch bus tour, woodcarving (including model boats), chainsaw sculptures, stone skipping contests, a Venetian boat parade, and fireworks over Lake Michigan.

From Manistee, Highway BR-31 is a straight shot to Ludington. Along the way, stop in at the **Nordhouse Dunes Wilderness**—the only federally designated wilderness in the Lower Peninsula. For information, contact the Huron-Manistee National Forest, (231) 723-2111.

FROM THE GALLEYS

Dinghy's Restaurant and Bar, 415 Main Street, Frankfort, Michigan 49635, (231) 352-4702, www.dinghysrestaurant.com. Friday Fish Fry, steaks, sandwiches, salads, soups. Local, lake-inspired décor with antique carferry signs, sailing memorabilia, and photos of old Frankfort.

The Manitou, 4349 Scenic Highway, State Highway 22 (nine miles north of Frankfort), Frankfort, Michigan 49635, (231) 882-4761. Enjoy broiled Lake Michigan whitefish, rack of lamb, sautéed perch, berry pie, regional wine and beer.

GRAVITY HILL

It takes a local to tell you about Gravity Hill, because there are no signs to direct you there. And once you do find it, there is no one to sell you tickets or trinkets. The official brochures don't even promote it. So you're on your own. But, hey, when was the last time you just took off in search of something unknown?

Gravity Hill is an unmarked, word-of-mouth mystery where your car, while in neutral, will go back up the hill that you have just driven down. To get there, drive north for a few miles from Arcadia on State Highway 22, then turn right onto Joyfield Road and drive a few more miles. At the church, turn right onto Putney Road and head to the bottom of the hill. Put your car in neutral, and see if it doesn't go back up the same way, reaching speeds up to 15 mph.

The preacher from the local church marvels at the phenomenon: "Five more this week. If they want miracles, why don't they come in here instead?"

At various sites on the Internet, though, others will tell you that Gravity Hill is nothing more than an optical illusion.

The Cabbage Shed, 198 Frankfort Avenue, Elberta, Michigan 49628, (231) 352-9843, www.cabbageshed.com. Historic 1867 setting on Betsie Bay, with some early ties to local shipping trade. Savor steaks, prime rib, whitefish, walleye, and the clams and oysters of the summer Raw Bar. Dine inside among the old sea charts and memorabilia, or outside overlooking the bay. Dinner only. Live entertainment.

TO THE DOCKS

Betsie Bay Inn, 231 Main Street, Frankfort, Michigan 49635, (231) 352-8090, www.betsiebayinn.com. Across the street from sparkling Crystal Lake sits this lovingly restored old hotel that has been completely and stylishly reinvented for contemporary sensibilities. It is not far, either, from the sands of Lake Michigan.

Harbor Lights Resort, 15 Second Street, Frankfort, Michigan 49635, (800) 346-9614, (231) 352-9614, www.harborlightsresort.net. Reserve a condo or motel room and make the private Lake Michigan beach your own. Indoor pool and spa, luxury suites with fireplaces, whirlpool tubs, and full-size kitchens.

Portage Point Inn, 8513 South Portage Point Drive, Onekama, Michigan 49675, (800) 878-7248, www.portagepointinn.com. There was a time when, if you traveled in certain circles, you might get a Christmas card from the Portage Point Inn as an invitation to be a guest. Decades later, it was said that local girls would go to pavilion dances to meet the sons of wealthy guests. A lot has happened here since 1903, and today, the inn artfully mixes classic resort styling with contemporary amenities. Nestled pleasantly along Portage Lake, the inn boasts calm waters, a sandy beach, and a deep-water marina for yachts to 100 feet. You can also walk out past the cottages to the Lake Michigan side. Choose from the variety of options, including a hotel, condo, townhouse, cottage, or dollhouse. Some date back to the beginning, others are newer additions; but all are in keeping with the historic look.

Riverside Motel & Marina, 520 Water Street, Manistee, Michigan 49660, (231) 723-3554, www.riversidemotelandmarina.com. A fisherman's favorite, this basic but clean motel puts you into a front row seat for river activity, especially from a patio chair outside your room. The row of charter and pleasure boats, nearby Riverwalk, and glorious evening colors will keep you entertained.

AIDS TO NAVIGATION

Benzie County Convention & Visitors Bureau, (800) 882-5801, www.visitbenzie.com.

Manistee County Convention & Visitors Bureau, (877) 626-4783, www.visitmanistee.com.

Hamlin Lake to Silver Lake

"The keepers always say they're paid in sunsets."
—Nancy Gerts, Executive Director, Big Sable Point Lighthouse Keepers Association

Hamlin Lake & Ludington

WELCOME TO SEVEN MILES of sandy shoreline, home to an active lighthouse, a U.S. Coast Guard station-cum-maritime museum," to "maritime exhibits, about 50 charter fishing businesses, a **Carferry Festival**, and even **Shoreline Cruises on the SS *Badger*** in June. You've arrived in the port town of Ludington—about 60 miles north of Muskegon and 30 miles south of Manistee—where you can find all these attractions and so much more.

From downtown Ludington, take Lakeshore Drive to State Highway 116, which takes you right into **Ludington State Park**, 915 Diana Street, Ludington, Michigan 49431, (231) 843-2423, (800) 447-2757 (call 800# for camping reservations), www.michigan.gov/dnr. You'll find yourself surrounded by dunes, and likely by people as well, as this is said to be Michigan's most popular camping destination. Fortunately, 5,300 acres of parkland spread everyone out nicely. Shining like the North Star, the still-active 1867 **Big Sable Point Lighthouse**, (231) 845-7343, www.bigsablelighthouse.org, is located near the park's north end; and to reach it, you will need to walk 1.5 miles. But it's worth the walk, as this could very well be the highlight of the park. There is an avail-

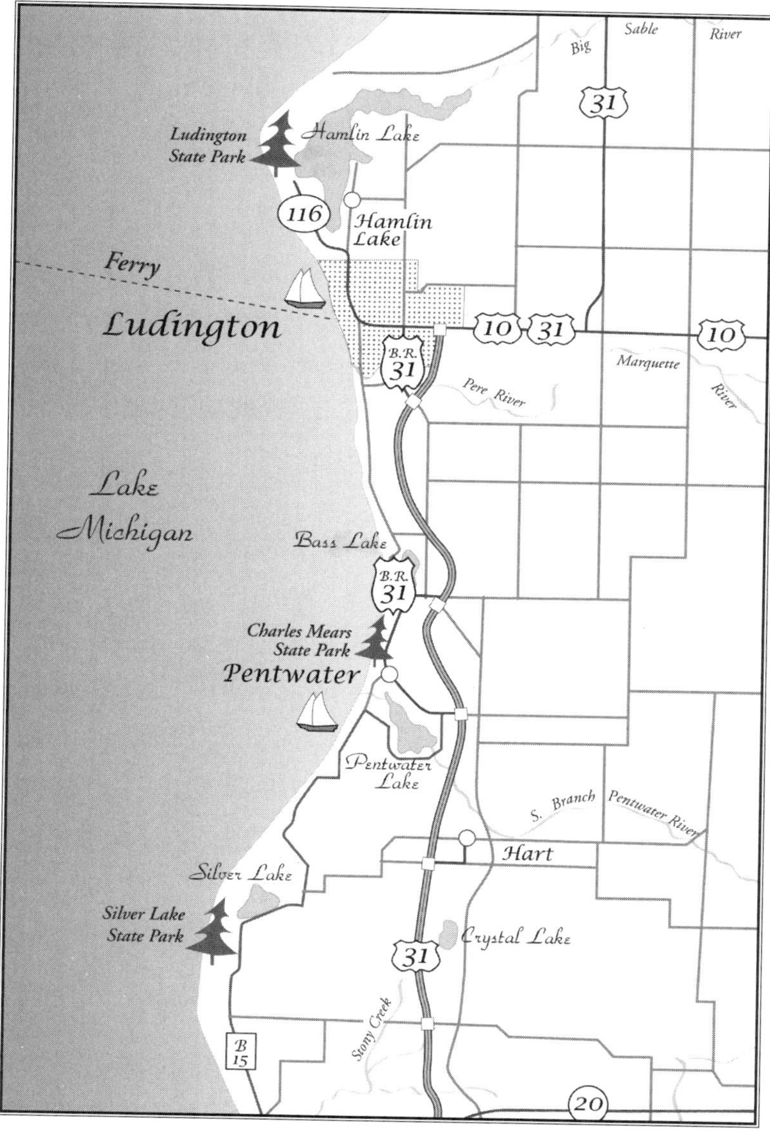

able footpath (look for the nautical history sign), but according to one park superintendent's advice, you should walk the beach at least one way. About three times a year, you can also take a bus for a nominal fee; either way, you will appreciate the small effort it takes to get there once you arrive.

The classic black-and-white brick lighthouse tower shoots 112 gorgeous feet into the sky. After watching an introductory film, it's time to climb the tower's 130 spiral steps. Don't worry; there are several catch-your-breath landings along the way, even if you don't need them. At the top, you can walk all the way around the lantern deck and enjoy 360-degree views of the lake and dunes, as well as ponds, wetlands, jack pine, and other vegetation typical of this environment. Since the state park collides with federal parkland, the view goes on forever. Time it right and you may be able to see the Mac Race, or simply wave to friends on the ground below.

You can learn a lot from the volunteer keeper who is stationed here, such as the fact that this site has long been significant to mariners as the midway point between the Straits of Mackinac and Chicago; or that it is the narrowest part of Lake Michigan, and also particularly treacherous. And if you thought your walk to get here was inconvenient, let the keeper tell you of a time when the lighthouse was accessible only by boat, before a road was constructed in the 1930s; and that before 1948, there was no indoor plumbing or central heating. The adjacent keeper's quarters still serves its original purpose, but with considerably greater turnover, because today each volunteer actually lives there for two weeks. Anyone can apply for the job, but in keeping with tradition, these folks work hard (10:00 a.m. to 6:00 p.m. every day!) to assure a great visitor experience. But the work indeed pays off. As volunteer lighthouse keeper Dale Painter said one October afternoon:

"This time of year it's really great because the sun is a little lower in the sky so you get the deeper colors. You kind of look out on the beach, hear the waves all night. Last night my wife and I were out walking on the beach, and the Milky Way was . . . oh, was it awesome!"

After your bird's-eye view, pop into the park's Great Lakes Visitor Center to learn about the unique natural features of all five Great Lakes. View the wall-size satellite image, learn about sand dune formation, and sign up for snowshoe-making classes (or stay at the Lamplighter B&B in Ludington and borrow their finished snowshoes). Take a dip in Lake Michigan or Hamlin Lake; explore the marked Canoe Pathway on Hamlin Lake; fish for salmon in the Big Sable River; hike along 18 miles of trails that lead you deeper into the wooded sand dunes where deer and other wildlife can keep an eye on you. Need more ideas? Why not sign up for great summer programs that take you canoeing, stargazing, or searching for the ghost lumbering town? How about an evening spent listening to folk songs straight out of the Great Lakes maritime past? There's just no room for boredom on these 5,300 acres.

Follow State Highway 116 south now to experience lakefront Ludington, then hit the downtown shops farther inland. The **House of Flavors**, 402 West Ludington Avenue, (231) 845-5785, www.houseofflavors.com, is always good for ice cream, while **Anna Bach Chocolates & Danish Bakery**, 102 West Ludington Avenue, (231) 843-9288, www.annabachchocolates.com, has been doing chocolate since 1949.

Big Sable Point Lighthouse, Ludington State Park, Ludington, Michigan

Like animals? Drive just four miles inland to the 130-acre **Amber Elk Ranch**, 2688 West Conrad Road, Ludington, Michigan 49431, (231) 843-5355, www.amberelkranch.com. Here you can hop onto a tractor-pulled wagon for an incredibly intimate experience with the farm's herd of golden brown elk. Bring your camera, because with fields and trees as a backdrop and at times no fence between you and the animals, you can get great shots of brawny bulls or sweet-faced calves. Observe the quiet tranquility—until the bulls shatter the silence with bugle calls and mock fights. Kids will love the tractor ride; the more water-logged ruts, the better. After the ride, take the whole family to the petting zoo and the Antler

Amber Elk Ranch, Ludington, Michigan

Shed, and then lose them all in the autumn corn maze.

As you continue south along the lakeshore, visit the 23-acre **Historic White Pine Village**, 1687 South Lakeshore Drive, Ludington, Michigan 49431, (231) 843-4808, www.historicwhitepinevillage. org, which is a collection of over 25 buildings that interpret county history, beginning in

THE SS *BADGER*, FROM STEM TO STERN

• She was built for $5 million in 1952 by the Christy Corporation of Sturgeon Bay, Wisconsin;

• She entered into service on March 21, 1953 under the ownership of the C&O Railroad;

• In 2003, she was re-christened in honor of 50 years of service on Lake Michigan;

• She can carry 620 passengers and 180 vehicles (semi-trucks are no problem for her) as she sails for four hours across the mid-section of Lake Michigan;

• Her average crossing speed is 18 mph, and she covers a total of 60 miles each crossing (492 crossings per season);

• She is the only coal-fired passenger steamship still operating in the U.S.; she burns no oil;

• The SS *Spartan*, permanently docked in Ludington, helps supply her with parts;

• Semaphore flags adorn some of the lounge walls. Find out where name of ship is secretly spelled out (hint: the first two flags are the same);

• She was built to handle Lake Michigan's tough year-round conditions, but her sailing schedule runs from mid-May through mid-October. Each May, she brings the promise of summer to the shorelines; but come October, she leaves a little wistfulness in her wake;

On the Ludington side, the lofty ramp at the dock is a relic of the railroad car transport days. Passenger vehicles used to be loaded from it onto the main deck, and while that is no longer the case, the company still uses it.

1850. The village is somewhat hidden among the back roads but well worth seeking out, and you can spend lots of time here. Learn that the carferries used to run year-round, and they were built so tough that they had the capability of tackling winter ice on the lake—a task that was no walk on the beach. For actual footage of a carferry doing battle with the ice, head to the Maritime Museum, which is one of the historic buildings, to watch *A Game All By Itself.* This stirring, 10-minute video is offered for sale in the gift shop. View artifacts including marine uniforms, the Big Sable Point Lighthouse's original third order Fresnel lens, a *City of Midland* carferry lifeboat, a 44-foot U.S. Coast Guard lifeboat that was used from 1965–2001, and the captain's chair from the SS *Spartan* (now used to supply parts for the SS *Badger*). Learn how lumbering fed the maritime trade with white pine that could be floated downriver to the waiting ships. See a 1901 sawmill still in operation and two original lumber camp buildings. Root for the Ludington Mariners that play "baseball" by 1860 rules.

During the off-season, you can go behind the counter of the village ice cream parlor and scoop it up "On Your Honor." You've heard of town bands, right? But a Clown Band? Watch a video of the Scott-ville Clown Band, which was formed in a local Michigan community in 1903 and has evolved into an outrageous yet professional outfit. The Web site, www. scottvilleclownband.com, reports that members do have day jobs—including everything from "doctor" to "horseshoer" to "criminal."

Power plants are not high on the list of vacation attractions, but as you continue south on shore-hugging County Road BR31 toward Pentwater, you'll probably be curious about the massive piece of engineering looming in the distance. It's one of the largest hydroelectric plants of its kind in the world, and it draws water up from Lake Michigan to satisfy the electrical energy needs of 1.4 million people in a way that is friendly to the environment. For you, its scenic overlook offers great lake views. Just up the road, make a stop at **Bortell's Fisheries**, 5528 South Lakeshore Drive, Ludington, Michigan 49431, (231) 843-3337. They have been smoking fish here since 1898, and you can get their hot fried fish, among other nautical delicacies, to go. A great place to eat, it is just across the road at **Summit Township Park**. Here you can dig your feet in the sand while enjoying lovely lake views; and you may even see a few Amish families enjoying a picnic lunch, too.

Pentwater

Sixteen miles south of downtown Ludington, you'll reach Pentwater, where you'll find a charming downtown with plenty of waterfront activity. Take a moment to read the roadside **Graveyard of Ships** signage that tells about the 70 vessels that have sunk along the 20 miles between the points of Ludington and Silver Lake, from the *Neptune* in 1848 to the vessels lost during the Armistice Day storm of November 11, 1940. That tragic day is chronicled on the signage:

"The most disastrous day in the history of Lake Michigan shipping. . . . With 75 mph winds and 20-foot waves, a raging storm destroyed three ships and claimed the lives of 59 seamen. Two freighters sank . . . a third . . . ran aground. . . . Bodies washed ashore throughout the day."

It is also noted that three Pentwater fishermen were later honored for having rescued 17 sailors. Other signage brings Pentwater's 1865–1900 lumbering era to life, so that you can almost smell the stacks of newly-sawn wood piled high and awaiting shipment to faraway ports. Find out what a lumber shover was, and how many freight and passenger vessels visited the Pentwater harbor in 1891.

Before you leave Pentwater, you may wish to stop in at the **Brass Anchor**, 500 South Hancock Street, Pentwater, Michigan 49449, (231) 869-4200, an intriguing store that caters to boaters but also deals, on a limited basis, in nautical antiques. Continue south now along County Road B-15 to Mears, which is the town that anchors Silver Lake. Mears is 24 miles south of Ludington and about 10 miles south of Pentwater.

Silver Lake

Silver Lake is so many things. It's like being in the desert, but with plenty of fresh water lapping all around. It's like playing in a sandbox, but in the realm of

giants. And when the water is still as glass after all the boats have gone, the dunes seem to double in height. This is the otherworldly beauty of Silver Lake.

WHEN LIGHTNING STRIKES, FULGURITES!

Did it storm last night? If so, then this morning is the perfect time to hike out onto the dunes of Silver Lake in search of fulgurites, or petrified lightning. In Michigan, Silver Lake is one of the few places you can find these fragile formations. They are created when lightning strikes the dunes and the heat from the powerful electrical charge melts a hole in the sand. The result is a smooth glass sheathed in melted sand, ranging in shape from tubes to miniature lightning bolts. Pick up a fulgurite and it will likely crumble in your hand. Leave it alone, and it will remain a signature in the sand.

But when it's not ethereal, it's sizzling. Get ready for a little hotspot that celebrates summer in classic style, complete with bumper cars and ice cream shops. Expect everything to be clean and small-town friendly without a hint of pretense.

Besides being out on the water and then flopping down to sunbathe, people come to drive on the sand, which is actually part of the **Silver Lake State Park**, 9679 West State Park Road, Mears, Michigan 49436, (231) 873-3083, www.michigan.gov/dnr. This is not the dune buggy culture that spilled over from the 1960s; rather, it goes way back to 1930. To keep things from getting too out of hand, the 2,936-acre parkland is divided more or less into thirds. The north end is the 450-acre off-road vehicle area and the only place in Michigan where you can drive a jeep, a dune buggy, or other sand-gobbling vehicles on the dunes. The south end is home to **Mac Wood's Dune Rides**, 629 North 18th Avenue, Mears, Michigan 49436, (231) 873-2817, www. macwoodsdunerides.com, where you can go on a seven-mile sojourn in an open-air, four-wheel drive truck—as people have done since 1930. The middle section is designated for quiet hiking and exploration. From the eastern shore of Silver Lake, the dunes look deceptively narrow, but once you've surveyed the scene from atop a dune, you may be surprised to discover just how much sand there still is between you and Lake Michigan. The dried-up, gnarly tree roots that you see in some spots are actually artifacts of the nineteenth-century lumbering days, and if you're lucky enough to find a jagged piece of glass, it just may be a fulgurite (see sidebar, page116).

A few miles south of Silver Lake, the **Little Sable Point Lighthouse** rises from the sand like a giant cinnamon stick. It was built in 1874 and still lights the way on the water. It is surrounded by a gorgeous stretch of beach and easily accessed from the parking lot. But the most exciting thing is that tours up the 139 cast iron steps are now offered to the public. Find out why the tower went from unpainted red brick to bricks painted white and then sandblasted back to red brick.

As you backtrack (the road south of the lighthouse dead ends) and then drive south on Scenic Drive (County Road B-15), you can catch several glimpses of Lake Michigan. Quintessential Michigan orchards decorate the roadsides with sturdy trees and colorful fruits. Beyond this bounty, more adventure and a treasure chest of local history await your arrival in the White Lake area.

FROM THE GALLEYS

PM Steamers, 502 West Loomis Street, Ludington, Michigan 49431, (231) 843-9555, www.pmsteamers.com. Savor various seafood and steaks on the waterfront. The Great Lakes Trio combines sautéed salmon, whitefish, and walleye with shitake mushroom sauce and matchstick vegetables. Nutty Walleye is rolled in pecans and brown sugar, then topped with Michigan dried cherry sauce. Deck dining available with full menu.

Scotty's Restaurant, 5910 West U.S. Highway 10, Ludington, Michigan 49431, (231) 843-4033, www.scottysrestaurant.com. Deep fried and lightly seasoned lake perch is a house specialty, along with marinated and charbroiled swordfish steak and seafood kabob. Or opt for steak, chicken, or chops.

TO THE DOCKS

Dunes Waterfront Resort, 1180 North Shore Road, Mears, Michigan 49436, (231) 873-5500, www.duneswaterfrontresort.com. Nestled on the waterfront of Silver Lake, this contemporary resort features a private beach and dock. The entire top floor has a 62-foot-long swimming pool, hot tub, sundeck, game room, and meeting room. Guest rooms have refrigerators.

The Lamplighter Bed and Breakfast, 602 East Ludington Avenue, Ludington, Michigan 49431, (800) 301-9792, www.ludington-michigan.com. If your ferry sails early in the morning, your hosts will be ready with shipboard breakfast vouchers; and if it docks in the evening, they'll have the lamps lit and pillows plumped. Fall in love with antique details such as the radiator with a muffin-warming box, the framed antique marriage certificate in the honeymoon suite, and thoughtful touches like cookies by the door and a TV in every room. Find out what Carrom is. Meet Maggie the Soft-Coated (and well-mannered) Wheaten Terrier who looks like a teddy bear and adores the guests. Breakfast is often a lively affair: guests gather around a lovely table along with the caring innkeepers, who have more than one story to tell. Enjoy fruit juice that is freshly blended and slightly slushy without being thick; warm half-grapefruit with berries; and sausage and German pancakes with locally produced maple syrup.

Hamlin Lake Cottage-Resorts. A host of cottage-resorts have anchored down on the woodland shores of both Upper and Lower Hamlin Lake, north of Ludington and adjacent to Ludington State Park. In anticipation of your stay, visit www.luding

toncvb.com for the complete list of details for each property. Weekly rentals are the norm. Many also rent out low-key boats such as canoes and pontoons.

AIDS TO NAVIGATION

Ludington Area Convention & Visitors Bureau, (877) 420-6618, www.ludingtoncvb.com.

Pentwater Chamber of Commerce, (866) 869-4150, www.pentwater.org.

Silver Lake/Hart Convention & Visitors Bureau, (800) 874-3982, www.silverlakecvb.org.

The White Lake Area & Muskegon

"The cottages kind of just stay in the family. Since I've been here, in the 22 years I think there are only maybe one or two that have actually gone up for sale outside of the family."

—Karen McDonnell, Curator, White River Light Station Great Lakes Maritime Museum

On White Lake

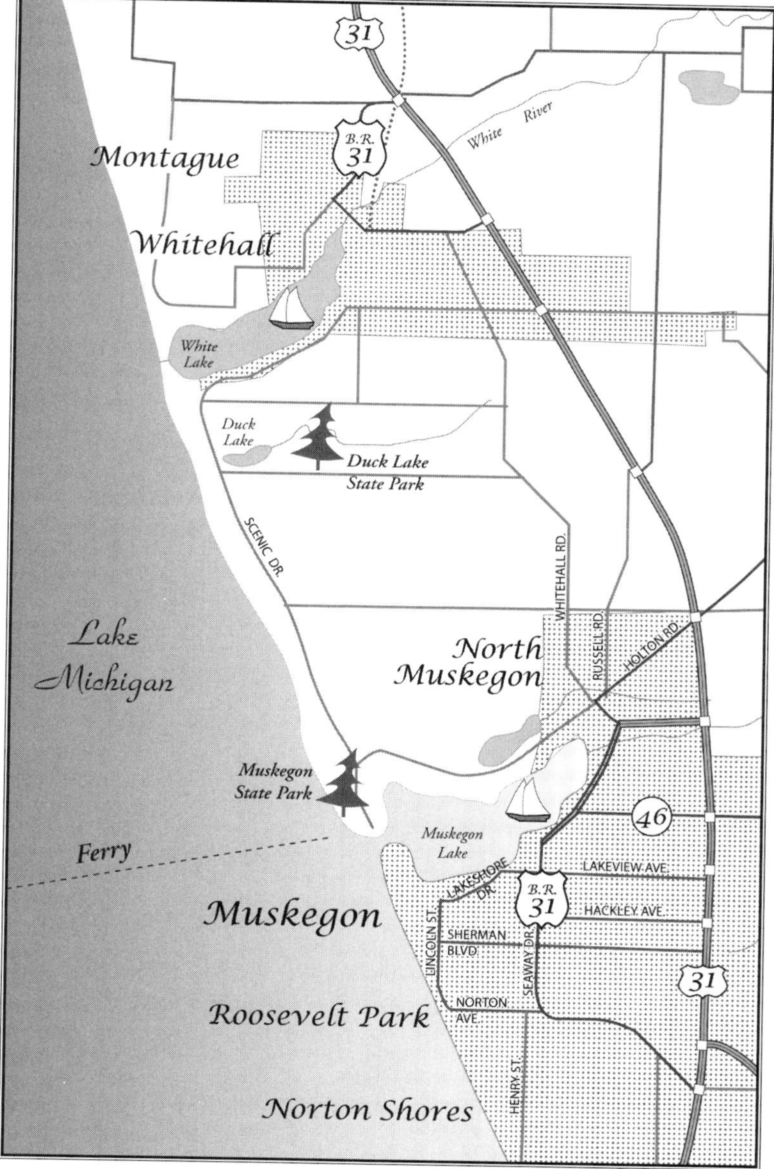

ONLY A CAUSEWAY over White Lake separates Montague to the north from Whitehall to the south, but both towns share spectacular sunsets and an abundance of fresh water. Dine or stay lakeside, because the views are lovely, the sand is sugary-soft, and the water is warm. There is history here, too, in the way of a lighthouse where a female curator has lived for almost a quarter century, and old resorts where families have summered for generations. Montague and Whitehall are about 43 miles south of Ludington.

As you continue south from Silver Lake, stay on Scenic Drive (County Road B-15), turn onto Highway BR-31, and drive the short distance to downtown Montague and the **World's Largest Weathervane**. The name makes it sound like one of those odd roadside attractions, but it is in fact a rather noble piece. The lumber schooner that crowns the weathervane's 48-foot summit honors the sunken *Ella Ellenwood.* The ship was built in 1869 and operated out of White Lake until 1901, when she went down north of Milwaukee, Wisconsin. Remarkably, her nameplate floated across Lake Michigan and was discovered on the shore of White Lake, her home port, the following spring. They say the lady had found her way home.

Ply the waters of White Lake from the seat of a kayak rented from **Powers Outdoors**, 4523 Dowling Street, Montague, Michigan 49437, (231) 893-0687, www.powersoutdoors.com. You can take Powers' two-hour class for a reasonable fee, then hit the calm waters where wildlife sightings are common.

Zip across the causeway to the Whitehall (south) side of White Lake, and drive seven pleasant miles along South Shore Drive, passing lakeside homes until you reach the **White River Light Station Great Lakes Maritime Museum**, 6199 Murray Road, Whitehall, Michigan 49461, (231) 894-8265, www.whiteriverlightstation.org. At this point you'll be very close to Lake Michigan, or "the Big Lake," as it's known to locals up and down the shore. Actually, the Native Americans used to call it that, too; the name originated as the Algonquian word *michigami* or *misschiganin,* meaning "big lake."

Built in 1875 of Michigan limestone and brick, the light station houses resident curator Karen McDonnell. She has lived here since graduating from college, taking care of the tower and the tourists, and raising her son in an enviably unique environment. Since the light has been decommissioned by the U.S. Coast Guard, McDonnell is technically not the lighthouse keeper—but she jokes that she does light housekeeping. This is no small feat, however. Since visitors are invited to climb the tower's 54 chocolate-brown spiral steps 38 feet to the top, McDonnell likes to keep the lantern glass smudge-free for picture taking. This service requires performing a somewhat alarming series of contortions through the lantern trapdoor. What's more, McDonnell readily assists those with ailments and anxieties so they can enjoy the view of Lake Michigan, the channel, and the sand dunes along with everyone else.

During your visit to this lighthouse museum, view the nautical and navigational artifacts and compelling photographs, including those of former keepers—one of whom, locals say, just might haunt the tower. While there is no official evidence, consider the tale of the blinking light bulb. After McDonnell installed a 200-watt light bulb into the tower, it began to blink in an oddly steady way, drawing the attention of the U.S. Coast Guard. The tower appeared to be transmitting a signal, which was not al lowed at a decommissioned lighthouse. The U.S. Coast Guard insisted the bulb be removed. But McDonnell pled her case, explaining that a dark tower would not do. She succeeded in convincing them to at least let her put in a mere 15-watt bulb. The replacement bulb, as it turned out, never blinked. Neither did the 200-watt bulb when it was later tested in a different socket.

At this point, a little fresh air may be in order. So after exploring the lighthouse and its mysteries, be sure to take advantage of the outdoor photo opportunities, and follow the channel walkway out to the beach and pierhead lights.

Next up, head 17 miles southeast to Muskegon.

Muskegon

In a city where nineteenth-century lumber barons harvested fortunes from the forests, you can tour two of the generation's most spectacular homes, then wander into a museum that illustrates the connection between Michigan's lumbering and maritime trades. Plan on staying in town a while, because you can board not one but three vessels that gallantly served twentieth-century America on the world's stage. Also board a steamer that ferried passengers on Lake Michigan as late as 1970, and a high-speed catamaran that has just begun its maritime run.

But first, are you up for adventure? Then head to **Michigan's Adventure/Wildwater Adventure**, 4750 Whitehall Road, Muskegon, Michigan 49445, (231) 766-3377, www.miadventure.com. This is the state's largest playground, and it will happily toss you about like a dinghy on Lake Michigan. Ride the menacingly graceful waves of the Shivering Timbers wooden coaster. Don't just study Michigan's logging era, *become* the log on the 1,500-foot Grand Rapids wild river ride, which first made a splash in 2006. Cruise into the

USS LST 393 camouflage ship, Muskegon, Michigan

Weathered lifeboat aboard *USS LST 393*, Muskegon, Michigan

new Coasters Drive-In for burgers, fries, and malts in vintage diner style.

Dry off and return to the lakeshore, following Scenic Drive south into **Muskegon State Park**, 3560 Memorial Drive, Muskegon, Michigan 49445, (231) 744-3480. The park's generous 1,165 acres of woodlands, windswept dunes, and sugary beaches invite you to hike, fish, picnic, swim, and unscramble your brains after the amusement park. The USS *Silversides* submarine is visible across the channel from the Muskegon Harbor Navigation Project, but you'll need to backtrack a little and drive all the way around Muskegon Lake to get there.

DUNE AFTERNOON

Why does the eastern shore of Michigan possess the world's largest mass of sand dunes along fresh water? How do these piles of sand form? How does plant life change them? Get the answers to all sorts of questions about the dunes at P. J. Hoffmaster State Park, 6585 Lake Harbor Road (at Pontaluna Road), Muskegon, Michigan 49441, (231) 798-3711, www.michigan.gov/dnr. The 1,130-acre park, located just south of downtown Muskegon along the Lake Michigan shore, reveals all inside its E. Genevieve Gillette Sand Dune Visitor Center, (231) 798-3573. Get comfortable in the 82-seat auditorium where multimedia presentations explain dune ecology and the principles of plant succession. Put your new-found knowledge to work on the Dune Climb Stairway and along 10 miles of trails. Occupy the kids by challenging them to build their own sand dunes on the beach.

Docked in front of the **Great Lakes Naval Memorial and Museum**, 1346 Bluff Street, Muskegon, Michigan 49441, (231) 755-1230, www.glnmm.org, is **USS *Silversides SS-236***, a 312-foot U.S. Navy submarine that ranks third among all subs in the number of enemy ships that it sunk during World War II. The price of a ticket grants permission to board as your guide shows you the guns, sail armaments, target and attack periscopes, torpedo loading skid, and escape trunk hatch. Go below, where you will actually be underwater amid a tangle of gauges, valves, hatches, switches, and torpedoes. Although the sub is in the water, it does not actually dive; but don't touch anything, because everything still works. Here you can imagine life for the servicemen who slept in bunks stacked three-high, some within inches of torpedoes, and ate meals prepared in closet-sized galleys—200 feet beneath the surface of the ocean. Cover your ears when the guide activates the recorded sound of the engines.

Your ticket also includes a tour aboard the nearby **U.S. Coast Guard Cutter *McLANE W-146***, which was built in 1927 to enforce Prohibition but likely also sunk an enemy sub during World War II. Her polished wood and brass fixtures contrast dramatically with the sub's cold metal surfaces.

Traveling eastward away from Lake Michigan, retrace your route along the south shore of Muskegon Lake to the **SS *Milwaukee Clipper***, 2098 Lakeshore Drive, Muskegon, Michigan 49441, (231) 755-0990, www.milwaukeeclipper.com. Tour this steamship that, from 1941 to 1970, carried thousands of passengers and their automobiles between Muskegon and

Milwaukee. Like so many historic vessels on Lake Michigan, she is currently being restored. Check the Web site for current information on shipboard tours.

The **Lake Express Ferry**, Muskegon Terminal, 1918 Lakeshore Drive, Muskegon, Michigan 49441, (866) 914-1010, www.lake-express.com, docks nearby. And a little over two miles northeast along Muskegon Lake, the ***Port City Princess***, 560 Mart Street, Muskegon, Michigan 49440, (800) 853-6311, (231) 728-8387, www.portcityprincesscruises.com, offers cruises of Lake Michigan, with reservations required. Take a scenic cruise, or save your appetite and taste for romance by choosing a lunch or dinner cruise.

Curious about that massive camouflage ship on the Mart Dock? She is the venerable **USS *LST 393***, 563 Mart Street, Muskegon, Michigan 49440, (231) 730-1477, www.lst393.org, a 1943 warship that won three Battle Stars for three World War II invasions in the Atlantic Ocean and Mediterranean Sea, including the Normandy Invasion. As a Landing Ship Tank, her job was to get the tanks where they needed to be, but with a cruise speed of only 8.5 knots per hour, the crew quickly nicknamed her Large Slow Target. The U.S. Navy built 1,148 LST's during the war; this is one of the two remaining.

With her hull painted government-issue camouflage, LST 393 looks ready for battle; but instead, her only mission is to thrill visitors. The tour takes you through the Tank Deck, the Berthing Deck where the crew slept, the Main Deck, and the Navigating Bridge. From the Berthing Deck, vertical escape hatches descend all

Townsend, World War II cement freighter, Muskegon, Michigan

Weathervane Inn, Montague, Michigan

the way to the bottom of the ship; but as scary as they look, the hatches allowed a fast escape to safety for the sleeping crew in the event of an attack. Although they're off limits to visitors, you can still descend to the steering gear room with its tangle of pipes and eerie sloshing sounds.

In the wheelhouse, a device called the Inclinometer measures the degrees of roll; it was manufactured by the John L. Chaney Instrument Company in Lake Geneva, Wisconsin. From the captain's quarters to the officers' mess to the bridge deck lifeboats, a tour of LST 393 is an absolute must during your Muskegon visit. The ship is bold, raw, and victorious; and as the brochure reads, "You have indeed walked where heroes have walked." Enjoy a growing list of special events like the **World War II Anniversary Commemoration**, which features a reenacted encampment, a big band orchestra, and other engrossing activities.

Two land-based museums, both located downtown, colorfully interpret the region's lumbering and maritime traditions. Hidden downstairs inside the **Muskegon County Museum**, 430 West Clay Avenue, Muskegon, Michigan 49440, (231) 722-0278, www.muskegonmuseum.org, is the superb Coming to the Lakes exhibit, which chronicles 10,000 years of history. Join the ancient People of the Three Fires as they ply the waters in dugout canoes, fishing through ice in winter and with nets and spears in summer. Learn that, in 1836, settlers thought 500 years would pass before they could cut down all of the magnificent Michigan white pine—and it ended up taking only 50. Learn about the life of river rats, those loggers who used pikes and peaveys to guide logs downriver to the sorting pens. Find out what barking spuds were good for. Learn how, in order to move sawn lumber to market, it had to be shipped by boat to Chicago railroads.

Walk three blocks to the **Hackley & Hume Historic Site**, 430 West Clay Avenue, Muskegon, Michigan 49440, (888) 843-5661, (231) 722-0278, www.muskegonmuseum.org. Once home to Muskegon's two most famous lumber barons, this site drips with delicious Queen Anne detail that is as rich as Swiss chocolate. There are two houses on the site. The Hackley House was built to sweeten the retirement years of lumber baron Charles H. Hackley (1837–1905). Its exterior is coated in 14 glossy colors, and its interior features Moorish arches, interesting keyhole designs, Japan-ese-inspired stenciling, and majolica tiles. The Hume House, which was built for Hackley's partner and his young family, is a little less lavish. It only has 12 exterior colors.

From the City Barn, your guide will sweep you into the Hackley House. Considering Hackley, a lumber baron, helped make the town known as "Lumber Queen of the World" and "the city that built Chicago and a hundred other prairie towns," his house is filled with beautiful woods. Every room has a theme: Look for the fishing and hunting motif in the dining room, and the figureheads of ships in the nautical-inspired library. By contrast, the Hume House presents a strikingly less ornate interior; but it's noticeably more spacious. Seven children grew up here, and the home stayed in the family until 1952.

Horse and history lovers alike should head to the **Fire Barn Museum, C. H. Hackley Hose Company No. 2**, Clay Avenue (between Fifth Street and Sixth Street, one block west of the mansions), (231) 722-7578, www.muskegonmuseum.org/fb_museum.asp. In the late 1800s, Charles Hackley built a fire barn, which now houses the museum, behind his home. When the fire bell shrieked, the horses inside the barn pushed open their stall doors and stood beneath harnesses that automatically dropped from the ceiling. For the upstairs firemen, the horses' well-trained readiness was a vital timesaver. Trace the history of firefighting from handcarts to horse-drawn hose carts to early fire trucks, and find out why Dalmatians have endured as a symbol of American firefighting.

And now that you've glanced far back into the past, it's time again to look toward the future, and your next stop along the Lake Michigan shore.

FROM THE GALLEYS

Dog 'n Suds Drive-In, 4454 Dowling Street, Montague, Michigan 49437, (231) 894-4991, www.dog-n-suds.com. Raise a frosty mug of root beer and bite into a juicy burger in honor of this, the last remaining Dog 'n Suds in all of Michigan.

Michillinda Lodge, 5207 Scenic Drive, Whitehall, Michigan 49461, (231) 893-1895, www.michil lindalodge.com. Soldierly pines and delicate flowers nod a welcome along the driveway that leads you to this classic Lake Michigan resort (its name, by the way, is a combination of Michigan, Illinois, and Indiana). Dine lakeside on salads, sandwiches, steak, chops, and chicken, as well as lake-fried perch, pan-fried trout, grilled walleye, and other fine fish selections. Do your part to help preserve the "Cookies at Sunset" tradition.

Rafferty's Dockside Restaurant, 730 Terrace Point Boulevard, Muskegon, Michigan 49440, (231) 722-4461, www.shorelineinn.com. Just steps from the Shoreline Inn & Suites and Muskegon Lake, this land and sea restaurant offers great surf, such as pretzel-crumb walleye hand-fried with whole-grain mustard sauce and herbed redskins, and great turf, like lumber-baron prime rib slow-roasted with herbs and served with garlic mashed potatoes.

Scales Fish House & Steaks, 302 South Lake Street, Whitehall, Michigan 49461, (231) 893-4655, www.scalesfish house.com. Dine under the umbrella of a patio table and enjoy the cool lakefront breeze. Lunch could be an ocean-fish taco or spinach salad with goat cheese, candied pecans, red onions, and raspberry vinaigrette. Try the smoked whitefish spread with grilled onion flatbread appetizer. Dinner entrées include lake perch and pecan crusted walleye, and Kansas City bone-in strip.

TO THE DOCKS

Cocoa Cottage Bed and Breakfast, 223 South Mears Avenue, Whitehall, Michigan 49461, (800) 204-7596, (231) 893-0674, www.cocoacottage.com. Take a break from the lake and stay in this charming bungalow. Perfectly restored in artistic style, this B&B features warm woods and amazing detail, such as the cherry, walnut, and oak-inlaid entry floor. And there's chocolate at every turn! The innkeepers make everyone feel at home with a friendly, approachable demeanor—so much so that they recently earned the #1 B&B/Country Innkeepers in North America award (*Arrington's Inn Traveler Magazine*).

Lakeside Inn Resort, 5700 North Scenic Drive, Whitehall, Michigan 49461, (888) 442-3304, (231) 893-8315, www.lakesideinn.net. This much-loved White Lake landmark keeps generations of vacationers returning for endless Lake Michigan views, proximity to sandy beaches and lighthouse tours, a variety of accommodation options, an outdoor pool, tennis courts, shuffleboard, and a relaxed atmosphere, courtesy of friendly hosts. It all began as a general store in 1855 and has been in the Groessl family since 1939. Inside the dining room, a seasonal menu offers creative choices such as Cherry Pork Loin with caramelized onions and Michigan cherry chutney, and Yellow Perch that is lightly battered and deep-fried. For dessert, order an Ice Cream Sundae Pie for yourself and the Cookie Monster for the kids, which they can decorate with edible paint.

Shoreline Inn & Suites, 750 Terrace Point Boulevard, Muskegon, Michigan 49440, (866) 727-8483, (231) 727-8483, www.shorelineinn.com. Victorian elegance soars 10 sumptuous stories toward a fresco of golden seashells. Ornately carved wooden furnishings, rich hues, balconies, a lakeside indoor pool and hot tubs, and panoramic lake views all attend to your needs. Complementary continental breakfast.

The Weathervane Inn, 4527 Dowling Street, Montague, Michigan 49437, (877) 893-8931, (231) 893-8931, www.theweathervaneinn.net. From your private balcony, you cannot only look out across the lake, but also down into the water—it's that close. And the nearest boat is docked just a few lily pads away. The Corner Suite features wrap-around windows and balcony with a generous helping of chairs, along with a double-whirlpool tub, a fireplace, a refrigerator, and additional luxurious amenities. Follow the property's boardwalk past native grasses and benches to the gazebo. If you love breezes, boats, and blue water, you would be hard-pressed to find a better spot than this. Complementary continental breakfast, specialty coffees, aromatherapy soaps, and lotions.

AIDS TO NAVIGATION

White Lake Area Chamber of Commerce, (800) 879-9702, www.whitelake. org.

Muskegon County Convention & Visitors Bureau, (800) 250-WAVE, www.visitmuskegon.org. Before the turn of the twentieth century, lumber baron Charles H. Hackley and other local developers constructed Muskegon Union Depot in Richardsonian Romanesque style to impress visitors. Fittingly, this railroad station now houses the CVB.

Grand Haven to Saugatuck

From the Guestbook of Harbor House Inn, Grand Haven:
"We are . . . checking out ports for next year's yachting trip. Grand Haven is a must. We can smell breakfast—can't wait to go downstairs."
—Christina & Mark

"We like to say that after the railroad arrived in 1870, the lake became less a lifeline and more a lifestyle."
—Joel Lefever, President, Holland Museum

"Has anyone told you about the green flash? When the sun is right at the horizon and when it sinks under, if atmospheric conditions are just right there's a neon green flash. It just goes right along the horizon. I've only seen it once and it's absolutely spectacular."
—Sally Hallan Laukitis, Executive Director, Holland Area Convention & Visitors Bureau

"Whenever one of us sees a freighter, we run through the house, 'Big boat! Big boat!'"
—Lois Sligh, resident

"Beginning in the 1880s they started raising fruit. They talk about the peach boats leaving Saugatuck, and you could see the little cloud of fruit flies after the boat disappeared over the horizon."
—Kit Lane, Saugatuck-Douglas Historical Society Museum

Grand Haven

Do you like sand? Then you will love Grand Haven's languidly long stretches of beach. Do you like bands? Then you will love the marching bands that resound every summer during Grand Haven's 10-day U.S. Coast Guard Festival. Life is grand in Grand Haven, a darling town that publishes its own sunset schedule, and boasts not only the longest river in Michigan, but also the third-largest of the Great Lakes. About 14 miles south of Muskegon, this beautiful lakeshore town is waiting—so come along, and, at least for a while, make it your haven.

South of the channel that links the river with the lake, **Grand Haven State Park**, 1001 South Harbor Drive, Grand Haven, Michigan 49417, (616) 847-1309, sprawls out along a lakeshore where RV campsites are paved into the sand. Summer is playtime here, for ambitious surfers and languid sunbathers alike. At night, the catwalk out to the **Grand Haven Lighthouses** radiates as if it were Christmas. The locals are particularly proud that their lighthouses retain the catwalk, as so many of their kind have been torn down. Catwalks were essential to nineteenth-century lightkeeping: during storms, when foamy waves broke over the cement walkways far below, the keepers still needed to access the pierhead lights—and this was the only safe form of passage. Today the catwalks are not open to visitors, but the memory of their importance lives on.

Follow the 2.5-mile **Boardwalk** away from the lighthouses and back toward downtown. You'll arrive at the Waterfront Stadium, which provides front-row seats for the seasonal nighttime **Musical Fountain** show. Built across the river where a ghost town once thrived, the fountain hides by day amid the dunes, only to explode with color and sound, and 90,000 gallons of water, beneath the night sky. It's the biggest fountain of its kind in the world, and home to over 75 thematic programs and a different dance nearly every summer night.

Continue on past the **Brass River** (which you can walk upon and not get wet) to the slips of **Chinook Pier Sportfishing**, 301 Harbor Avenue, Grand Haven, Michigan 49417, (800) 782-5369, (616) 842-2229. From this point, any of Chinook Pier Sportfishing's 15 vessels can take you out on the lake in hot pursuit of salmon and other desirable fish. Captain Willis, who has been landing them for almost four decades, says that salmon downrigger fishing, which is what charters do, is very different from almost any other kind of fishing. So, once aboard the boat, an educational session is in order. But when the rod pops, Captain Willis jokes, new fishers typically forget everything they have been told, which makes for great stories afterward.

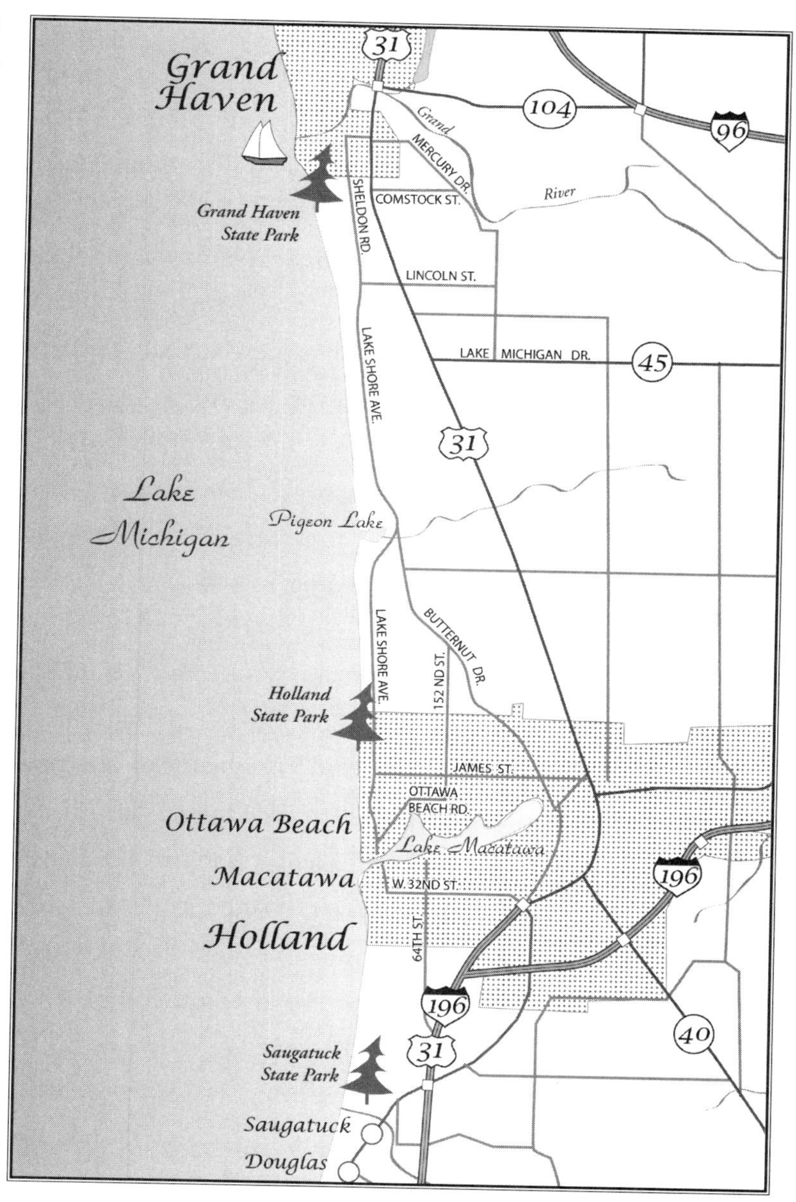

You can also make a stop at the nearby 1870 railroad depot that now houses the transportation section of the **Tri-Cities Historical Museum**, 1 North Harbor Drive, Grand Haven, Michigan 49417,

(616) 842-0700, www.tri-citiesmuseum.org. Follow the historical timeline through northwest Ottawa County's fur trading, lumbering, shipping, and railroading eras, as well as the arrival of the tourists to the old mineral springs hotels. Artifacts abound, including a fourth order Fresnel lens from the Old Grand Haven Lighthouse, which catches the sunlight and ignites a rainbow of color. U.S. Coast Guard memorabilia explain Grand Haven's unique connection with this military branch, a link that goes back to the late 1700s. A collection of stunning model ships, many under full sail, tells a fascinating maritime story. Here you can also learn the nautical origin of common terms, such as "going berserk," which originally referred to Viking sailors who fought without shirts on, or "baresark," meaning "bare of shirt." Being "three sheets to the wind" originally meant that when any three of a sailing vessel's sheets (lines, or ropes) were waving in the wind, the vessel became out of control.

After leaving the depot, walk two blocks southeast to the museum's other location at 200 Washington Avenue. Fittingly, it was built in 1871 by a lumberman and shipbuilder. Early history comes alive inside the walk-in dioramas, including a wigwam covered in birch bark, a log trading post from the Voyageurs era, and a logging camp bunkhouse.

Afterward, stroll and shop downtown Grand Haven's other finely restored buildings, including **The Schooner**, 211 Washington Avenue, Grand Haven, Michigan 49417, (888) 616-8673, (616) 842-6048, www.schooner-gifts.com, which sells a delightful collection of nautical artifacts.

As you head south toward Holland, reconnect with the lakeshore in 164 acres of lofty beauty at **Rosy Mound Natural Area**, Ottawa County Parks, 13925 Lakeshore Drive, Grand Haven, Michigan 49417, (616) 738-4810, www.co.ottawa.mi.us. It was here that locals, who had left generations of childhood memories atop a sand dune called Rosy Mound, witnessed the systematic shrinking of their mountain at the hand of a sand mining company. Follow the boardwalk trails through sequential stages, from backdune forest and interdunal wetland to the foredune and beach zones. As you make your way down to the Lake Michigan beach, stay on the boardwalk trails rather than "off-roading" through the dunes in order to help protect the legacy of Rosy Mound.

Holland, Macatawa

Back in 1860, without the help of government funds, the Dutch settlers of Holland dug their own channel between Lake Macatawa and Lake Michigan. This vital link enabled barge access at a time when the shipment of goods across water was far more practical than trying to go overland. Fast forward to 1939, when legendary boatbuilding company Chris-Craft expanded operations and selected Holland as a new location, largely for the skill of its craftsmen, who were renowned furniture makers. After World War II, the company's famous Cabin Cruisers became a symbol of the postwar "good life." Holland's boatbuilding tradition has come a long way, and continues to produce popular, high quality yachts to this day.

Holland's Dutch heritage is symbolized by the imported eighteenth-century windmill that still grinds grain. You can also experience Dutch culture inside the factories that produce wooden shoes, Delft china, and carved candles; at a nostalgic theme park; and during the wildly colorful Tulip Time Festival that welcomes spring each May.

Pick up threads of both Dutch and maritime heritage inside the **Holland Museum**, 31 West 10th Street, Holland, Michigan 49423, (888) 200-9123, www.hollandmuseum.org. The story begins with the arrival of the first Dutch settlers in 1847. These were primarily farmers who knew as well as anyone how to reclaim land from water, and thus developed the western Michigan swamps into plentiful farmland.

The maritime story resumes in the 1880s, with the dawn of the glory days of passenger steamers, grand resorts, and summers of privilege. While wealthy guests came from Midwestern cities, their lifestyles were a world apart. Randy Vande Water, a former editor of the *Holland Sentinel*, recalls that the summer job he took in one of these resorts—even as late as the 1940s—was an eye-opener.

Dennis Swartout with 4th Order Fresnel lens from Old Grand Haven Lighthouse, Tri-Cities Historical Museum (depot), Grand Haven, Michigan. Originally lit with whale oil.

In the summer of 1949, Vande Water worked as a night clerk at the Waukazoo Inn. More than half a century later, he still remembers two things about a wealthy guest from Cincinnati. First, the man paid his $1,000 bill with something Vande Water had never before seen—$100 bills. Second, he would stop to talk baseball with the night clerk. The most famous of the resorts was the Ottawa Beach Hotel, which was said to have 1,000 rooms that sparkled on the waterfront until it all went up in flames in 1927.

But fun on the water was not just for vacationers; locals also got their share. According to popular accounts, young men came up from Saugatuck to watch Dutch girls ice skate on the frozen lake. Bob Sligh, who grew up and learned to water ski on Lake Macatawa, got his picture in a 1946 issue of *Life* and won the national water-skiing championship the next year. Eventually, though, the resort era faded away, and none of the area's old resorts remain.

View from deck of *Star of Saugatuck II*, Saugatuck, Michigan

Don't miss the Holland Museum's passenger/car goship displays. The "Sinking of the *Alpena*" illustrates the 1880 tragedy that killed everyone on board during the storm that came to be known as "The Big Blow." Steamed out of Grand Haven and bound for Chicago, the *Alpena* never made it. And although the wreck itself has never been found, it is thought to have sunk near Holland because of all the debris that later washed ashore—including lumber, a piano, and thousands of bobbing apples. Especially poignant is an actual ticket that was issued to a doctor who missed the boat; his descendants donated the fateful bit of paper to the museum.

Finally, see the remaining artifacts from the *Alabama*, which cruised the Great Lakes and moored in Holland for the winter. What was billed as a "hotel afloat" has been reduced to bits and pieces: a mahogany railing, a luncheon menu, various china, a fancy stateroom key, and a plastic Please Do Not Disturb sign.

Take a brisk walk to the museum's 1867 **Settler's House**, 190 West 9th Street, where Thomas Morrissey, an Irish-Canadian ship's carpenter, lived with his wife and five children in only 800 square feet of space. Early maps displayed on the walls illustrate the design and location of local shipyards. The crudeness of the house stands as testament to the hard life that the Morrissey family undoubtedly led.

If you drive west from downtown Holland for seven miles along the north shore of Lake Macatawa, you'll come to **Tunnel Park**, 66 Lakeshore Drive North, Holland, Michigan 49424, (616) 738-4810, www.co.ottawa.mi.us, which is distinctive for the tunnel that is cut into a sand dune. You can access Lake Michigan from here or two miles to the south at **Holland State Park**, 2215 Ottawa Beach Road, Holland, Michigan 49424, (616) 399-9390, www.michigan.gov/dnr. With 142 acres, the park is comparatively small; but the view of **Hol-**

land Harbor Lighthouse, which sits across the channel, its gabled roof proudly symbolizing the local Dutch heritage, makes up for the size. After the U.S. Coast Guard ordered all navigation aids located on the right side of any harbor entrance to be red, locals quickly nicknamed the lighthouse **Big Red**. Take a good long look, for it has become virtually impossible to reach Big Red from its own pier, despite a paved walkway. Private interests have installed not one but two gates, in addition to a guard.

Yet anyone here at the right time can thrill to the sight of sailboat races or 700-foot freighters "silently gliding by," as schoolteacher and *Holland Sentinel* columnist Bob Vande Vusse puts it, with their loads of raw material moving through the channel that Dutch settlers dug so long ago.

Continue south toward the neighboring cities of Saugatuck and Douglas, 11 miles south of Holland and 75 miles north of the Michigan-Indiana border.

Saugatuck-Douglas

The luxury yachts, the sparkling waters, the brimming creativity—Saugatuck-Douglas is a pretty picture indeed, and you can jump right into the canvas by boarding the ***Star of Saugatuck II***, 716 Water Street, Saugatuck, Michigan 49453, (269) 857-4261, www.saugatuckboatcruises.com. This pert paddle-wheeler cruises down the Kalamazoo River and, weather permitting, out onto Lake Michigan. On nice days, everyone heads for the upper deck, which is partly canopied for shade or sun. The bow is a great place to hang out, not only for the unobstructed view, but also for proximity to the water. Stake your claim and enjoy the ride.

Along the riverbanks, the busy shopping and dining scene gives way to quaint

THE COAST IS CLEAR

You've seen them all around Lake Michigan, the tidy U.S. Coast Guard stations with their reassuringly removed presence behind high-security fences. Maybe you've heard the crisp call of reveille as you gulped morning coffee outside your hotel, or seen a cutter leave the harbor for another search-and-rescue drill out on the lake.

But in Grand Haven, for 10 days each summer you can get closer to understanding the U.S. Coast Guard than you can anywhere else, or at any other time. For Grand Haven is Coast Guard City USA; and each year as July becomes August, the town celebrates a unique link with this distinctive branch of the military.

"The festival salutes and honors the men and women of the U.S. Coast Guard. It originated out of a love of the U.S. Coast Guard way back when," says Commander M. J. Smith, USCG (Ret), Executive Director of the festival. "In 1999 by an act of Congress, Grand Haven was officially designated Coast Guard City USA, and it's the only one."

Join the thousands of people who attend the festival's National Memorial Service, board active cutters, and stand a little straighter as the U.S. Coast Guard Band rings out with military precision and pride. Significant to the Memorial Service is the story of the first Escanaba, which sank in the Atlantic Ocean in 1943, a disaster that took the lives of 101 crewmen. One of the only two survivors, Raymond F. O'Malley, Seaman First Class, USCG, has returned to the festival for the past half-century.

You might not expect a town that is situated on an inland sea to be designated as Coast Guard City USA, but it comes as no surprise to Commander Smith.

"We have very daring rescues here; there are very treacherous waters here. We've lost lots of people off the pier and swimming, because there are tidal effects on the water. The wind across a small-surface [body of] water like Lake Michigan creates a huge water effect, which becomes a wave and causes lots of damage if you're not a seasoned boater.

"Weather changes quickly over the lake," he cautions. "All you need is a heavy fog, a lot of rain, and waves to turn your day into a nightmare."

Thank goodness for the U.S. Coast Guard.

cottages and the occasional heron. Out on the lake, forested and sandy dunes seem to roll on forever, while seagulls glide by with graceful calm. Throughout the cruise, well-timed narration draws your attention to points of interest like the hand-cranked chain ferry that once carried horses across the river, the Scottish-built SS *Keewatin* that was once cut in half, and the prime real estate of a yacht-building family. You'll also hear of things you can only imagine, such as the lumber-era ghost town that got buried beneath the sands, and the 1909 Big Pavilion dance hall that lit up the night for the last time when it burned to the ground 51 years after its construction.

No doubt the shops of Saugatuck are calling; but first, how about boarding another boat? You could rent something small and speedy, or tour the huge **SS *Keewatin*,** Blue Star Highway and Union Street, Douglas, Michigan 49406, (269) 857-2464 (in season), www.keewatinmaritimemuseum.com, which is moored upriver from the *Saugatuck II*, on the southern bank just south of the Saugatuck-Douglas Bridge. This 350-foot, steam-powered overnight luxury liner once transported twentieth-century passengers to summer dreamlands around the upper Great Lakes. She could carry 288 passengers with a crew of 86, but her glory days ended in 1965 when she was thrown onto a scrapyard, as it was feared she would catch fire. Fortunately, she has been reborn as a museum, designed to whisk you away on a voyage of discovery. Take the new and improved Grand Tour and peek into the areas that once served the passengers and crew. These include the passenger staterooms, Bridal Suite #168, the former Musicians' Room, the Ladies' Drawing Room, the Men's Lounge, the Captain's Suite, the crews' quarters, dining and lounge areas, food preparation areas, the wheelhouse, and engine rooms. View displays of fashion, accessories, brochures, dolls, and toys of the period 1907–1965.

Other nearby sites to explore include **Oval Beach** on Lake Michigan; **Mount Baldhead,** the 236-foot sand dune; **Fishtown Trail**, which winds through a forested dune to an overlook to the site of a ghost fishing village; and the **Saugatuck-Douglas Historical Society Museum**, 735 Park Street, Saugatuck, Michigan 49453. Housed in a turn-of-the-twentieth-century red brick water pumping station, this tiny museum features local history exhibits and, in the gift shop, a wealth of books and the infamous "I Climbed Mount Baldhead" t-shirt. Outside, get a great view of the river and read signage about the environment that is so beautifully laid out before and—in the case of Mount Baldhead—above you.

FROM THE GALLEYS

Bil-Mar Restaurant, 1223 South Harbor Drive, Grand Haven, Michigan

49417, (616) 842-5920. House specialties include perch and prime rib. Great daily specials such as broiled lemon-pepper walleye with seasonal squash and wild rice. Right on the beach and just steps from Lake Michigan.

Boatwerks Waterfront Restaurant, 216 VanRaalte Avenue, Holland, Michigan 49423, (616) 396-0600, www.boatwerksrestaurant.com. Located near the Immigrants Statue that honors Dutch settlers and donated in 1997 by the Dutch province of Drenthe, this new waterfront eatery serves up innovative, contemporary fare based on ingredients that are locally sourced as much as possible. Enjoy the scenery as you munch on sandwiches, burgers, pastas, and house specialties such as crispy chicken with lemon and artichokes, or beer battered halibut with a tarragon-caper remoulade and jalapeno coleslaw. Décor is also locally sourced, with design cues taken from vintage boats and summers on Lake Macatawa.

The Kirby House, 2 Washington Avenue, Grand Haven, Michigan 49417, (616) 846-3299, www.thekirbyhouse.com. Relax in comfort beneath the two-story tin ceiling and rich woods of The Grill Room (The Kirby Grill and K2 Pizzeria round out the dining choices). Built as a hotel in 1873, this showplace once hosted visitors who arrived by passenger steamer. Savor the atmosphere as you enjoy fresh seafood, steaks, and chops.

Mermaid Bar & Grill, 340 Water Street, Saugatuck, Michigan 49453, (269) 857-8208. Opt to dine and people-watch outdoors on the boardwalk. American and Mexican fare.

The Piper Restaurant, 2225 South Shore Drive, Macatawa (west of Holland near Lake Michigan), Michigan 49434, (616) 335-5866. Sunlight glitters like diamonds off the waters and yachts of Lake Macatawa. Enjoy a creative atmosphere and tasteful artwork while you savor delicious American fare with ethnic influences.

Remember When Café, 1146 South Shore Drive, Macatawa, Michigan 49423, (616) 355-8422. Nothing fancy, but the food is delicious at this breakfast place that locals love. Flavorful omelets, toasted coconut French toast, and more.

TO THE DOCKS

Harbor House Inn, 114 South Harbor Drive, Grand Haven, Michigan 49417, (800) 841-0610, (616) 846-0610, www.harborhousegh.com. Had it been built in 1897, this Victorian-style charmer most certainly would have accommodated wealthy Chicagoans arriving by steamship. But today's guests are surprised to learn that the inn dates not to 1897 but to 1987! Let the 17 spacious guestrooms delight you with classic style and contemporary comforts such as canopy beds, fireplaces, and balconies. Superb home-baked treats are always coming out of the ovens, from white chocolate-cherry cookies in the evening, to specialty breads for the continental breakfasts, which also include cold cuts and cheeses in European fashion. Inside your room, you'll discover a small gift basket awaiting your arrival, filled with delicious surprises like rich and creamy hand-made caramels. They'll disappear quickly no doubt; fortunately, you can purchase more to prolong the pleasure. From the screened veranda, enjoy a close-up of the Musical Fountain.

Looking Glass Inn, 1100 South Harbor, Grand Haven, Michigan 49417, (800) 951-6427, (616) 842-7150, www.bbonline.com/mi/lookingglass. Hop the 1948 electric trolley up the hill to this B&B cottage that takes its decorating cue from the elevated lakeside location. Finished in sunny yellows and cool blues, the Beach Room delights guests with touches such as hand towels rolled up in a child's sand pail, and a watercolor depicting bathing beauties of a certain age. The innkeepers say that guests from England always seem to end up in the Americana Room, although they're never sure why. During your stay, you can also loll about on the deck, which features sweeping lake and lighthouse views, or in the hot tub nestled within a wooded dune. Served as a buffet with your choice of private or shared seating, breakfast is an indulgent affair of hot entrées such as French toast or quiche, as well as cereals and homemade breads.

Ship 'n Shore Motel-Boatel, 528 Water Street, Saugatuck, Michigan 49453, (269) 857-2194, www.shipnshoremotel.com. The same views you fell in love with during the day can be yours at night, as well. Swim in the outdoor pool and Jacuzzi or relax in the fireplace-filled lanai; choose from 40 units that have in-room refrigerators, and awaken to a lovely continental breakfast.

AIDS TO NAVIGATION

Grand Haven/Spring Lake Area Convention & Visitors Bureau, (800) 303-4096, www.visitgrandhaven.com.

Grand Haven Coast Guard Festival, www.ghcgfest.org.

Holland Area Convention & Visitors Bureau, (800) 506-1299, www.holland.org.

Saugatuck/Douglas Convention Visitors Bureau & Chamber of Commerce, (269) 857-1701, www.saugatuck.com.

South Haven to Michiana

"Our complex of buildings is right here in the harbor along the Black River—it's where the maritime heritage was, so it really does give you a feel for the water. We're adjacent to remnants of the Jensen Fisheries, which was the last commercial fishing business in South Haven. We're unique for other reasons, too. Nowhere else in the United States can you see in one place the three types of Coast Guard surf boats that we have. And, the best view of the harbor is from the keeper's house, which is home to our Great Lakes research library."

—Ellen Sprouls, Executive Director, Michigan Maritime Museum, South Haven

South Haven

Drop anchor in a waterfront village located 19 miles south of Saugatuck-Douglas and 58 miles north of the Michigan-Indiana border. See million-dollar pleasure boats docked alongside antique fishing tugs, and a brand-new replica of a very early nineteenth-century, single-masted sloop named ***Friends Good Will***. Board her for a day sail you will never forget, and act fast when a crew member asks you to help hoist the mainsail. *Friends Good Will* is the most exciting addition to the **Michigan Maritime Museum** campus, 260 Dyckman Avenue (at the bridge), South Haven, Michigan 49090, (800) 747-3810, (269) 637-8078, www.michiganmaritimemuseum.org. Experience a living history here, beyond that of a traditional museum, with multiple buildings to explore and vessels to board, all in a bustling harborfront setting. What's more, *Friends Good Will* expands your visit out onto the waters of Lake Michigan—and back in time to when the Great Lakes

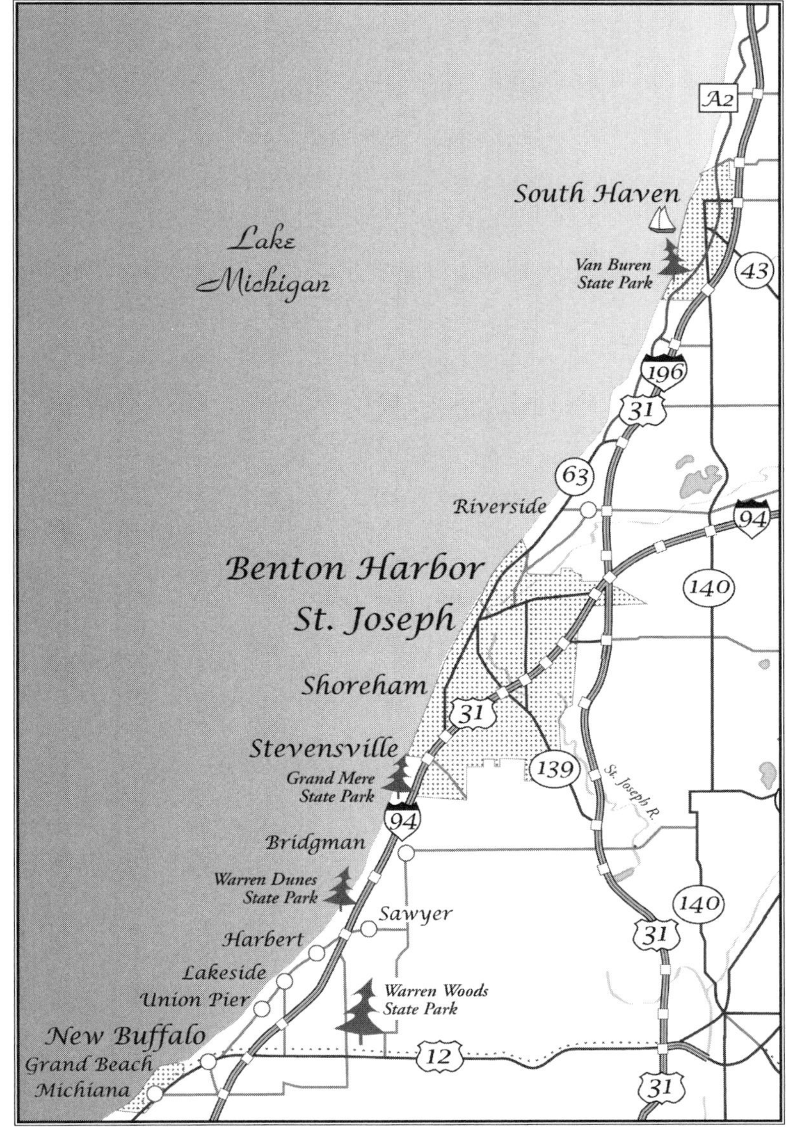

played a role in the War of 1812.

The story begins in 1810 when Oliver Williams, an American entrepreneur living in Detroit, decided to boost his commercial opportunities by building a boat that could haul inventory for his dry goods store. In the summer of 1812, Williams agreed to carry supplies to Fort Mackinac for the Federal Government. What he and his captain and crew did not realize, though, was that the fort had been captured by the British, who were flying false colors from its ramparts in order to deceive American mariners. Held at gunpoint, the Williams party was taken prisoner, and *Friends Good Will* was pressed into service for the Royal Naval Squadron on the upper Great Lakes. During the last months of 1813, she was recaptured by the Americans when Commander Oliver Hazard Perry, U.S.N., issued this famous dispatch:

"We have met the enemy and they are ours: Two ships, two brigs, one schooner, and a sloop." That sloop was *Friends Good Will.* Learn what happened next aboard the remarkably detailed replica that has single-mastedly transformed the South Haven waterfront.

Jump ship now and head to the main building of the Michigan Maritime Museum, which houses provocative exhibits on the Great Lakes. One display interprets the Native American use of the Great Lakes, which involved travel by dugout, and, later, birch bark canoes. Watch a video on the demise of Great Lakes commercial fishing; by watching another video, you can join a commercial fishing family of Door County, Wisconsin as they haul in gill nets that are heavy and writhing with fresh-caught fish. By now, you'll have heard a lot about the parasitic sea lamprey that wreaked havoc on the native lake trout population, and the zebra mussel that hitched rides aboard freighters and reproduced like crazy. Here you can see what they look like.

Walk outside to the replica U.S. Coast Guard Station where early lifesaving vessels have been gorgeously restored and await your inspection. Hear the story of the surfboat that was found in a cornfield. Admire the courage it took for coast guardsmen to row out across waters made frothy and treacherous by pounding surf, knowing they would tip over at least once, in order to rescue mariners in distress. Such surfboats have long since been retired, replaced by search-and-rescue helicopters.

Experience the sights, sounds, and smells of wooden boatbuilding inside the Padnos Boat Shed, where the line between museum and boatyard blurs like the horizon in fog. Museum volunteers, for instance, go about their work as if in a real boatyard. Become part of the scene by signing up for Family BoatBuilding, a multiday class in which you build your own boat to take home.

You can also board the *Evelyn S*, a 1939 commercial fishtug that was fully equipped to serve gill net fishermen. Everyone wants to "captain" the tug, and you can, too, by taking a gentle turn at the wheel and looking out through the surprisingly small portholes of the pilothouse. The limited view makes you appreciate how well those captains must have known their craft.

Visit the **South Haven Center for the Arts**, 600 Phoenix Street, South Haven, Michigan 49090, www.southhavenarts.org. Behind the arched windows of this 1905 Neoclassical Revival building there are exceptionally well-chosen exhibits that typically showcase regional artists. Sign up in advance for accompanying hands-on workshops.

Pop into **Arbor Antiques**, 527 Phoenix Street, (269) 639-8866, for nautical antiques, and **Hale's Clothing**, 257-263 Center Street, (269) 637-8456, for gorgeous organic cotton sweaters and maybe a chat with the fifth-generation owners of this oldest family-owned clothing store in all of Michigan.

South Haven welcomes walkers. Poke around the marinas and boat storage yards for intimate views of all manner of watercraft. Read the "Aids to Navigation" along the three-quarter-mile **HarborWalk**, which escorts you up and down both sides of the channel and out to the lighthouse. Learn boatloads of stuff about the maritime history of this port, including the passenger steamship era of 1880–1940, when first-class passengers enjoyed hotel-like comforts while everyone else was left to wait it out on deck throughout the five-hour trip from Chicago. Enjoy HarborWalk's picnic tables, sandy beaches, and sometimes high swells in the channel. When night falls, admire the delicate white lights that trace the lines of the 1925 steel-frame catwalk that leads all the way out to the lighthouse.

Offshore, the **Southwest Michigan Underwater Preserve**, www.michiganpreserves.org, lures divers deep into the cold, fresh waters of Lake Michigan. It stretches from just north of Holland to Bridgman near the Indiana border. Here in South Haven, plunge below to see the 92-foot yacht ***Verano***, whose keys remain in the ignition. She was sailing up from Chicago when heavy seas overtook her and dropped her 55 feet to the bottom of the lake. Divers can also enjoy exploring the **South**

Lighthouse and catwalk, South Haven, Michigan. Fisherman had just caught a salmon to cheers from a passing fishing boat.

Haven Clay Banks, an amazingly vast underwater geological formation.

On your way south to the neighboring port towns of Benton Harbor and St. Joseph, visit **Van Buren State Park**, 23960 Ruggles Road, South Haven, Michigan 49090, www.michigan.gov/dnr, where you can enjoy 400 acres and nearly a mile of Lake Michigan frontage.

Benton Harbor St. Joseph

It is about 20 miles south from Van Buren State Park to downtown Benton Harbor. Be sure to visit **The Morton House**, 501 Territorial Road, Benton Harbor, Michigan 49022, (268) 925-7011. The house, which dates back to 1849 and is the city's oldest, has ties to four generations of the Morton family, the owners of the Graham & Morton Transportation Company, which operated passenger steamships. Costumed guides lead you through the period rooms and local past. In Benton Harbor you can also freighter-watch from Tiscornia Park.

The busy city of St. Joseph (St. Joe to the locals) is 32 miles north of the Michigan-Indiana border. St. Joe is perched high on a bluff where old hotels look down upon a century of commemoration in **Lake Bluff Park**. Monuments, memorials, and markers punctuate the park with a range of expression, from the solemnity of the **Revolutionary War Cannon** that saw action in 1780, to the softness of the 1872 **Maids of the Mist Fountain**. Down at lake level, where the St. Joseph River flows into Lake Michigan, a twenty-first century piece, "**And You, Seas**," by Richard Hunt, blends the forms of lighthouses and waves into one stainless steel spire. From here you can view the **North Pier Historical Lighthouse and Catwalk**, as well as **Silver Beach**, where a magical thing is happening. Beginning in 1910, a spirited carousel twirled here until 1971. Two years later, it was sold intact to a collector. But a campaign to "Help Bring the Horses Back to the Beach!" is leading to the creation of a replica carousel and the reawakening of the entire waterfront area. Check www.silverbeachcarousel.org for the latest updates.

Current exhibits at **The Heritage Museum and Cultural Center** (formerly The Fort Miami Heritage Society), 708 Market Street, St. Joseph, Michigan 49085, (269) 983-1191, www.fortmiami.org, are mostly maritime-oriented. These folks will take you on a tour of local maritime sites including the St. Joseph's lighthouses, the U.S. Coast Guard Station, and the U.S. Lighthouse Depot that once housed supplies for Michigan lighthouses.

Take your kids to the **Curious Kids' Museum**, 415 Lake Boulevard, St. Joseph, Michigan 49085, (269) 983-CKID, www.curiouskidsmuseum.org. This hands-on museum is conveniently located at Silver Beach, just across the street from Lake Michigan. The SS *Cruizer* ship exhibit invites kids to send signal flags to shore; navigate the ship using the captain's wheel, compass, and navigational charts; load cargo; fish off the deck and learn about Great Lakes fish; feed the crew; and dive into the captain's trunk. Learn a thing or two yourself about the historic Port of St. Joseph.

North of the river, make **Tiscornia Park**, Marina Drive, and the lake your picnic and freighter-watching headquarters.

Harbor Country: Sawyer to Michiana

The Indiana border draws near, but Michigan's southernmost shoreline has a few more things to show you first. They call the area Harbor Country. It is one of Chicago's favorite escape hatches, and it has always been this way. As you arrive from St. Joe, drive 2.5 miles south of Bridgman to the town of Sawyer, where you'll find **Warren Dunes State Park**, 12032 Red Arrow Highway, Sawyer, Michigan 49125, (269) 426-4013, www.michigan.gov/dnr. If you like to hang glide, hike, swim, or cross-country ski, you can do it on these 1,952 acres of lofty dunes and two miles of shoreline. On the way, though, you may wish to pop into **Sawyer Market**, 5868 Sawyer Road, Sawyer, Michigan 49125, (269) 426-4646, for gourmet picnic fare such as deli meats, freshwater fish, imported cheese, fresh produce, a bottle of Michigan wine, and a freshly-baked pie.

RESTORED: THE STORY OF A SURFBOAT

"After these boats were decommissioned, no longer in use by the Coast Guard, [they] were usually dragged out into the field and burned, because who has six friends who would get hold of an oar and go out on a Saturday afternoon and enjoy a row?"

Frank James, a volunteer at the Michigan Maritime Museum, said his son-in-law often drove by a farm on his way to work and notice a wooden boat out back of the barn. One day Frank asked the farmer about it, who said it was too far gone to be of any use—but his neighbor had a better one in his barn. Frank took a look.

"Anything that was brass was gone, but it was in pretty good shape. I was going to put a motor on it and make a little putt-putt to go on the lake and have some fun with it," Frank said. "Then I couldn't do it once I found it had value to the museum. You have to imagine the curator's face when I started describing the boat. He said something like, 'You couldn't have one of those! We've been searching through all the networks the museum has.' He said this museum had given up finding one and had commissioned one to be built from drawings.

"And that's how I got introduced to the museum. It was about 15 years ago, and I've been hanging around here ever since. It's not my boat, but I can talk about it and pet it any time I want to."

Want to catch a wave on Lake Michigan? Pop into New Buffalo's **Third Coast Surf Shop**, 22 South Smith Street, New Buffalo, Michigan 49117, (269) 932-4575, www.thirdcoastsurfshop.com. They sell locally made surfboards that are specially designed for Great Lakes waves, and even give surf lessons. Given the proximity to Chicago, New Buffalo's waterfront is packed with condos, which appeals to some but not others.

From rolling waves and dunes that pile up to the sky, to glorious sunsets that are often the only entertainment you need, Michigan is hard to leave. But there on the horizon is the Indiana border, where you can almost see the windswept tip of a dune called Mount Baldy. Ready to test your climbing ability?

FROM THE GALLEYS

Chocolate Café & Museum, 300 State Street, St. Joseph, Michigan 49085, (269) 985-YUMM, www.sbchocolate.com. It's all about chocolate-drenched beverages and desserts, so what more do you need to know? How about these tempting little details? The Lake Effect Mocha is espresso with white chocolate and steamed milk; Chocolate LaSalle is made with regionally produced mint oil; and the Lighthouse Shake comes with a chocolate lighthouse and is lit by a sweet Michigan cherry. Come get your fix.

Clementine's, 500 Phoenix Street, South Haven, Michigan 49090, (269) 637-4755, www.ohmydarling.com. Dark woods and high ceilings set the tone for comfort within this gorgeously restored eatery. Try the Mess of Perch (lightly dusted and pan fried), Drunken Sailors (beer steamed shrimp), or Tin Pan Walleye (potato crusted and pan fried in an iron skillet) from the Dockside menu. Plenty of grilled choices and pastas, too.

Phoenix Street Café, 524 Phoenix Street, South Haven, Michigan 49090, (269) 637-3600. Sure they know how to make great beef sandwiches in Chicago, but wait until you try the piled-high hot Reuben Roast Beef Sandwich with slaw dressing on lightly grilled, thick-sliced multi-grain bread. Will you ever go back to the Windy City? Homemade soups and desserts, and breakfast anytime.

TO THE DOCKS

The Harbor Grand, 111 West Water Street, New Buffalo, Michigan 49117, (888) 605-5900, www.harborgrand.com. Live luxuriously in rooms with harbor views, fireplaces and whirlpool baths, one-bedroom suites with wet bar and micro-wave, indoor pool/spa with harborside sun deck, fitness center, complementary bicycle rentals, and continental breakfast in bed.

The Last Resort, 86 North Shore Drive, South Haven, Michigan 49090, www.lastresortinn.com. Artistry abounds within this vast, intriguing inn, which, built in 1883, was the first resort in South Haven. Fourteen guestrooms and huge penthouse suites offer lake views on one side, harbor views on the other, and bear the names of Great Lakes ships. Let the innkeepers' passion for color, texture, and music transport you to their favorite continents. Enjoy breakfasts of gourmet treats such as oversized muffins and freshly cut fruit, orange juice, and coffee. Relax outdoors on a large front deck that overlooks a tangled garden, only steps away from a golden Lake Michigan beach.

Sandpiper Inn, 16136 Lakeview Avenue, Union Pier, Michigan 49129, (800)

351-2080, (269) 469-1146, www. sandpiperinn.net. This waterfront B&B collects kudos like a child collects shells on the beach. Elegant verandas, fireplaces, Jacuzzi tubs, and a private beach will have you singing its praises, too.

AIDS TO NAVIGATION

South Haven Visitors Bureau, (800) SO-HAVEN, www.southhaven.org.

Southwestern Michigan Tourist Council, (269) 925-6301, www.swmichigan.org.

Harbor Country Chamber of Commerce, (800) 362-7251, www.harborcountry.org.

INDIANA

OVER HALF OF Indiana's state border is water, but Lake Michigan accounts for only a fraction of that. Even so, the Hoosier state knows how to wring the most fun possible from its piece of the lake. About 25 miles of the shore-line is preserved as a national lake-shore—one of only two on the entire lake—and thus dedicated entirely to parkland. It comes in pieces spanning three counties, from Michigan City to the east side of Gary, with smokestacks, chimneys, and a cooling tower interspersed through-out. But with a total area of about 15,000 acres, you will find no shortage of places to play. Among all national parks, this one ranks seventh for native plant diversity, and its variety of habitats includes beaches, dunes, wetlands, forests, and a bog. And nowhere else on the Lake Michigan shore-line will you find a view of the Chicago skyline quite like this. From here, the soaring skyscrapers seem to rise from an island in the lake like a collection of little lighthouses. So come for the beaches like most everyone else does, but stay for the park ranger programs, trails, and things you will see absolutely nowhere else.

Michigan City

"It's Indiana's only federal lighthouse and one of the first on Lake Michigan. The present building was built in 1858, replacing an earlier one from 1836. It was home to keepers even after they moved the lighthouse itself out to the pierhead light. We have the original 5th order lens that was upstairs in the lantern room."

—Jackie Glidden, Director, Michigan City Old Lighthouse Museum

THE FIRST STOP ALONG the Indiana shoreline tour is Michigan City, located about 10 miles southwest of New Buffalo, Michigan and about 60 miles from downtown Chicago, Illinois. Incorporated way back in 1836, Michigan City is just now rediscovering its enviable location on the lake. Here you will find a 600-slip marina, a swimming beach, and an unexpectedly diverse set of small cultural venues. You'll also find Washington Park, which blankets 90 acres of Michigan City waterfront in a rich shade of green that has been embroidered with old stone statues, picnic tables, a flower-festooned gazebo, and other trimmings. Contact **Washington Park & Beach**, Six on the Lake, Michigan City, Indiana 46360, (219) 873-1506, www. michigancityparks.com. Located in the park, just inland from the pierhead lighthouse and its distinctive catwalk, the **Michigan City Old Lighthouse Museum**, Heisman Harbor Road, Washington Park, Michigan City, Indiana 46361, (219) 872-6133, www.oldlighthousemuseum.org, sheds light on its own history. Extensive museum exhibits include the story of Harriet Colfax, who served as keeper from 1861–1904. Wrought iron gates frame this beacon, which was built in 1858 and has since been gorgeously restored with forest-green trim and bricks the color of cream. A most attractive and unusual feature is the half-moon porch and balcony above. The structure's colorful history also teaches visitors about nineteenth-century squatters, twentieth-century vandals, and its preservation.

Walk or drive over to the **Washington Park Zoo**, 115 Lakeshore Drive, Michigan City, Indiana 46360, (219) 873-1510, www.washingtonparkzoo.com, which began in the 1920s with a bear named Jake. Jake was a brown bear whose retired trainer brought him to the new park on the lake, where he quickly began to draw crowds. Other exotic animals were soon introduced from the local firehouse, where they had been accumulating. It was not long before a zoo was built on a nearby sand dune, and guests of the area's resorts came to visit the new attraction. Stairwells, buildings, landscaping, and indeed the entire design reflect the zoo's 1930s heritage. Native plants have been re-introduced both for environmental reasons and to enrich the lives of the animals. At only 19 acres, this small but delightful sanctuary is home to 100 different species from South America, North America, Africa, and Asia—from big cats to binturongs. Shifting sands do present some challenges to the zoo folks, but tourists love the location. Climb the observation tower to get a view of the zoo from above.

Nearby, the nondescript, yellow-brick exterior of the **Jack & Shirley Lubeznik Center for the Arts**, 101 Avenue of the Arts (West 2nd Street), Michigan City, Indiana 46360, (219) 874-4900, www.lubeznikcenter.org, belies the richness within. Enjoy exhibitions of local and regional artists.

Indiana Dunes National Lakeshore

"When I was young I wanted to save the world,
In my middle years I would have been content to save my country.
Now I just want to save the dunes."

—Senator Paul H. Douglas

AS YOU DRIVE WEST from Michigan City along U.S. Highway 12, the **Indiana Dunes National Lakeshore**, 1100 North Mineral Springs Road, Porter, Indiana 46304, (800) 959-9174, (219) 926-7561 x225, www.nps.gov/indu, begins with a bang at **Mount Baldy**. You are both invited and challenged to climb this 123-foot sand pile that is called a living dune—because it moves inland, toward the highway, at a rate of four feet per year. Follow the trail past the dramatic site of half-buried trees and choose your route to the top. It's true that walking on sand dunes hinders plant growth that would otherwise help to stabilize them, so climbing them is not always recommended. But people will climb dunes anyway, so if you're going to do it once, do it here.

Don't bother shaking the sand out of your shoes just yet. Head westward to **Central Beach**, or go a bit farther to the lakeside enclave of Beverly Shores and the interpretive overlook and beach area called **Lake View**. After parking, you can walk south along the beautiful beach for glimpses of the five **Century of Progress Homes** that were

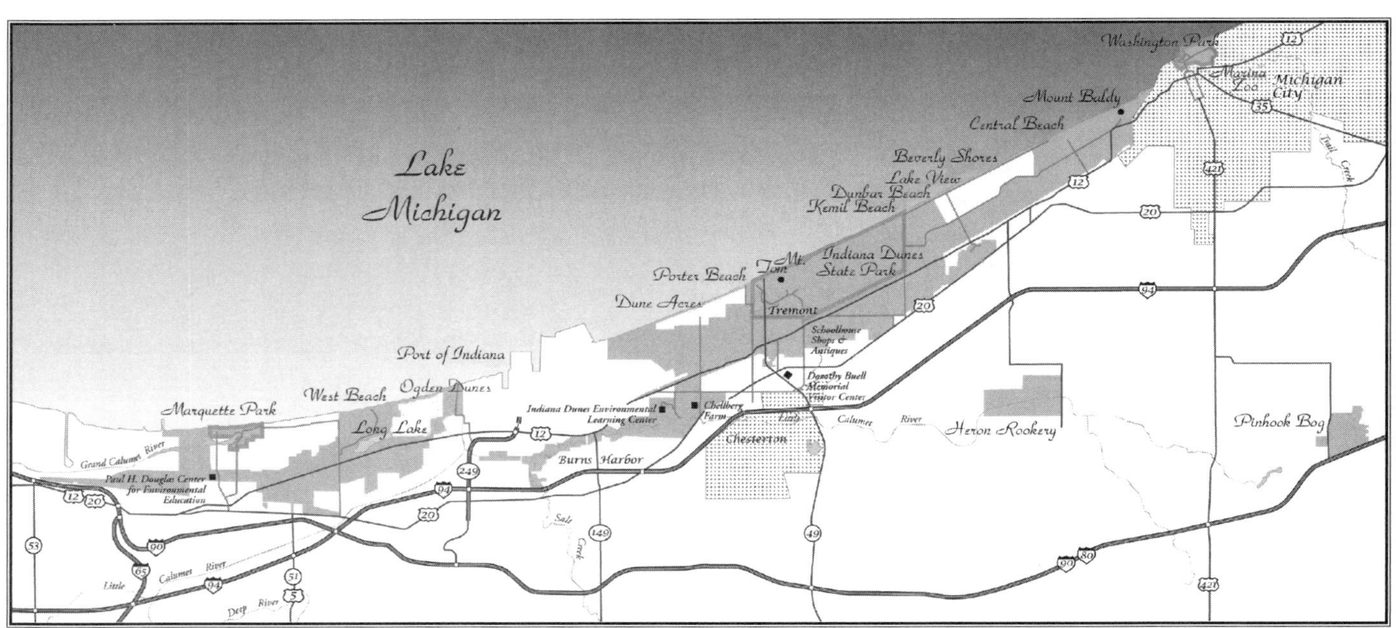

built to demonstrate modern architecture and materials at the 1933 Chicago World's Fair. For better views, hop back into your car and drive a short distance south along Lake Shore Drive (also called Lake Front Drive) past the homes. Their story is as unique as their architecture.

In 1935, Robert Bartlett—you could call him a dune tycoon—transplanted the model homes here by barge to attract buyers to his new resort community of Beverly Shores. After years in horrible disrepair, funding finally came through and restoration is currently progressing. There's something intriguing and exciting about these homes, perched on this lonely stretch of lakeshore. From east to west, the houses include the Cypress Log Cabin, House of Tomorrow, Florida Tropical House, Armco-Ferro House, and Wieboldt-Rostone House. More than any of the others, the Florida Tropical House connects with the sand and the lake, while the House of Tomorrow is most visually interesting for its perpetual look to the future.

Stop in at the **Dorothy Buell Memorial Visitor Center**, U.S. Highway 12 and Kemil Road, Beverly Shores, Indiana 46301, www.nps.gov/indu/. Here you can learn about the world you've been passing through, a world where the Ice Age left its signature in the extraordinary variety of plants that coexist here. Drive west on Kemil Road and turn left on Furnessville Road to the **Schoolhouse Shops & Antiques**, 278 East County Road 1500 North, Chesterton, Indiana 46304, (219) 926-1551, www.schoolhouseshop.com. Nestled in the forested dunes, this two-room schoolhouse dates from 1886 and makes for a delightfully refreshing stop, as it is

Boardwalk through the dunes, Indiana Dunes National Lakeshore

Indiana Dunes National Lakeshore

packed to the rafters with lovely items for you and your home. Stock up on gourmet goodies from the Magic Pantry, which offers the most charming outdoor seating beneath leafy trees and umbrellas the color of wild mushroom caps. Owner Roy Krizek says this is the southernmost place you can go to get authentic Cornish pasties that are actually made in the Upper Peninsula of Michigan. Here they are sold frozen to go and ready for your oven.

Returning to U.S Highway 12, drive a short distance west to the **Indiana Dunes State Park**, 1600 North 25 East, Chesterton, Indiana 46304, (219) 926-1952, www.state.in.us/dnr, where you'll find a lovely beach and campground. At 192 feet, Mount Tom is the tallest of the Indiana Dune Country dunes, and a trail takes you to its summit. Discover the tree graveyard along Trail 10, which parallels the lakeshore for about half of its 5.5-mile length.

Continue driving westward through the Indiana Dunes National Lakeshore, which encircles the State Park, and try the Cowles Bog Trail or visit the **Chellberg Farm & Bailly Homestead**, on Mineral Springs Road between U.S Highway 12 and U.S. Highway 20, Porter, Indiana. Two distinct eras of human history, one of fur traders, the other of Swedish immigrant farmers, come alive in this beautiful woodland, partially cleared for crop fields, livestock pastures, and rustic buildings. Feeding time is fun for everyone, not just the animals. Hidden trails wind up and down ravines and out to an enigmatic family cemetery.

Backtrack to State Highway 49 and follow it south to the sleepy charm of downtown Chesterton. Discover the photographic dunescapes of Craig Berg at **Dunes Photography Gallery & Gifts**, 206 South Calumet Road, Chesterton, Indiana 46304, (219) 926-6637, www.dunesphotos.com, as well as the works of over 100 regional artists inside the **Chesterton Art Center**, 115 South 4th Street, Chesterton, Indiana 46304, (219) 926-4711, www.chestertonart.com.

At the **City Marina**, 1200 Marina Way,

WHY CAN'T MOUNT BALDY STAND STILL?

One of the most dramatic sites at the 123-foot Mount Baldy is seen even before you get to the top—the half-buried trees on the dune's south side. The dune that gave the trees a place to root is also burying them alive. Here's why:

"The primary wind comes from the north, so the strong winds come off the lake and . . . push the top [of the dune]," says Mark Bluell, Supervisory Park Ranger of Indiana Dunes National Lakeshore.

"It happens as long as the sand is not grounded anywhere, so if there's no vegetation to hold it in place, the prevailing wind continues to push it until it runs up against something. So with that kind of wind action that we get, it usually moves about four to five feet southward a year. That varies depending upon how much strong wind we get that year, and it varies based upon the amount of vegetation it runs into."

"If you go there," he continues, "you'll see it seems to be gradually moving toward the parking lot. We understand that maybe someday . . . we'll have to deal with sand being on top of the parking lot."

Bluell goes on to explain that if people stopped walking on the dune, there would be vegetation that would normally take place over the course of time called plant succession, and that then perhaps the movement would be slowed.

"However," he adds, "we understand the park is here for recreational purposes, too, and when people ask us, 'where can we walk on the dunes?' rather than sending them to all of the dunes that we have, we have something that I refer to as the sacrificial lamb, and that is Mount Baldy."

State Highway 249 and Burns Waterway, Portage, Indiana 46368, (219) 763-6833, www.ci.portage.in.us, launch your boat onto Lake Michigan or opt to fish from the pier. **CMS Marine**, Port of Indiana-Burns Harbor, 1305 Crisman Road, Portage, Indiana 46368, (219) 762-2666, rents out powerboats for fun and fishing. The **Port of Indiana-Burns Harbor**, which is one of the Great Lakes' newest and most modern ports, covers 560 acres and serves commercial vessels with direct access to the Atlantic Ocean via the St. Lawrence Seaway. Both Great Lakes bulk carriers (lakers) and ocean-going vessels (salties) call at this port for transit of iron, steel, grain, and other goods. There is no public access to the commercial port.

Sweeping sands, shiny grasses, a sparkling beach, and a boardwalk to the sky—**West Beach** has it all. To get there from the Port of Indiana-Burns Harbor, continue west on U.S. Highway 12 and go north for a quarter mile on County Line Road. Make plans to grill out, too, because the beach's attractive shelters offer protection from the elements while remaining open to the view. Whatever you plan for lunch, don't miss the fresh blueberries from a nearby orchard. Finally, if you want to take the road less traveled, head to a part of the Indiana Dunes National Lakeshore that many people miss: the wetlands area of Miller Beach. Here the trail system eventually leads to Lake Michigan and greets visitors with cheerful spring wildflowers, interdunal ponds surrounded by forest, unusual plant life, and a path that parallels the South Shore Line. Park rangers highly recommend this route for spectacular fall colors.

Now that you have thoroughly explored one of Lake Michigan's two National Lakeshores, how about stopping in town for lunch?

FROM THE GALLEYS

A Token of Friendship, 107 South Second Street, Chesterton, Indiana 46304, (219) 926-5100. Get cozy with a vast range of teas from all over the world; mutan white, for example, has twice the antioxidants of green tea. Tasty sandwiches feature the freshest possible ingredients and amazing attention to detail. The turkey cranberry is a large, golden, flaky croissant generously stuffed with real turkey breast, cranberry chutney, cream cheese, cucumber, and lettuce. Service is as warm and wonderful as the food.

Dockside Café, 1 Washington Park Marina, 200 Heisman Harbor Drive, Michigan City, Indiana 46360, (219) 871-0645. Savor lake and lighthouse views over casual waterfront lunches and breakfasts.

Sunset Grill, 1305 Crisman Road, Portage, Indiana 46368, (219) 763-9772. Daily specials and fresh fish, just off Lake Michigan and next door to CMS Marine.

TO THE DOCKS

Beachwalk Vacation Rentals, 208 Beachwalk Lane, Michigan City, Indiana

46360, (219) 879-7874, (800) 814-7501, www.beachwalkresort.com. Do summer the way you have always dreamed—in an ice-cream colored cottage with beach grasses waving beside your front porch, and a 400-foot boardwalk that leads you down to the lakeshore. Instead of trying to conquer the precious environment found here, the designers of Beachwalk have chosen to celebrate it—and have been hugely successful. Just read this excerpt from the guest information book:

"Look closely at the sand to see tiny flecks of red, yellow, black, and blue colors. These small bits of other Michigan minerals are part of the history of Lake Michigan and tell us that a warm, tropical saltwater sea once covered this area." Hike the sandy nature trail on Beachwalk's 160 acres; swim or fish in either the resort's 26-acre lake, in Lake Michigan, or in the outdoor pool; and build your own miniature beach cottage out of sand. Summer rentals by the week, off-season two-night minimum, additional reservation fee.

Duneland Beach Inn, 3311 Pottawattomie Trail, Michigan City, Indiana 46360, (800) 423-7729, (219) 874-7729, www.dunelandbeach.com. Walk one block to a private Lake Michigan beach.

Springhouse Inn, 303 North Mineral Springs Road, Porter, Indiana 46304, (219) 929-4600, www.springhouseinn.com. The 50 oversized rooms inside this rambling, rustic inn combine lodge amenities with B&B charm. Deluxe, fireside continental breakfast features make-your-own waffles with toppings. Get a room facing the woods, where you can step out onto your private balcony and feel as if you are in a treehouse. Indoor pool, gas fireplace, and huge whirlpool. Sitting porch on every floor. Couldn't be closer to the Chellberg Farm.

AIDS TO NAVIGATION

Lake County Indiana Convention & Visitors Bureau, Indiana Welcome Center, 7770 Corinne Drive (I-80/94 and Kennedy Avenue South), Hammond, Indiana 46323, (800) ALL-LAKE, www.alllake.org. Talk about form following function—the architectural design of this center is a symbolic snapshot of the very place you are visiting—from lake to dunes to industry to farms. Beyond brochures, the wave-inspired exhibit hall and the gift shop showcase area artistry.

LaPorte County Convention & Visitors Bureau, 1503 South Meer Road, Michigan City, Indiana 46360, (800) 634-2650, www.visitlaportecounty.com.

Porter County Convention, Recreation & Visitor Center, 1120 South Calumet Road, Suite 1, Chesterton, Indiana 46304, (800) 283-8687, www.casualcoast.com.

ILLINOIS

ILLINOIS MAY HAVE the smallest stretch of lakeshore on the Lake Michigan tour, but lack of mileage is certainly made up in experience. Chicago alone, with some of the most varied and interesting culture—and arguably the best pizza—in the country, is reason enough to come. But don't let the Windy City be your only stop: from a fantastic lighthouse in Evanston to a lovely beachside park in Zion (and not to mention all those fabulous North Shore mansions along the way), the Illinois lakefront has a lot to offer.

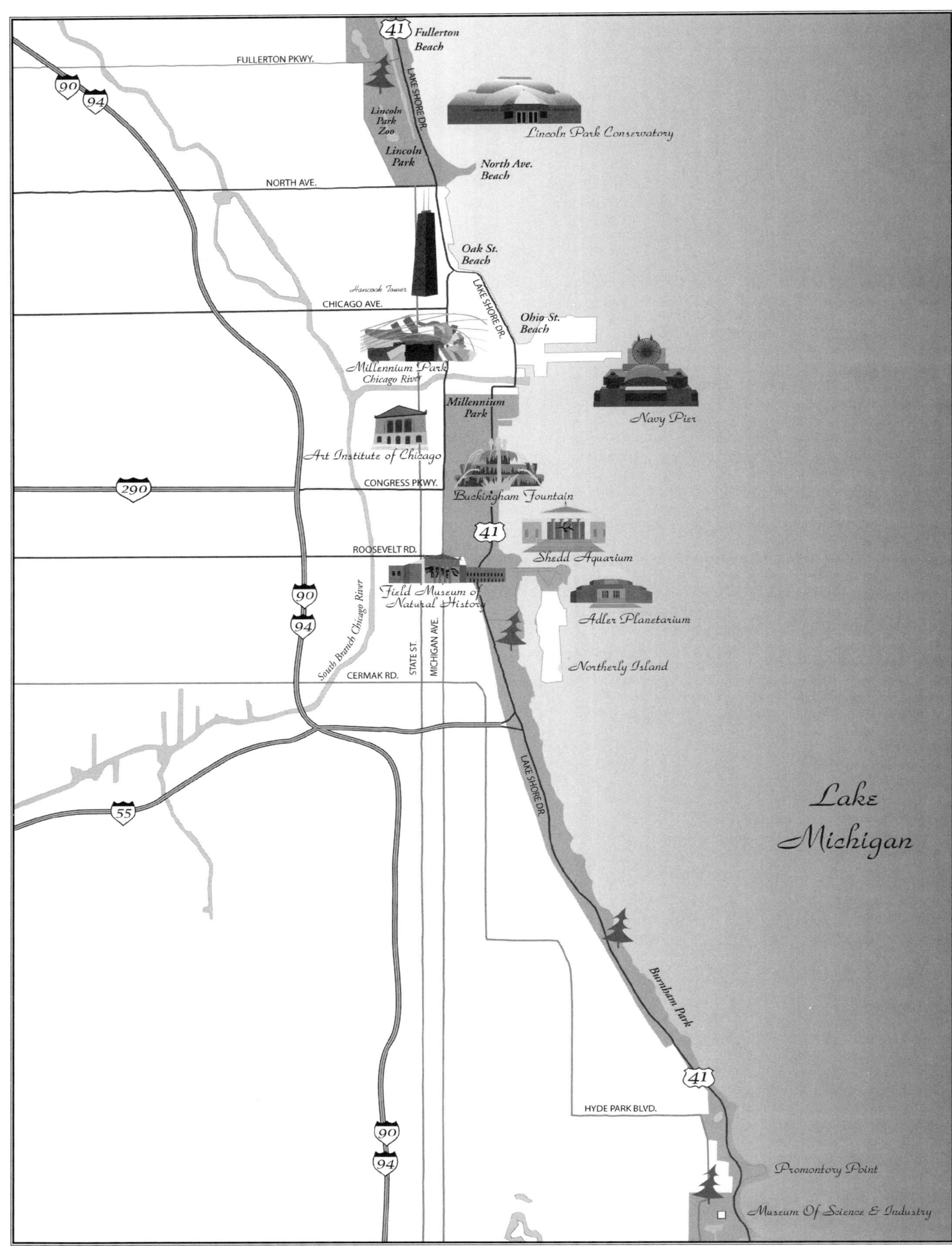

41
Fullerton Beach
FULLERTON PKWY.
90
94
LAKE SHORE DR.
Lincoln Park Zoo
Lincoln Park Conservatory
Lincoln Park
North Ave. Beach
NORTH AVE.
Oak St. Beach
Hancock Tower
CHICAGO AVE.
LAKE SHORE DR.
Ohio St. Beach
Millennium Park
Chicago River
Navy Pier
Millennium Park
Art Institute of Chicago
CONGRESS PKWY.
290
Buckingham Fountain
41
Shedd Aquarium
ROOSEVELT RD.
Field Museum of Natural History
90
94
Adler Planetarium
South Branch Chicago River
STATE ST.
MICHIGAN AVE.
Northerly Island
CERMAK RD.
55
LAKE SHORE DR.
Lake Michigan
Burnham Park
41
HYDE PARK BLVD.
90
94
Promontory Point
Museum Of Science & Industry

Chicago Lakefront

"The lakefront and its waterways tell the history of Chicago."

—Jerry Thomas, Chicago Maritime Society

WELCOME TO CHICAGO, the biggest and boldest settlement ever to explode onto the Lake Michigan scene. Home to the tallest skyscraper in the country, the longest pier on the planet's fifth-largest body of freshwater, the world's largest indoor marine mammal pavilion, the world's only backward-flowing river (that turns green for St. Patrick's Day), the largest collection of Impressionist art outside of the Louvre, the largest Polish population outside of Warsaw, and the best pizza in the universe. A bustling, exciting city spread across Lake Michigan's southwest shore, Chicago has never done anything in a small way.

As you would expect, things cost more in Chicago, including hotel taxes that can often jack up your bill. In a city this size, you'll pay for things that you might not pay for elsewhere, namely parking. But there are many options to help reduce cost. If Chicago's infamous traffic and sky-high parking fees are too intimidating, consider the city's variety of public transportation choices, from trains to trolleys. Use them whenever possible to cut down expenses and perhaps have a chance to chat up the locals. Whether driving or commuting, transportation in Chicago can be confusing, time-consuming, and a bit frustrating. Your best bet is to plan ahead, expect some transportation setbacks that can make for great stories, and invest in a Chicago City Pass, www.citypass.com.

Allow plenty of time for Chicago. Depending on your interests, a museum visit could take two hours or two days. Find out what time museums open and be there then, because lines can stretch to alarming lengths in the afternoon. With all that Chicago has to offer—great restaurants, events, and neighborhoods —you could easily be here a week or longer. Knowing what you want to see, figuring out how to get to the sights before you leave home, and allowing extra time for wrong turns will make for a much happier trip.

A great way to lose yourself in the magic of the neighborhoods is with **Chicago Neighborhood Tours**, (312) 742-1190, www.ChicagoNeighborhoodTours.com. Neighborhoods are a big deal in Chicago, as each one is a cultural concentration within a finite number of city blocks. From historic to hot, from ethnic to elegant, relax and enjoy the ride as someone else does the driving. The result is over 20 tours of exploration, including Historic Bronzeville, the Pullman Historic District, Little Italy, Threads of Ireland, and Summertime Sampler Tours. New in 2006, The Olympics that takes care of sightseeing and lunch on one jolly jaunt. All tours conveniently meet on Saturday mornings at the **Chicago Cultural Center**, 78 East Washington Street (at Michigan Avenue near the Art Institute of Chicago), Chicago, Illinois

BRIAN MORRISON

Chicago Skyline and Buckingham Fountain

White City tour highlights sites of the 1893 World's Columbian Exposition. A tour of Wicker Park and Bucktown, which are two of Chicago's hottest neighborhoods, whisks you through an area that evolved from a midcentury Polish enclave into a trendy lifestyle center with edgy eateries and boutiques, and gorgeous restorations of old Victorians. Chicago is a great food town, so savor the flavors on "Taste of the Neighborhoods," an eating 60602. Don't miss the bus!

Consider a spin around the Chicago lakefront and hotspots aboard a vintage fire truck with **O'Leary's Chicago Fire Truck Tours**, (312) 287-6565, www.olearyfiretours.com. These narrated, one-hour, advance-reservation tours board at Michigan Avenue and Illinois Street.

For boaters, the Chicago Park District—from Jackson to Lincoln, and every park in between—provides nine lakefront harbors that accommodate 5,000 boats. For slip information, contact (312) 742-8520 or www.chicagoharbors.info.

Museum of Science and Industry

Still standing from the 1893 World's Columbian Exposition is the Palace of Fine Arts—now the Museum of Science and Industry. Long before "interactive" became de rigeur in the museum world, the **Museum of Science and Industry**, 57th Street and Lake Shore Drive (Hyde Park neighborhood about six miles south of the Museum Campus), Chicago, Illinois 60637, (773) 684-1414, www.msichicago.org, was inviting kids of all ages to turn cranks, push buttons, pick up telephones, and run happily amok among the exhibits that had learning down to a science.

Exhibits come and go in a museum such as this, as it must not only preserve history, but also keep pace with cutting-edge technology and discovery. The "Ships Through the Ages" exhibit features a climb-on quarterdeck of a nineteenth-century tall ship, and teaches about vessels that make it possible to lay cable on the ocean floor. But familiar fans of the museum will be happy to discover that the chicks are still hatching, the miniature trains are still running, the Foucault Pendulum is still swinging, and the coal mine train is still lurching around in the blackness. From beneath the headlamp of her hardhat, a coal-mine guide warns folks to keep all body parts inside the train, because the museum uses any stray ones for science experiments. Is she kidding? Hard to tell; it's so dark down there.

The Museum of Science and Industry's new *U-505 Submarine* offers a story for the ages. Like a huge gray whale reflecting swirls of light off the water, this captured World War II German U-boat boasts 35,000 square feet of subterranean strength. Most significant about the capture was that it provided access to two M4 Enigma Machines and German Codebooks. This development was so critical to the Allied war effort that the seamen involved were forced to sign letters swearing secrecy about the discovery—on pain of death. Following capture, they had to tow the sub 2,500 nautical miles across the Atlantic Ocean, and they did so, rather miraculously, without detection. The gripping exhibit offers a monumental story of national security, human drama, courage, and heroism on the high seas. Throw yourself into the action and undergo dive training; e-mail a coded message to someone you know; and test your ability to control the depth of a vessel. Find out why the sub arrived in Chicago. Tour it for an additional fee.

Just north of the museum, head to Burnham park, where you'll find **Promontory Point**, Burnham Park, 5491 South Shore Drive, which was created by landfill in the 1920s. Its fieldhouse opened in 1937. Built of Wisconsin Lannon stone, it looks strikingly—but deceptively—like a lighthouse. The park's **Wallach Memorial Fountain** graciously supplies water to both people and pets. A bronze fawn snoozes at its summit, and its base is made of two-billion year-old granite.

Museum Campus

Enjoy long views of Lake Michigan as you drive north on Lake Shore Drive to the heart of the city. You'll soon pass **Soldier Field**, home of the Chicago Bears, and the **Museum Campus**, which links three iconic institutions: The Field Museum, John G. Shedd Aquarium and Oceanarium, and Adler Planetarium & Astronomy Museum. Cars once zoomed between the Field and the Shedd until quite recently, when much of Lake Shore Drive was rerouted so that this stretch of the original route could be reserved for pedestrians.

So park your car at Museum Campus Parking and start at the Field. Mummies, dinosaurs, fauna, flora, Native American artifacts—they are all here inside **The Field Museum**, 1400 South Lake Shore Drive, Chicago, Illinois 60605, (312) 922-9410, www.fmnh.org. Over 16 million specimens lurk behind the stately white columns to teach about anthropology, botany, geology, and zoology. Climb the smooth marble steps—glancing back for glimpses of the lake—and enter this realm of riches from natural and native worlds. Everyone wants their picture snapped with Sue, the meat-eating *T. rex*. Simultaneously frightening and friendly, Sue helps to fill the vastness of the cavernous main hall, where you can purchase tickets and pick up a floor map. Exhibits surround the main hall on three levels; and even though the Field encompasses over 300,000 square feet, it is easy to navigate.

Start at the Upper Level to examine Sue's real skull, which, at 600 pounds, proved too heavy for her skeletal structure to support. At "Traveling the Pacific and Pacific Spirits," discover the difference between island sand and Chicago beach sand. Museum traditionalists will be pleased to find that the Field retains much of its classic nobility, which can be seen in the polished wooden cases of "Plants of the World." In the "Hall of Gems," mysteries of star sapphires and other fabulous stones are demystified.

Moving down to the Main Level, you'll come face to face with the man-eating Lions of Tsavo. The two males, curiously lacking manes, have been re-created from their original skins, which were sold to the museum in 1924. The creatures killed over 140 railway workers during a nine-month period in 1898, and although the story is no longer news, it still chills the blood of visitors who crowd the display case. Don't miss the towering totems and other Native American artifacts, 1,000 of which were on display at the 1893 World's Columbian Exposition.

On the Ground Level, break for burgers and fries at the museum-based McDonald's, then gaze into the black eyes of Bushman, the famous Lincoln Park Zoo gorilla. A small but fascinating display of local archeology—gleaned from the landfill that descends 35 feet beneath the museum—catches the eye with simple pieces of Chicago history. There is plenty more to explore in the Field Museum, including special ticketed exhibitions; but before you leave, stop to help an Egyptian farmer irrigate his land using a shaduf, and reward yourself with chocolate river rocks from the gift shop.

Go deep at the **John G. Shedd Aquarium and Oceanarium**, 1200 South Lake Shore Drive, Chicago, Illinois 60605, (312) 939-2438, www.sheddnet.org. Home to the world's largest indoor collection of aquatic creatures, the Shedd teems with underwater life. An Australian lungfish has been drawing breath here since 1933. The huge fishbowl called "Caribbean Reef" swirls with tropical colors and a diver's friendly patter. The aquarium's newest exhibit, "Wild Reef: Sharks at Shedd," features 30 toothy sharks swimming in 750,000 gallons of water. A short elevator ride spills visitors into this exhibit's colorful coral reefs; one tank features garden eels that plant themselves into the sand and wave like grasses in the wind. Coral-scrubbing divers keep things clean, and sea rays ripple under the glass beneath your feet.

The Oceanarium embraces both the land and sea of the Pacific Northwest. Beluga whales, dolphins, Alaskan sea otters, seals, and penguins command center

THOMAS BARRAT

Museum of Science and Industry, Chicago

RITU MANOJ JETHAN

Japanese Sea Spider, Shedd Aquarium, Chicago

stage against a rocky backdrop that frames a postcard view of Lake Michigan. Don't miss a presentation that combines important education and dolphin hijinks, with a suggestion to learn more from the Great Lakes Forever campaign, at www.greatlakesforever.org. Most of the Shedd features saltwater species, but the Great Lakes gallery showcases walleye, perch, and other native fish—along with the invasive species. They've got these bad guys—the zebra mussels, gobi, and sea lamprey—locked up in their own tank. Visitors gather and gawk as if all the old Chicago mobsters had been thrown in there. Learn that over 170 invasive species have made their home in the Great Lakes, changing the waters forever.

GEMMAV D. STOKES

Art Institute of Chicago

AGA

Millennium Park at night, Chicago

Finally, before you leave the Shedd, stop in the gift shop for Belgian chocolate seashells, and see if you can spot the octopus-draped lamps.

Next, blast off to the **Adler Planetarium & Astronomy Museum**, 1300 South Lake Shore Drive, Chicago, Illinois 60605, (312) 922-STAR, www.adlerplanetarium.org. Adler is special on the campus, and in the city, because it sits at the end of a long drive that sticks out into Lake Michigan, and honors Polish astronomer Nicolaus Copernicus—who long ago did the math to patiently explain to the rest of us that the earth revolves around the sun. As America's first planetarium, Adler can fully explain the science of astronomy over time. The StarRider Theater and the Sky Theater present a changing array of exciting shows. Plan to take in at least one, but also allow plenty of time to explore the universe of exhibits, many of which are interactive. Starting downstairs, take in the animation of a Hubble deep-space image, learn more about the Big Bang theory, and admire the 1864 Dearborn Telescope encased in walnut veneer. You do not necessarily have to understand the old astronomy instruments in Adler's collection, some of which date back to twelfth-century Persia; for most visitors, it's enough just to admire their timeless beauty.

Upstairs, exhibits teach specific principles of the solar system and the Milky Way galaxy using professional science fair projects. Visitors of all ages gravitate to them like magnets, especially the one that involves smashing an asteroid into a powdery surface. Be sure to step out onto the Skywatchers' Terrace for a look through a real telescope. Most afternoons, a guide will focus the telescope on the only star you can see in the daytime: the sun. On clear days, sunspots may be visible; but even if it is overcast, the sight of clouds swirling before the sun is impressive. Upstairs you will also find a panoramic view of Lake Michigan. Sailboats, yachts, wave runners, and the occasional nineteenth-century replica schooner play in the water just beyond the wraparound glass. Stop for lunch or snacks at Galileo's Café and savor the view along with gourmet fare. Before leaving the Adler Planetarium, shoot into the Infinity Gift Shop for books, clothing, toys, and freeze-dried mint chocolate chip astronaut ice cream.

Adler Planetarium is located on **Northerly Island**, which extends south past the 12th Street Beach and east of the Burnham Park Yacht Harbor. Part of the original city plans and home to Chicago's second World's Fair, the island was the brainchild of famous

AGA

"The Bean," Millennium Park, Chicago

THOMAS BARRAT

Sunset over the Chicago River

ANDRÉ KLAASSEN

Tall Ship, Chicago

NOEL POWELL

Navy Pier, Chicago

architect Daniel Burnham. Although man-made, the 91-acre peninsula is mostly devoted to nature, with pleasant park space, strolling paths, and unbeatable views of the skyline and the lake.

Still on the Museum Campus, meet up with **City Segway Tours**, (877) SEG-TOUR, www.CitySegwayTours.com, and take a tour of the city while standing on two wheels. It's not cheap, but it's a lot of fun to glide along with your personally guided group heading north to Millennium Park.

One of the world's largest fountains, the famous and recognizable **Buckingham Fountain** spouts on the lakefront in Grant Park, east of Columbus Drive at the head of Congress Parkway near Monroe Harbor. Built in 1927, its water is circulated and replenished through an elaborate pumping system. Four identical pairs of bronze seahorses—weathered to a delicate aqua green—symbolize the four states that border Lake Michigan.

If one fountain is just not enough, take a short walk southwest through Grant Park to 11th Street and Michigan Avenue to the **Rosenberg Fountain**. Here the Greek goddess Hebe, daughter of Zeus and Hera, graciously hands down the gift of water, as she has since 1893.

Art Institute of Chicago

Continue north to the city's greatest art museum, the **Art Institute of Chicago**, 111 South Michigan Avenue (just south of

PETER TAMBRONI

Looking skyward, Sears Tower, Chicago

Monroe Street), Chicago, Illinois 60603, (312) 443-3600, www.artic.edu. Before going inside, take a moment to view the 1913 Lorado Taft sculpture **Fountain of the Great Lakes**, located at the south wing. It depicts five female figures arranged so that water flows from their shells in the same way it courses through the five Great Lakes. The piece resulted from a remark made during the 1893 Columbian Exposition by chief consulting architect Daniel Burnham, who complained that the event's sculptors were not looking to the surrounding area for their subject matter. Walk around to the east side of the building to see a geometric fountain that represents two essential, natural forms—an upright tree and a horizontal spring.

Inside in three buildings and on three levels, the Art Institute showcases a variety of works from the ancient to the contemporary, from paintings to paperweights. See Hopper's famous *Nighthawks* on the first level. European masterworks fill the Second Level galleries, including the recently acquired *Water Lilies* oil by Monet, and Seurat's timeless *A Sunday on La Grande Jatte*. The gallery's many guards can be helpful aids, but keep your floor plan handy, as navigating can become tricky. It helps to know that on the First Level, Gallery 140 (or Gunsaulus Hall) is the main connecting corridor to all three levels, and will take you to the Lower Level restaurant and café. Since Gallery 140 serves as the institute's main hub, it tends to be a bit noisy; but the silent intensity that resounds from the gallery's retired armor and swords more than makes up for the clamor. The First Level also houses ancient and classical art from almost every continent.

Here's a tip for parents: save the Lower Level for last. This is where the food is, so when crankiness and tired feet finally triumph over great art, head downstairs. After lunch, check out the Thorne Miniature Rooms, created in the mid-twentieth century to depict rooms spanning the sixteenth to the twentieth centuries. From the microscopic letters that spell "London" on the face of an inches-high grandfather clock to the tiny velvet chairs of drawing rooms, the attention to detail never fails to fascinate.

Millennium Park

Just north of the Art Institute and neatly squaring off Grant Park is the shiny new **Millennium Park**, Michigan Avenue (between Randolph and Monroe Streets), (312) 742-1168, www.millenniumpark.org. Highlights include the Crown Fountain's 50-foot faces, some of which spout water to play in; see the city and yourself reflected in the 66-foot stainless steel "Cloud Gate" sculpture, which locals have affectionately nicknamed "The Bean"; and check out the BP Bridge, which meanders like a silver stream toward the lake. The Lurie Garden combines nature and urban edginess with a playful approach to water. The garden's Dark Plate landscape symbolizes the area's pre-settlement shoreline.

The Chicago River

Chicagoans have been monkeying with their river for a long time, from making it flow away from Lake Michigan to dying it green for St. Patrick's Day; but the **Centennial Fountain** celebrates in the river in a way that is at once respectful and playful. Not far from the 333 West Wacker building is the site of the 1915 *Eastland* disaster, which killed 825 Western Electric employees and their families who were about to set off on a company outing. The boat had not even steamed away from the dock when it rolled over and sank to the river's muddy bottom, trapping most of its passengers inside.

Order tickets in advance for an architectural cruise aboard **Chicago's First Lady**, Michigan Avenue and Wacker Drive, Chicago, Illinois, (312) 902-1500, www.cruisechicago.com. The top deck offers the best seats in the house, with 360-degree views of some of the most magnificent and historically groundbreaking skyscrapers in the world, along with close-ups of 24 different bridges. On a rainy day, though, head for the boat's enclosed salon, complete with black piano, full-service bar, cloth-draped tables, and water-level views that include weathered pilings, shorebirds, and the occasional passing barge.

Delivering amazing quantities of information, volunteer docents of the venerable Chicago Architecture Foundation interpret the growth and development of Chicago along its river. Glide past over 50 structures and sites of the Chicago School of Architecture, such as the 1913 Great Lakes Building, the Wrigley Building, the graceful arc of 333 West Wacker, and the notorious Trump Tower. You'll likely hear wry commentary on the proliferation of riverside condos, which is hardly what draws the international crowd to this tour, but offers

THE CHRISTMAS TREE SHIPS

A century ago, not all of the wood that was shipped down from the great northern forests was stripped of its fragrant green glory. Some of it—the pines, to be precise—arrived intact, just in time for Christmas. The schooners that brought the trees came to be known as the Christmas Tree Ships.

It's hard to imagine the excitement that must have surrounded the arrival of the most legendary Christmas Tree Ship, the Rouse Simmons, at the dock near Clark Street Bridge. It was from this vessel that people could buy trees directly. How the people of the city must have celebrated the sight of trees that they would soon dress with candles and ornaments and cranberry garland. Today, the artists, writers, singers, and performers of Chicago can tell us what it was like. Gather 'round their Web sites and let them introduce you to the century-old story of the Christmas Tree Ships. Here are some great places to go to experience the sights and sounds:

Clipper Ship Gallery, 10 West Harris Avenue, LaGrange, Illinois 60525, (800) 750-7327, (708) 352-2778, www.charlesvickery.com. Glorious paintings to view and purchase.

Website of historian Fred Neuschel: http://christmastreeship.homestead.com/index.html.

Website of Great Lakes region singer-storyteller Lee Murdock: www.leemurdock.com/html/christmasship.html.

Annual stage performance by the Bailiwick Repertory Theatre, 1229 West Belmont Avenue, Chicago, Illinois 60657, (773) 883-1090, www.bailiwick.org.

A new chapter of the Christmas Tree Ship story began in 2000, when the Chicago marine community raised funds to buy thousands of trees for disadvantaged families, and saw to it that they arrived in the traditional way. The Mackinaw made a 350-mile journey with her cargo from northern Michigan; and as she came into view at Navy Pier, a brass band played and well-wishers welcomed the arrival of the trees. And although the Mackinaw is now retired, the Christmas Tree Ship tradition lives on.

insight into the contemporary resurgence of residential life along this corridor.

As you explore the riverfront, keep your eyes open for several pieces of artwork that honor the city's connection to its waterways. On the south bank at Wacker and Lake Shore Drive where the river meets the lake, the **Riverwalk Gateway** is a circa-2000 visual narrative of 28 painted ceramic tiles beginning with the journeys of Jacques Marquette and Louis Jolliet in 1673. Chicago's largest public artwork, it connects the riverwalk to the lakefront path.

A few blocks north and east of the mouth of the river, the illustrious **Navy Pier**, 600 East Grand Avenue, Chicago, Illinois 60611, (800) 595-PIER (outside Chicago), (312) 595-PIER, www.navypier.com, juts out into Lake Michigan as it has since its debut in 1916. Airman George Bush trained here in the 1940s. By 1964, Navy Pier was accommodating 250 overseas vessels a year, making it one of the world's greatest inland ports. Today locals and tourists alike enjoy the pier's happy jumble of carnival rides, museums, ice skating rink, theater performances, children's entertainment troupe, eateries, specialty shops, IMAX theater, weekly fireworks, and sensory waterfront promenade. Inside the pier's **Chicago Children's Museum**, (312) 527-1000, www.ChiChildrensMuseum.org, the kids will have a blast scaling the three floors of rigging aboard the Climbing Schooner, making a splash as they navigate their boat down the WaterWays river and past the miniature Buckingham Fountain. For the really little ones, Treehouse Trails lets kids angle for plastic fish.

Best of all, Navy Pier really is a pier, with a long history of naval service and a delightful fleet of token-operated remote boats, tour boats, dining cruise ships,

CROWDS, CAPTAINS, AND CREWS

It is July in Chicago. Once again, as it does every year, the Chicago to Mackinac Race is about to set sail from Navy Pier. It will be an estimated two days and 333 miles across unpredictable miles of cold Lake Michigan waters to Lake Huron. Storms may kick up the waves that have sunk many ships. Seasickness may turn faces green. There may be headwinds or no winds. But all too soon the race will come to an end. And there at the fabled Mackinac Island, the promise of glory and the trading of stories over drinks at the Pink Pony awaits.

Visitors gather to witness the start of the event. They surge to the edge of the pier and hop onto picnic tables to see nearly 300 luxury yachts parading around like expensive thoroughbreds. One after another the boats float by as cameras click and binoculars focus. Heat mixes with coconut-scented sunscreen and rises in waves off the concrete. One lady manages to look cool in a straw hat and sea-green linen pants. A little boy scuttles forward to squeeze himself into a coveted spot at the rail. An announcer's patter bathes the crowd and the racers in jovial excitement.

The crowd eagerly reaches out to the racers, and the energy flows both ways. It is all hands on deck as the crews wave and shout out to the audience. One delivers a dirge on the bagpipes, while another sports jaunty pirate bandanas. All participants seem anchored together by a collegial competition. Most of the yachts are at least 27 feet long; many fly "brag flags" that demonstrate prowess in races gone by.

In a race that began over a century ago, tradition runs deep. Many of the sailors represent returning generations of families and friends. Those who have sailed in at least 25 Mac Races have earned the right to be called Island Goats.Hours after the parade begins, the last yacht leaves the pier to join the others that have unfurled their sails out beyond the breakwaters. On the pier, the crowd begins to disperse and move on. But whatever exciting Chicago attraction they may be heading to see, nothing will quite compare to this.

speedboats, and tall ships.

Sail aboard the tall ships ***Windy*** or ***Windy II***, (312) 595-5555, and enjoy a sort of celebrity status on the inland seas. Once under full sail, these four-masted replica ships command the attention from everyone on land. *Windy* is a 148-foot schooner, and *Windy II* is a 150-foot barquentine. On occasion, a yacht posing as a pirate ship will aim cannon fire (friendly, of course) at the tall ships, which are perfectly capable of returning fire should they choose to do so. Such moments are a thrilling throwback to the nineteenth century. Also thrilling are the rescue drills that the crew might decide to practice while you are on board. At a shout of "Man overboard!" the crew springs into action to "rescue" a buoy. Your job is to stay out of the way and cheer their success. Feel the wind in your hair as you help raise a sail. And once the engine shuts off and the ship clears the pierhead lights, as you watch the city skyline recede from your stern, know that it is only the wind that moves you.

Chicago's legendary wind comes in handy each August during **Tall Ships Chicago**, www.tallshipschicago.net, when masted sailing ships gather in port to evoke nineteenth-century maritime Chicago. Visitors enjoy the spectacle of life in the mast lane, and can board the majestic vessels that dock at Navy Pier, the Chicago River, and the DuSable Harbor. Not an annual event, Tall Ships Chicago only occurs every three years.

Board the fastest elevator in North America for the most panoramic view of the lake in the city. Spanning up to 80 miles and four states, the view from **The John Hancock Observatory**, John Hancock Center, 94th Floor, 875 North Michigan Avenue, Chicago, Illinois 60611, (888) 875-VIEW, (312) 751-3681, www.hancockobservatory.com, is not to be missed. From Navy Pier, the observatory is about one mile north. "Big John" is so close to the lakefront that most of what you see to the east is lake. Signage pinpoints the locations of offshore shipwrecks such as the schooner *Evening Star* (1894) and the coal cargo schooner *Wings of the Wind* (1866). The northern shoreline view is especially picturesque; that vessel sunken into the sand is not a wreck but the café of North Avenue Beach. Fun features include the wind-in-your-hair Skywalk, the Soundscopes talking telescopes, and personal audio Sky Tours.

To reach even greater heights, head to the **Sears Tower Skydeck**, 233 South Wacker Drive, Chicago, Illinois 60606, (877) SKY-DECK reservations, (312) 875-1632, www.theskydeck.com. Let the elevator whisk you up 103 floors for breathtaking views of the lake, the city, and neighboring states. Ground was broken for the 1,450-foot-tall tower in 1970, but the story really began when Sears and Roebuck started their legendary catalog business in 1886. Learn what role cigarettes played in the design of the tower, as well as the number of years Sears Roebuck & Co. was actually headquartered there. Ultimately eclipsed in height by a tower in Taiwan, the Sears Tower still has the tallest antennas in the world. On sunny summer weekends, be prepared for long waits that are at least broken into segments including a theater presentation. One good option is to go at the dinner hour or later for sunsets and city lights.

Points North

Leave the skyline behind and hit one, or several, of Chicago's lakefront beaches. Over at **North Avenue Beach**, North Avenue and Lake Shore Drive, (312) 742-PLAY, www.chicagoparkdistrict.com, a boathouse sports the Castaways Bar & Grill on its top deck. From here, you can thrill to the **Chicago Air & Water Show**, which thunders along the lakefront from Fullerton Avenue to Oak Street each August. Billed as the largest free show of its kind in the country, it supplies a heavy dose of high quality entertainment including the U.S. Navy Blue Angels and extreme wave riders.

Also in the vicinity, the Chicago Park District's **Theater on the Lake**, 2401 North Lake Shore Drive, (312) 742-7994, www.chicagoparkdistrict.com, entertains with summer-long productions by professional Chicago theater companies. Nestled near the 18-mile **Lakefront Bike Path**, this is a cultural must-see in the summer. Every Halloween, the theater building becomes the Haunted Sanitarium—visitors enter at their own risk.

Maritime Chicago

Chicago's maritime heritage keeps a surprisingly low profile; but things are changing thanks in large part to the Chicago Maritime Society and the revamped **Chicago History Museum**, 1601 North Clark Street, Chicago, Illinois 60614, (312) 642-4600, www.chicagohis tory.org. Find the museum in trendy Lincoln Park (which, for a bit of trivia, was originally to be named Lake Park). Formerly named the Chicago Historical Society, this museum was revamped and reopened in 2006. Hear the history of Chicago waterways in the "City on the Make" exhibit, which explains how the Chicago River, Lake Michigan, and the Illinois and Michigan Canal served as routes of transportation and commercial trade. Artifacts include a model of nineteenth-century ships being loaded with grain at the Newberry & Dole Warehouse, a hand-carved eagle head stem timber, caulking chisels, and the captain's megaphone from the schooner *Mary Gregory.*

And if you think lusty pirates, sailors of luxury yachts, swashbuckling singers, underwater archeologists, air traffic reporters, ancient voyageurs, U.S. Coast Guard personnel, and displeased environmentalists don't belong in the same room, the **Chicago Maritime Festival**, www.maritimefestival.org, will make you think again. Every year in March, the Chicago Maritime Society throws all these folks together for a celebration of all things maritime. Chicago, they say, has a great maritime story to tell. If you want to hear the story from an amazing variety of perspectives, then be in Chicago during this weekend event. You will be treated to informative lectures on everything from tall ships to nautical archeology, as well as spirited musical performances featuring songs of the sea, and children's boat-building activities.

The Nature of Chicago

Continue north from the Chicago History Museum (it is a somewhat ambitious walk through the park or an easy bus or trolley ride) to the free-of-charge **Lincoln Park Zoo**, 2400 North Cannon Drive (at Fullerton Parkway), Chicago, Illinois 60614, (312) 742-2000, www.lpzoo.org. Watch dwarf crocodiles and pygmy hippos swim in rainforest pools while seals flow through their infinity edge pool as if they were made of water. Also outdoors, the shorebird pond teems with splashing ducks, stately swans, and statue-like flamingos.

In the zoo's Regenstein Center for African Apes, a mother gorilla flops back onto straw and holds her baby aloft, while a silverback male gazes stoically out a window. See an ape swoop down from a tangle of climbing ropes, grabbing a handful of carrots and entertaining the crowd. At "Farm in the Zoo," damp-eyed cows munch hay and watch visitors like humans watch television.

Have lunch in any number of zoo cafés, shop the Wild Things! gift shop, ride the Endangered Species Carousel that offers glimpses of Lake Michigan, and rent a swan paddleboat in the South Lagoon.

Tuckered out as you may be, take a few more steps to the (also free) **Lincoln Park Conservatory**, 2391 North Stockton Drive, Chicago, Illinois 60614, (312) 742-PLAY, www.chicagoparkdistrict.com, with its four greenhouses and 50-foot rubber tree that first took root in 1891.

How about one more stop? Located just across the street, the **Notebaert Nature Museum**, 2430 North Cannon Drive, Chicago, Illinois 60614, (773) 755-5100, www.naturemuseum.org, is definitely worth a visit. This gem of a museum focuses on nature in the Midwest—including that of the Great Lakes. Special emphasis on crawling bugs, soggy marshes, and the chaos of the climate keeps kids engaged.

The RiverWorks water lab is probably designed for kids; but if you, too, want to see what happens when you dam the river, by all means dive right in. You can always justify your involvement by reading the interpretive signage, including information on Chicagoland's newest—and invisible—waterway. Take the stairs up past the pebble pool to alight in the warm and wonderful world of wings and waterfalls. Here on any given day, over 1,000 butterflies and moths sip nectars and fruit juices, bask in the sunlight, and live in harmony with the fish and flowers. Did a fairy just peek out from behind those rocks? It seems almost possible in this magical realm. If the moist, 80-degree heat starts making you wilt, head upstairs to the rooftop deck's open-air catwalk for views of pond and prairie. Afterward, pop into the gift shop for all things creepy-crawly, including a lollipop that looks like amber with a lifelike insect trapped inside.

One Last Look

If you leave the city by way of Chicago Midway International Airport, take one last look at Lake Michigan—in the form of a unique sculpture. Suspended from the airport ceiling, **The Body of Lake Michigan** is a fiberglass and steel sculpture that was developed using scientific data from the National Oceanic and Atmospheric Administration and the National Environmental Satellite, Data, and Information Service. It displays the lake's volume as shaped by the underlying topography of the earth's surface. It is truly a lake view you will find nowhere else.

But if you are continuing north along the lake, the next chapter will guide you to the best sites along the rest of Illinois' short but significant shoreline.

FROM THE GALLEYS

Catch Thirty Five Seafood & Steaks, 35 West Wacker Drive, Chicago, Illinois 60601, (312) 346-3500, www.catch35.com. Whether charcoal grilled, pan seared, or oven baked, the freshest possible seafood lands here. Consider entrées along the lines of grilled yellowfin tuna with ginger-sesame sauce or baked Atlantic salmon in puff pastry with lemon-dill sauce.

Hugo's Frog Bar and Fish House, 1024 North Rush Street, Chicago, Illinois 60611, (312) 640-0999, www.hugosfrogbar.com. From crab cakes to frog legs, the preparations are delicious and the selections are as fresh as they get.

Shaw's Crab House, 21 East Hubbard Street, Chicago, Illinois 60611, (312) 527-2722, www.shawscrabhouse.com. This time-tested favorite specializes in fresh seafood that is flown in daily from around the world and the Great Lakes. Selections range from Planked Lake Superior Whitefish to BBQ Eel & Avocado.

Embassy Suites Hotel, 511 North Columbus Drive, Chicago, Illinois 60611, (312) 836-5900, www.chicagohilton.com. Close to the places you want to be, this 455-suite hotel sits between Navy Pier and the Magnificent Mile (Michigan Avenue). Only a short walk to the John Hancock Observatory, beaches, and upscale shopping. Stay in a two-room suite, unwind at the nightly manager's reception, and wake up to a complementary, cooked-to-order breakfast.

Hilton Chicago, 720 South Michigan Avenue, Chicago, Illinois 60605, (312) 922-4400, www.chicagohilton.com. Overlooking Grant Park, Buckingham Fountain, the Museum Campus, and Lake Michigan, this 1,544-guestroom hotel is almost a city itself and a beloved Chicago landmark. Relax in old-world style and elegance, from lobby grand pianos and floor-to-ceiling drapes to Italian marble bathroom fixtures and impeccable service. Not to be outdone by newer properties, the Hilton keeps up with the times with contemporary conveniences.

Sheraton Chicago Hotel & Towers, 301 East North Water Street, Chicago, Illinois 60611, (312) 464-1000, www.sheratonchicago.com. Riverfront mega-hotel with 1,209 guestrooms. Restaurants and eateries, indoor pool, health club, sundeck, and style.

AIDS TO NAVIGATION

Tourism Visitor Centers (south to north):

Chicago Cultural Center, 77 East Randolph Street, Chicago, Illinois 60602.

Navy Pier Information Center, 600 East Grand Avenue, Chicago, Illinois 60611.

Chicago Water Works Visitors Center, 163 East Pearson Street at Michigan Avenue, Chicago, Illinois 60611.

Illinois Department of Commerce and Economic Opportunity: www.gochicago.com; www.cityofchicago.org/ExploringChicago; www.877chicago.com; (877) CHICAGO.

Free Trolley: (312) 744-3565.

Chicago Greeter: www.chicagogreeter.com.

City of Chicago Stores: www.chicagostore.com.

Chicago Yacht Club (coverage of the Chicago to Mackinac Race): www.chicagoyachtclub.org/racetomackinac.

Chicago CityPass: www.citypass.com

FlagShip Integration Services, Inc. (provides live tracking of the Chicago to Mackinac Race): www.fistracking.com.

CTA Visitor's Pass: www.transitchicago.com.

Go Chicago Card: www.gochicagocard.com.

Evanston to Zion

"How glorious to see this grand old mansion alive again through the Evanston Historical Society. So much history and passion can be felt within these walls."

—review of the Charles Gates Dawes House

FROM EVANSTON TO ZION, the drive is easy on the eyes. Your other senses will not object either as you savor the sounds of seagulls, the fragrances and tastes of restaurants, and the touch of fine European linens against your suntanned skin. Coming from Chicago's Lake Shore Drive you can pick up Sheridan Road, which also hugs the lakeshore and takes you past the fabulous homes of the North Shore. North of Glencoe, you'll enter the aptly named Lake County, which ends at the Wisconsin border.

Only 18 miles north of Chicago, Evanston has 4.5 miles of lakefront with five beaches for swimming, sailing, windsurfing, and boating. You can do all this within a distinctly culture-drenched suburb located on the lakeshore. One of the beaches stretches out in front of the Charles Gates Dawes House, which is a good first stop as you drive up from Chicago. Once home to the 30th vice president of the United States, the **Charles Gates Dawes House** is a chateau-style mansion that has overlooked Lake Michigan since the 1890s. Today it is home to the **Evanston Historical Society**, 225 Greenwood Street, Evanston, Illinois 60201, (847) 475-3410, www.evanstonhistorical.org. View relics from an 1860 shipwreck and immerse yourself in the history of a suburb that stands out for maintaining its traditional culture amid suburban streets. The population is diverse and so are the shops, and the presence of Northwestern University's lakefront campus infuses it all with hip energy.

But as long as you're on the maritime trail, take Sheridan Road all the way to the must-see **Grosse Point Lighthouse**, 2601 Sheridan Road, Evanston, Illinois 60201, (847) 328-6961, www.grossepointlighthouse.net. Just over half a mile north of the Charles Gates Dawes House, the lighthouse overlooks accessible Lake Michigan beachfront, and sits on a point of land that early French explorers named grosse, or great. The light was built in 1873 in response to the wreck of the *Lady Elgin*. Today, it continues to warn mariners of shoals (shallow areas) and guide them toward the harbors of Chicago. The picturesque, cream-colored structure features an above-ground passageway from the keeper's quarters to the tower that rises 113 feet and houses a rare second order Fresnel lens. Enjoy seasonal tours of this active light, and explore the surrounding art center, butterfly and wildflower gardens, parkland, and sandy swimming beach.

As you leave the lighthouse, head west away from the lake to **The Mitchell Museum of the American Indian**, 2600 Central Park Avenue, Evanston, Illinois 60201, (847) 475-1030, www.mitchellmuseum.org. Permanent exhibits portray cultures of the Woodland, Plain, Southwest, Northwest Coast, and Arctic regions of North America. The Woodlands Galery includes artifacts and interpretation of the native Great Lakes cultures. Highlighting this is a birchbark canoe, along with exhibits of fishing, hunting and gathering, and adornment such as moosehair embroidery. Ever seen a walrus intestine parka? You will now.

As you leave Evanston, head east along Central Street and north to neighboring Wilmette. This is indeed one of Chicagoland's coveted suburbs, featuring 1925 street lights, **Plaza del Lago** shopping on the lake, **Gillson Park's** sandy beaches, and, of course, those posh homes. Unique along the entire Lake Michigan shoreline is the magnificent **Baha'i House of Worship**, 100 Linden Avenue, Wilmette, Illinois 60091, (847) 853-2300, www.us.bahai.org. Although the groundbreaking began in 1912, the structure was not completed until 1953. It pays homage to the oneness of God, the oneness of mankind, and the oneness of religion. All are welcome to enjoy the unique lacelike structure, which was achieved by casting concrete made of quartz crystal and white cement. The final result is a breathtaking, 135-foot filigree dome. Learn the tenets of the Baha'i world faith in the downstairs Visitors' Center, have a private moment in the auditorium, and stroll the outdoor gardens along round pools of water and intricately-designed landscape.

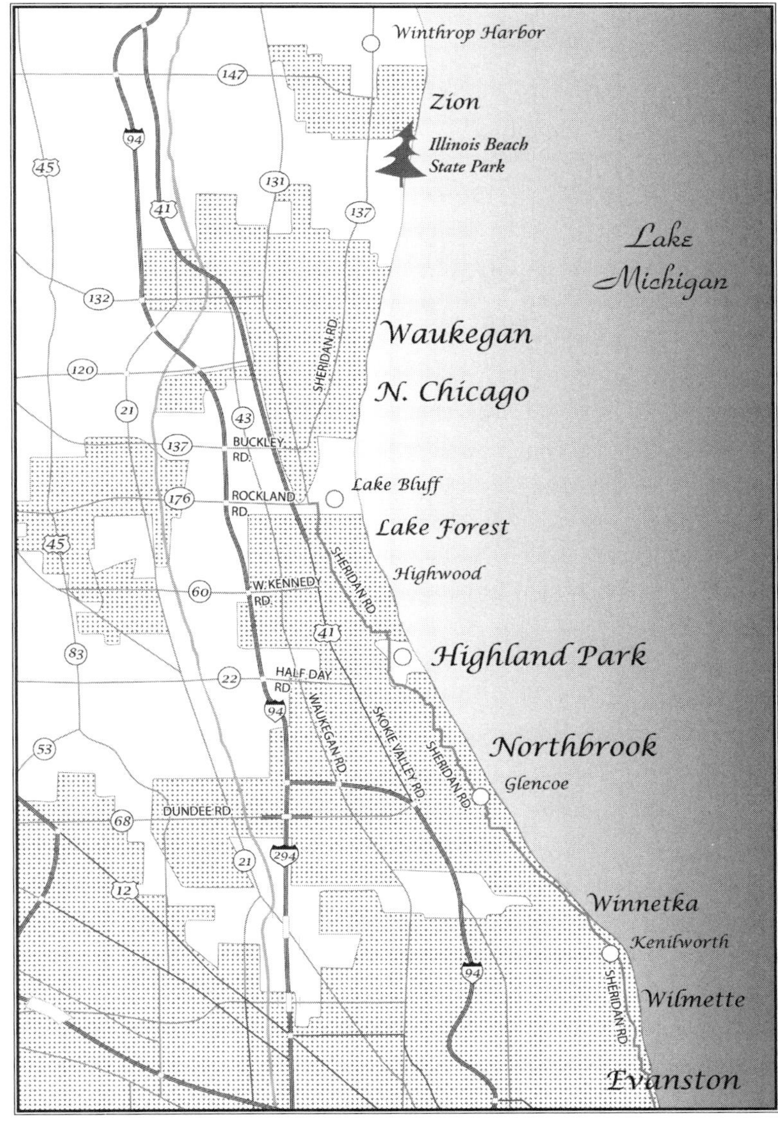

Continue north on Sheridan Road and turn west onto Lake Cook Road for a little side trip into paradise. This is the **Chicago Botanic Garden**, 1000 Lake Cook Road, Glencoe, Illinois 60022, (847) 835-5440, www.chicagobotanic.org; and if you like beautiful things, you definitely do not want to miss it. The beauty is not only in the colors, textures, and scents of the plant collections, but also in the ways they are presented. As gardens go, this one overflows not only with flora but also with water, ranging from postcard-quality lakes and fountains to delightful features that invite your touch. In fact, across the Chicago Botanic Garden's 385 acres, there are 81 acres of waterways, 10 bridges, nine islands, eight miles of shoreline, and tens of thousands of aquatic plants. Swans, herons, egrets, geese, and ducks patrol it all.

So where do you start? Hop aboard the tram for a narrated overview, then return on foot to favorite areas. Climb the 45-foot Waterfall Garden, whose rushing waters tumble over boulders and rest in pools. In the Enabling Garden, push your fingers into the wall of falling water to feel its softness. Have a seat in a summer chair on the brick-and-stone deck of the McGinley Pavilion to experience the serenity of Evening Island and the Great Basin. After lunch at the Garden Café and perhaps a turn through the Garden Shop, you will want to explore everything else, for the beauty is in full bloom across the 23 gardens and three native habitats of the Chicago Botanic Garden.

After the sights of the garden, move less than a mile northeast to the sounds of another world-class outdoor site. For almost four warm months throughout each year, the renowned **Ravinia Festival**, 200 Ravinia Park Road, Highland Park, Illinois 60035, (847) 266-5100 (seasonal), www.ravinia.org, rolls out nationally acclaimed acts on the starlit North Shore lakefront. Ravinia is big, and, like all great Chicago events, draws big crowds. You need to plan ahead, especially for the big names. But Ravinia is unlike any other concert venue: it is as much about an extravagant feast on the lawn as it is about the music onstage. So pack a gourmet picnic and enjoy the show.

At this point in your journey, you can continue driving Sheridan Road to Lake Bluff, or cut over onto I-94 (which continues into Wisconsin) for a faster trip north. Interstate 94 is a good choice if you plan to dive into the Six Flags Great America theme park and its newer **Hurricane Harbor** waterpark (which is included in the price of admission). Get wet, get wild, and have a blast with more than 25 water slides, the world's largest family water playground, and a vast wave pool. For information, contact: **Six Flags Great America**, 542 North Illinois Route 21, Gurnee, Illinois 60031, (847) 249-4936, www.sixflags.com. Plan to spend the entire day—or two.

Horse lovers will not want to miss a rare opportunity to lose their hearts to

The Tempel Lipizzans, Tempel Farms, 17000 Wadsworth Road, Wadsworth, Illinois 60083, (847) 623-7272, www.tempelfarms. com. Drive north for just under six miles on U.S. Highway 41 from Six Flags to see the amazing spectacle of dancing horses. A classic Viennese tradition imported to the North Shore, this is an art that dates back to sixteenth-century Austria. For the horses, training begins at age four and lasts up to five years. The horses are white, but the dark foals among them demonstrate that the breed's coat actually turns white as the animal matures. Horses are carefully selected to perform specific jobs, from carriage driving to the coveted "Airs Above the Ground"—a series of movements that are breathtaking to watch and difficult for the horses to perform. The various leaps and rearing positions represent specialized, advanced maneuvers not typically presented in competitive dressage.

Illinois Beach State Park

"We're the last remaining beach ridge along the Lake Michigan shoreline, and the first nature preserve in the state. We have more endangered and threatened species than anywhere else in the state, including prickly pear cactus and bearberry, which is an Arctic shrub that one of the glaciers brought down. Bearberry survives in this climate because of the lake's cooling effect."

—Bob Feffer, Site Assistant Superintendent, Illinois Beach

THE LAST STOP on this tour, just before you reach the Wisconsin border, is the **Illinois Beach State Park**, 1 Lake Front Drive, Zion, Illinois 60099, (847) 662-4811, www.dnr.state.il.us/lands/landmgt/PARKS/R2/ILBEACH.HTM. To get there from the horse farm, drive east on Wadsworth Road for just under nine miles to the main entrance (South Unit). Enjoy the park's 6.5 miles of sandy lakeshore for swimming and sunning. The 4,160 acres offer a little over five miles of trails through the varied terrain that is characteristic of successional areas. If you're not familiar with the concept of succession, here is your chance to learn all about it.

As you roam about the parkland, check out points of interest such as the Visitor Center, the North Point Marina, the Power House Museum (just north of the Zion Power Plant that services Chicago), and the cultural history of Camp Logan, which was a Civil War Union prisoner of war camp. Spend the night at a campsite or at the park's own comfortable and contemporary beachside resort.

From a nineteenth-century lighthouse and a glittering city to dancing horses and a beachside state park, Chicago's fabled North Shore and its surrounding lakefront towns ensure that you are never far from fun along Lake Michigan.

FROM THE GALLEYS

Bonefish Grill, 1905 Cherry Lane, Northbrook, Illinois 60062, (847) 509-0661, www.bonefishgrill.com. Enjoy flown-in fish cooked over a wood-burning grill. Taste the freshness of this Florida-based chain that serves nautical delicacies such as corn chowder with lump crab, pistachio parmesan crusted rainbow trout, and a range of grilled fish from grouper to swordfish.

Davis Street Fishmarket, 501 Davis Street, Evanston, Illinois 60201, (847) 869-3474, www.davisstreetfishmarket.com. Seasonal seafood chowders, spiced pecan & blue cheese salad with shrimp, chicken, or salmon, North Carolina-inspired breaded clam strips, New Orleans shrimp & crawfish étoufée, lobster, crab, steak, fish, and chicken.

Don's Fish Market Grill & Tavern, 9335 Skokie Boulevard, Skokie, Illinois 60077, (847) 677-3424, www.donsfish

market.com. What could be more fitting for summer than a selection from the "Chilled Seafood for the Grill" menu? Go all-out with the sampler, which is loaded with jumbo shrimp, clams, smoked salmon, oysters, and blue crabmeat cocktail. Try seafood specialties such as broiled lemon sole or grilled striped bass with field greens; or consider regionally-caught fish such as brook trout from Idaho or whitefish from the cold waters of Lake Superior.

TO THE DOCKS

Emanuelson Inn Bed and Breakfast, 1241 Shiloh Boulevard, Zion, Illinois 60099, (877) 872-8488 x119, (847) 872-8488 x119, www.emanuelsoninn.com. This unmistakably Victorian inn combines traditional style with thoughtful amenities and proximity to Illinois Beach State Park. Fourteen of the 17 bedrooms have private baths. You can also choose to stay in one of two cottages. In addition to starting the day with a delicious breakfast, guests are welcome to enjoy afternoon refreshments or evening nightcaps and conversation. Bicycles are available.

Hotel Orrington, 1710 Orrington Avenue, Evanston, Illinois 60201, (847) 866-8700, www. hotelorrington.com. Sophistication meets renovation in these 269 rooms and suites. Enjoy lavish furnishings including special attention to bedding and bath products to pamper you silly. Check out the on-site dining options.

Illinois Beach Resort & Conference Center, Illinois Beach State Park, One Lake Front Drive, Zion, Illinois 60099, (866) ILBEACH reservations, (847) 625-7300, www.ilresorts.com. Located right on the lakeshore, surrounded by sandy beach

LIGHTHOUSES

Lighthouses have a funny way of getting into people's hearts—and it's a love not even the U.S. Coast Guard can control. Up and down the lakeshore, the Coast Guard has decommissioned many old beacons that served mariners in their day. Rather than snuffing out the lights, the Coast Guard automated them, which was highly efficient but also removed the human element with the finality of a slammed door.

Little did the Coast Guard know, however, that following in their wake were the preservationists, the historians, and the hopeless romantics who could not bear to see the old towers fade from the Great Lakes maritime scene. What was the attraction? Was it the towers' lonely position on the edge of land? Was it their rock-solid dependability, their strength in keeping watch over those at sea? Or was it their unapologetic linear beauty that pointed to the sky through the brightness of each day and the darkness of each night?

Whatever the reason, instead of fading into history or crumbling into the lake, lighthouses have come around to fulfill an entirely new mission, one that would undoubtedly baffle the nineteenth-century builders and even some mariners. For today the old towers light the way for people who may never even set foot on a boat. These are the schoolchildren who file in with giggles and whispers and wide eyes. These are the couples who hold hands and hardly hear a word of the tour guides' narratives. And these are the retirees who lived through the old days and feel a private camaraderie with the towers themselves.

More recently, the Coast Guard has put up some, well, spindly towers that light themselves but that no self-respecting ghost would bother to haunt. So, the question must be asked. A century from now, when the Coast Guard starts thinking about decommissioning its newer towers, will the preservationists, the historians, and the hopeless romantics follow in their wake with visions of museums and tours?

Probably.

Lighthouses represent the water, and they represent the past. Lighthouses serve as a memorial for those who've died at sea; and as such, they garner an enduring, unparalleled respect. And no matter how much decommissioning occurs or how maritime culture may change, one thing is certain: that respect will never fade. The lights of these old towers will continue to shine well after all the ships have passed.

and state forestland. Enjoy the modern design of guestrooms and suites, and stay all day at the beach that rolls just outside your door. Indoor pool, health club, and room to roam.

The Margarita European Inn, 1566 Oak Avenue, Evanston, Illinois 60201, (847) 869-2273, www.margaritainn.com. Sink into one of 42 guestrooms and suites amid antiques; curl up in the English library; savor evening cocktails in the Grand Parlor; see glittering nightlights from the flower-festooned outdoor roof deck. Savor the flavors of the on-site Va Pensiero restaurant. Start the day right with complementary deluxe continental breakfast.

AIDS TO NAVIGATION

Chicago's North Shore Convention & Visitors Bureau, (847) 763-0011 x22, www.visitchicagonorthshore.com.

Lake County Convention & Visitors Bureau, (800) LAKE-NOW, www.lakecounty.org.

THE MAGIC OF THE FERRIES

LAKE MICHIGAN currently has two cross-lake ferries that get passengers from one side of the lake to the other. Having two ferries offers so many more options when planning a lakeshore route, including the option to cross over on one and back on the other.

But incorporating a ferry ride into a lakeshore journey also greatly enhances the experience of the lake. This is more than an opportunity to get somewhere faster than by driving around; it is also the chance to spend more time on the water. Land quickly disappears, and most of the journey is simply you and the lake—and snacks and Bingo and all the rest, of course.

Express Yourself

"The temperature is 64 degrees, the winds are out of the northeast at nine knots, the barometer reads three-zero-decimal-one-zero. There is a short-term weather advisory over Milwaukee this afternoon, the line of thundershowers has been reported moving to the east ... so we may see a little of that .... We're currently up at our transit speed of 32 knots, and I'm showing an ETA for the breakwall over in Milwaukee of five minutes after the hour .... Please sit back and enjoy your trip across the lake with us today. Thank you for choosing the Lake Express, *and welcome aboard."*

—Lake Express

Views of Muskegon, *Lake Express* ferry, Muskegon, Michigan

THE *LAKE EXPRESS* zooms between Milwaukee, Wisconsin and Muskegon, Michigan, taking about 2.5 hours each way. Farther north, the SS *Badger* steams between Manitowoc, Wisconsin and Ludington, Michigan on a four-hour crossing. Beyond these essential differences, the onboard experiences are comfortable, safe, and enjoyable, but differ vastly in style.

It's like being aboard an excursion boat as the twin-hulled ferry slips across Muskegon Lake at 4:45 p.m. Family, friends, and the terminal crew on land wave goodbye, then begin to quickly recede. On board, it's as if all the little stresses of the passengers seem to drift away with the lakeshore. Attention flits from the *Milwaukee Clipper* to the Shoreline Inn to a police boat that seems to be escorting the ferry. The day remains cloudy, but the weak play of sunlight on the lake seems beautiful in a way it did not on land. Once in the channel, those keeping watch on the sun deck begin to zip up jackets. They snap photos of the USS *Silversides* submarine.

Suddenly the air feels almost too cold to breathe. The sun deck empties.

Those who have paid for the Premier Class upgrade settle down to complementary beverages, newspapers, larger seats, no kids under 12, and other amenities in their forward lounge.

Most passengers return, with jackets and sweaters, to the standard lounge seats they have claimed. Still, the lounge is comfortably spacious with a variety of seating choices and aisles for toddlers to practice walking on short, stiff legs. The center seats, which are generally the least desirable on an airplane, have been cleverly crafted with tables. These are already cluttered with laptops and snacks. To either side are the window and aisle seats. As land disappears, there is nothing but the lake, which, on this ordinary summer afternoon, is calm.

The snack bar faces all of the standard lounge seats like a movie theater screen. During the next 2 hours, the food is, for most passengers, the main attraction. Passengers order soups, salads, warm sandwiches, snacks, coffee, soft drinks, wine, and beer.

Is it 6:00 p.m. already? The ride is half over, and, according to the map, it's time to turn back the watch and gain an hour. Perfect for watching a sailboat race before dinner in Milwaukee. There is still time to return e-mails and check voicemail on the cell, maybe even read about the ferry. She was the first high-speed automobile and passenger ferry built in the United States to operate a domestic route. At 292 feet, she carries up to 46 cars, 12 motorcycles, and 253 passengers. Her transit speed is about 34 knots (40 mph). Added in 2005, stabilization wings have improved her ability to remain on an even keel. They still sell motion sickness solutions at the terminals, but passengers have welcomed the smoother ride.

Lake Express made a splash during her June 1, 2004 debut, and it has been smooth sailing ever since, although her list of unexpected adventures is growing. In 2005 she proved not only to be a timesaver, but also a lifesaver. The *Milwaukee Journal Sentinel* reported that when Captain Rick Hopper spotted something in the water a few miles away, his gut instinct prompted him to change course despite the schedule. It turned out to be a capsized powerboat, its owner struggling in the water. The man's body temperature had fallen to 92-degrees Fahrenheit, and passengers assisted as he was treated for hypothermia. About 40 minutes later, the ferry returned to Milwaukee so the man could be taken to a hospital there. Other adventures followed, and it was in April of 2006 that members of the Marquette University Waterski Team got the ride of their lives—not on the ferry, but in its wake.

Lake Express may be new, but the concept of ferrying people across the lake is merely history repeating itself. Throughout much of the nineteenth century, schooners and later steamships were the transportation mode of choice. For a long time, Lake Michigan, and indeed all the Great Lakes, *were* the highway. Today, these ancient waters have become a refreshing alternative to the congestion of overland roads.

Land appears, along with the S/V *Denis*

Sullivan gently rocking offshore. By this time, many aboard the *Lake Express* have ventured back onto the decks. Does the sight of a three-masted schooner replicated from the 1880s make their hearts leap? Do they wonder, even just briefly, at the glory of the old days? Perhaps. But as the ferry maneuvers toward her dock, they hurry down to the car deck, squeezing past all the side view mirrors to their own cars and their own lives, leaving the lake behind.

AIDS TO NAVIGATION

Lake Express Ferry, (866) 914-1010, www.lake-express.com. **Milwaukee Terminal**, 2330 South Lincoln Memorial Drive, Milwaukee, Wisconsin 53207. **Muskegon Terminal**, 1918 Lakeshore Drive, Muskegon, Michigan 49441.

A Classic Crossing

Striking Up a Conversation on the SS *Badger:*

"What's the difference between people who sit forward and people who sit aft?" asked a passenger who seemed to have the sun baked an inch thick into his face. The question sat there on the deck like a line that had just been cast. It got a bite almost right away.

"It's the difference between those who want to see where they're going, and those happy enough to look back on where they've been," came the reply. There was silence for a time as everyone sort of nodded and wished they'd thought of that one.

Having caught his fish, the sun-baked passenger grinned. "Less wind aft," he said, before walking away.

AT 410 FEET and 4,244 tons, the SS *Badger* was launched in 1953 as the largest coal-fired carferry ever built, and she served for 37 years. But she almost didn't make it into the twenty-first century. The term *carferry* once referred to railroad cars, which were transported between ports on Lake Michigan. But with the building of interstate highways, it became easier to ship goods by truck, and soon carferries became the buggy whips of their time. On November 16, 1990 the SS *Badger* set sail from Wisconsin to Michigan. It was to be her last crossing. She was the last of the Lake Michigan carferries.

But that all changed in 1991, when Charles Conrad (1917–1995) bought and refurbished her and gave her a new job—transporting people and their vehicles. Today the laughter of children and gleeful shouts of "Bingo!" ring out across the SS *Badger's* many decks, lounges, and staterooms. Passengers savor hot, freshly cooked meals, and drinks from a bar. They lounge on deck chairs, watch the water, and find all kinds of spots for strolling or striking up conversations.

When you board the SS *Badger,* you are not just crossing from one state to another; you are venturing out into the vastness of the lake, between two time zones, with no land in sight. You are entering, if only for a

SS *Badger* steaming in to port, Manitowoc, Wisconsin

while, an entirely new world.

As she steams into port, your heart might begin to race. After all, she is an impressive seven stories high. Little ones jump up and down, and inside, so do you. Cameras click. The stern gate opens wide like the mouth of a whale as passengers disembark and loved ones reunite amid smiles and wriggling pets. The crew wastes no time unloading cars and garbage cans.

"The lake? I just like being on it."

—Mike Braybrook, Junior Engineer, SS *Badger*

Mike Braybrook makes his living on Lake Michigan. Here is a firsthand account of how he fell in love with the sea, and decided to build his life there.

"I was 12 or 13 years old," he began. "I found a book in the school library about a young kid that started sailing on a tramp steamer. I remember starting to read it; it was one of those books that grabs your attention and you can't put it down. I was mad when I got to the end of the book. Two evenings and it was done."

"From then on," Mike fondly recalls, "it was so intriguing to me. I wouldn't read anything else. It had to be something to do with sailing: the Navy, merchant ships, tramp ships, Great Lake steamers—it didn't matter, that's about all I would read. And that's what got me into it."

If it is the Wisconsin side, a dump truck piled high with black coal rolls onto the car deck as the ship prepares for her next sailing. Take your cue from veteran passengers and bring a jacket and maybe a hat. Take everything out of your car that you may need, but keep it to a minimum, because you will want to move about the ship. Leave keys in the ignition so they can drive your vehicle on and off the car deck.

It's quiet in the pilothouse when the captain issues orders to navigate the SS *Badger* out of the harbor at Manitowoc. One long blast of the steam whistle signals that she has left the dock. When waters are choppy, the captain says, they'll change course to keep the ship from rolling too much—although he adds that Lake Michigan is not difficult to navigate. Those who have gathered out at the pierhead light wave bon voyage, then recede into the horizon.

The galley crew keeps hot meals coming for buffet-style service in the Upper Deck Café. Each morning, the fragrance of golden eggs, crispy bacon, sizzling sausage, and toast lures passengers up the stairs. Steaming pots of coffee help, too. First Cook Irv Fulker, who came out of retirement for this job, says afternoon passengers enjoy hearty lunches aboard ship, including soups, salads, and hot entrees such as baked chicken, hamburgers, BBQ pork, and Philly steak sandwiches. Home-baked cookies come out of the galley, too. Down on the Main Deck, the deli-style Badger Galley has entrée salads, sandwiches, pizza slices, chicken wings, hot dogs, big pretzels, yogurt, and other snacky foods on the line.

Is Badger Bingo starting in the Main Lounge? Grab your lucky card, its cardboard layers softened by countless hopeful fingers. Take care when moving the red cellophane windows, because the older these cards get, the more nostalgic value they will have for all the passengers who come after you. Go as many rounds as you wish, then go exploring.

The Museum/Quiet Room combines historic photographs and signage with plush seats where some folks nod off. Browse for logowear, reading materials, keychains, and a variety of other gifts in the Boatique. See what's playing in the movie or TV lounges, try your hand in the video arcade; and if you are sailing with little ones, check out the action in the kids' playroom. Back in the main lounge, find out exactly how far along you are in the crossing with a glance at the GPS chart.

A stateroom is nice to have, but the vintage brass key they hand you is priceless. Staterooms are neither spacious nor luxurious, but for privacy, staging areas for belongings or babies, and refreshing naps, they can't be beat. Passenger housekeeping staff takes pride in keeping the 42 staterooms ship-shape. When it comes to making beds, Carolyn Cater and Geri Bietz say the tighter the better, and you need to be able to bounce a coin on the sheet. On occasion the staff finds interesting articles left in the staterooms, but they aren't talking.

Four hours later, you arrive at your destination and join the others at the rail who are eager to disembark. It's likely you'll leave carrying a few more things than you boarded with: a captain's hat won in Bingo, a book about Great Lakes lighthouses, a tiny pewter carferry, a connection with the lake and the breezes and the sun—and with the SS *Badger* herself.

AIDS TO NAVIGATION

Lake Michigan Carferry, 701 Maritime Drive, Ludington, Michigan 49431, (888) CAR-SHIP, (231) 845-5555, www.ssbadger.com.

APPENDIX 1
Attractions and Accomodations by Category

FOUNTAINS

LIGHTHOUSES (includes stations, keepers' quarters)

MARITIME SITES

MARITIME MUSEUMS

MUSEUMS

Art, Craft, Art Centers

History

Maritime

LAND-BASED

LIGHTHOUSE-BASED

VESSEL-BASED

OTHER

PARKS, BEACHES, DUNES

(Also see Waterparks)

Federal

Other

State

RESTAURANTS (FROM THE GALLEYS)

Illinois

Indiana

Michigan

Wisconsin

SAILING

SHIPS

See Boats: Tour, Cruise, Rental; Charter Fishing Museums; Maritime; Sailing; Submarines; Tall Ships

SHOPS, MARITIME

Also see Fish Markets

SHOPS, OTHER SPECIALTY

Wisconsin

WALKING, BICYCLE TRAILS

See Trails, Riverwalks

WATERPARKS

WINERIES, VINEYARDS

ZOOS

APPENDIX 2

Surf the Web for Boatloads of Information

Going Somewhere?

www.beachtowns.org – Michigan Beachtowns Association – North to south, it's Ludington to Harbor Country, a stretch of 151 miles of shoreline, 59 public beaches, 53 marinas, 7 lighthouses, 104 shipwrecks

www.cruisersyachts.com – Wisconsin-based boat builder

www.enjoyillinois.com – Illinois Department of Commerce and Economic Opportunity

www.gochicago.com – Illinois Department of Commerce and Economic Opportunity

www.great-lakes.org – Great Lakes Sport Fishing Council

www.greatlakescruising.com – Great Lakes Cruise Company: cruise the Great Lakes including Lake Michigan itineraries featuring ports of call

www.in.gov/enjoyin diana – Indiana Office of Tourism

www.lake-express.com. – The Lake Express ferry (cross-lake Muskegon-Milwaukee)

www.micharterboats.com – Michigan Charter Boat Association

www.michigan.org – Michigan Economic Development Corporation

www.michigan.org/drivingtours - select "Maritime Tours"

www.ssbadger.com – Lake Michigan Carferry (cross-lake Ludington-Manitowoc)

www.travelwisconsin.com – Wisconsin Department of Tourism

www.wisconsinharbortowns.org – Wisconsin Harbor Towns

www.wmta.org – West Michigan Tourist Association

In-Depth

www.boatnerd.com – Need more explanation?

www.greatlakesfor ever.org – Great Lakes Forever c/o Biodiversity Project – what can visitors do to help keep the future clean and bright?

www.lakemichigan.org – Alliance for the Great Lakes

www.maritimetrails.org – Wisconsin Historical Society, Maritime Preservation and Archaeology Program – Highlights the state's most interesting and accessible maritime attractions

www.michiganpre serves.org – Michigan Underwater Preserves

www.wisconsin shipwrecks.org – Shipwrecks off Wisconsin shores

National Park Service (for Sleeping Bear Dunes National Lakeshore & Indiana Dunes National Lakeshore) www.nps.gov

State Departments of Natural Resources (DNR)

www.dnr.state.il.us – Illinois

www.dnr.state.wi.us – Wisconsin

www.in.gov/dnr – Indiana

www.michigan.gov/dnr – Michigan

United States Coast Guard boating safety www.uscgboating.org

INDEX

D

E

F

G

M

N

O

P

R

S

T

U

V

Y

MORE GREAT TITLES FROM TRAILS BOOKS

ACTIVITY GUIDES

Biking Illinois: 60 Great Road and Trail Rides, *David Johnsen*
Biking Iowa: 50 Great Road and Trail Rides, *Bob Morgan*
Biking Wisconsin: 50 Great Road and Trail Rides, *Steve Johnson*
Great Iowa Walks: 50 Strolls, Rambles, Hikes and Treks, *Lynn L. Walters*
Great Minnesota Walks: 49 Strolls, Rambles, Hikes, and Treks, *Wm. Chad McGrath*
Great Wisconsin Walks: 45 Strolls, Rambles, Hikes, and Treks, *Wm. Chad McGrath*
Paddling Illinois: 64 Great Trips by Canoe and Kayak, *Mike Svob*
Paddling Iowa: 96 Great Trips by Canoe and Kayak, *Nate Hoogeveen*
Paddling Kansas: 61 Great Trips by Canoe and Kayak, *Dave Murphy*
Paddling Northern Minnesota: 86 Great Trips by Canoe and Kayak, *Lynne Smith Diebel*
Paddling Northern Wisconsin: 82 Great Trips by Canoe and Kayak, *Mike Svob*
Paddling Southern Minnesota: 85 Great Trips by Canoe and Kayak, *Lynne and Robert Diebel*
Paddling Southern Wisconsin: 82 Great Trips by Canoe and Kayak, *Mike Svob*
Walking Tours of Wisconsin's Historic Towns, Lucy Rhodes, Elizabeth McBride, *Anita Match*a,
Wisconsin's Outdoor Treasures: A Guide to 150 Natural Destinations, *Tim Bewer*
Kansas Outdoor Treasures: A Guide to 60 Natural Destinations, *Julie Cirlincuina*
Wisconsin Underground, *Doris Green*

TRAVEL GUIDES

Classic Wisconsin Weekends, *Michael Bie*
Explore Wisconsin Rivers, *Doris Green*
Great Indiana Weekend Adventures, *Sally McKinney*
Great Iowa Weekend Adventures, *Mike Whye*
Great Midwest Country Escapes, *Nina Gadomski*
Great Minnesota Taverns, *David K. Wright & Monica G. Wright*
Great Weekend Adventures, *the Editors of Wisconsin Trails*
Great Wisconsin Winter Weekends, *Candice Gaukel Andrews*
Minnesota Waterfalls, *Steve Johnson and Ken Belanger*
Tastes of Minnesota: A Food Lover's Tour, *Donna Tabbert Long*
The Great Indiana Touring Book: 20 Spectacular Auto Trips, *Thomas Huhti*
The Great Iowa Touring Book: 27 Spectacular Auto Trips, *Mike Whye*
The Great Minnesota Touring Book: 30 Spectacular Auto Trips, *Thomas Huhti*
The Great Wisconsin Touring Book: 30 Spectacular Auto Tours, *Gary Knowles*
Twin Cities Restaurant Guide, *Carla Waldemar*
Wisconsin Family Weekends: 20 Fun Trips for You and the Kids, *Susan Lampert Smith*
Wisconsin Gardens and Landscapes, *Mary Lou Santovec*
Wisconsin Lighthouses: A Photographic and Historical Guide, *Ken and Barb Wardius*
Wisconsin's Hometown Flavors, *Terese Allen*
Wisconsin Waterfalls, *Patrick Lisi*
Up North Wisconsin: A Region for All Seasons, *Sharyn Alden*

GIFT BOOKS

Badger Brain Twisters: Wisconsin Trivia, Games, Puzzles and More, *Kelly Whitt*
Madison, *Photography by Brent Nicastro*
Milwaukee, *Photography by Todd Dacquisto*
Spirit of the North: A Photographic Journey Through Northern Wisconsin, *Richard Hamilton Smith*

HOME & GARDEN

Creating a Perennial Garden in the Midwest, *Joan Severa*
Design Your Natural Midwest Garden, *Patricia Hill*
Eating Well in Wisconsin, *Jerry Minnich*
Midwest Cottage Gardening, *Frances Manos*
Northwoods Cottage Cookbook, *Jerry Minnich*
Potluck! Home Cooking from Wisconsin's Community Cookbooks, *Toni Brandeis Streckert*
Wisconsin Almanac, *Jerry Minnich*
Wisconsin Country Gourmet, *Marge Snyder & Suzanne Breckenridge*
Wisconsin Garden Guide, *Jerry Minnich*
Wisconsin Wildfoods: 100 Recipes for Badger State Bounties, *John Motoviloff*

SPORTS

After They Were Packers, *Jerry Poling*
Baseball in Beertown: America's Pastime in Milwaukee, *Todd Mishler*
Badger Sports Trivia Teasers, *Jerry Minnich*
Before They Were the Packers: Green Bay's Town Team Days, *Denis J. Gullickson and Carl Hanson*
Blood, Sweat and Cheers: Great Football Rivalries of the Big Ten, *Todd Mishler*
Boston Red Sox Trivia Teasers, *Richard Pennington*
Chicago Bears Trivia Teasers, *Steve Johnson*
Cold Wars: 40+ Years of Packer- Viking Rivalry, *Todd Mishler*
Denver Broncos Trivia Teasers, *Richard Pennington*
Detroit Red Wings Trivia Teasers, *Richard Pennington*
Green Bay Packers Titletown Trivia Teasers, *Don Davenport*
Mudbaths and Bloodbaths: The Inside Story of the Bears- Packers Rivalry, *Gary D 'Amato & Cliff Christl*
New York Yankees Trivia Teasers, *Richard Pennington*
No Bed of Roses: My Sideline View of the Wisconsin Badgers' Return to Greatness, *Chris Kennedy*
Packers By the Numbers: Jersey Numbers and the Players Who Wore Them, *John Maxymuk*
Vagabond Halfback: The Life and Times of Johnny Blood McNally, *Denis J. Gullickson*

LEGENDS & LORE

Got Murder? The Shocking Story of Wisconsin's Notorious Killers, *Martin Hintz*
Haunted Wisconsin, *Michael Norman and Beth Scott*
Hunting the American Werewolf, *Linda S. Godfrey*
The Beast of Bray Road: Tailing Wisconsin's Werewolf, *Linda S. Godfrey*
The Eagle's Voice: Tales Told by Indian Effigy Mounds, *Gary J. Maier, M.D.*
The Poison Widow: A True Story of Sin, Strychnine, & Murder, *Linda S. Godfrey*
Strange Wisconsin: More Badger State Weirdness, *Linda S. Godfrey*
The W-Files: True Reports of Wisconsin's Unexplained Phenomena, *Jay Rath*

For a free catalog, phone, write, or visit us online.

Trails Books
A Division of Big Earth Publishing
923 Williamson Street, Madison, WI 53703
800.258.5830 · www.trailsbooks.com